Eleven Short Stories
Undici Novelle

Eleven Short Stories
Undici Novelle
A Dual-Language Book

Luigi Pirandello

TRANSLATED AND EDITED BY
STANLEY APPELBAUM

DOVER PUBLICATIONS, INC.
New York

Acknowledgment

The publisher and the translator wish to thank Ms. Lauren Lee for her careful review of the translation and for numerous suggestions that have been gratefully adopted. Any flaws that remain are not imputable to Ms. Lee, but to the translator's lapses of judgment or skill.

Copyright

Copyright © 1994 by Dover Publications, Inc.

Published in Canada by General Publishing Company, Ltd., 30 Lesmill Road, Don Mills, Toronto, Ontario.

Published in the United Kingdom by Constable and Company, Ltd., 3 The Lanchesters, 162–164 Fulham Palace Road, London W6 9ER.

Bibliographical Note

Eleven Short Stories/Undici Novelle, first published by Dover Publications, Inc., in 1994, consists of a new selection of Pirandello stories, reconstituting the Italian text of the very first publication of each (see the Introduction for bibliographical details), accompanied by new English translations prepared specially for the present edition, with new introductory matter and footnotes.

Library of Congress Cataloging-in-Publication Data

Pirandello, Luigi, 1867–1936.
    [Short stories. English & Italian. Selections]
    Eleven short stories = Undici novelle / Luigi Pirandello ; translated and edited by Stanley Appelbaum.
        p.   cm.
    Italian text and English translation on opposite pages.
    ISBN 0-486-28091-8
    I. Appelbaum, Stanley. II. Title. III. Title: Undici novelle. IV. Title: 11 short stories. V. Title: 11 novelle.
PQ4835.I7A225   1994
852'.912—dc20   94-9455
                                                                 CIP

Manufactured in the United States of America
Dover Publications, Inc., 31 East 2nd Street, Mineola, N.Y. 11501

Contents

Introduction

THE MAN AND HIS WORK

A towering figure among early twentieth-century writers, winner of the 1934 Nobel Prize for literature, Luigi Pirandello (1867–1936) stood aloof from the literary currents of his day—Futurism, Surrealism and other more local movements—and was particularly hostile to the estheticism, self-heroization and political adventurism of Gabriele D'Annunzio. Nevertheless, recent Italian literary historians group Pirandello's work with that of his adversaries, classifying his oeuvre as one aspect—a major one—of the so-called Decadent period: the era in which the solid middle-class values and the ultimate appeal to human rationality typical of the late nineteenth century were being challenged and assailed from many directions and in many ways.

Pirandello's personal contribution, based on his belief that the progressive ideals of the liberators and unifiers of Italy in the 1860s and 1870s had been betrayed by the complacent bourgeois now entrenched in power, was to point out social inequalities (not through muckraking or sociological analysis, but by shedding sympathetic light on numerous individual cases) and, even more significantly, to dethrone reason by questioning the most basic assumptions about the way that people perceive the outside world and themselves. His writings are concerned with failure to communicate, disintegration of personality and the impossibility of arriving at a definitive truth.

These goals were accomplished in a vast oeuvre of poems, essays, short stories, novels and plays. Once Pirandello's career was under way, he never fully abandoned any of these genres, although the general progression of emphasis was: poetry (in his youth), short stories and novels (particularly in his thirties and forties) and plays (the best dating from his fifties, and bringing him international fame). The same ideas and subject matter interpenetrate all the genres. There is hardly a play of which all or part is not based on an earlier short story or segment of a novel. The short stories (which are of particular concern in the present volume) exhibit many traits of poetry (refrain-like verbal repetitions used structurally, highly colored descriptive passages), of essays (theoretical considerations

of psychology or the writer's craft expounded at length, with the "plot" sometimes acting merely as an illustrative anecdote) and especially of plays (long stretches of lively dialogue, with the connecting narrative often serving as "stage directions"). Humor is never lacking, though it can become acrid.

All of Pirandello's works are indissolubly linked to his own life and experiences. Born in 1867 near Girgenti (now Agrigento), Sicily, he studied at Palermo, Rome and Bonn (where he learned German well and received his degree in Romance philology). He settled in Rome, and Rome (with its huge variety of walks of life and its urban sophistication) and his native Sicily (with its parched landscape, poverty and its kaleidoscope of fixations and repressions) became the two poles of his mental world. In 1897 he began a decades-long career as instructor of Italian literature at a women's teachers college. Already known for his poetry, Pirandello was encouraged by Luigi Capuana, one of the deans of the Italian naturalist movement, to try his hand at stories and novels, and was immediately successful.

The flooding of his father's Sicilian sulphur mine in 1903 had far-reaching repercussions. Not only was Pirandello's income from home permanently cut off (so that he had to undertake extra tutoring and to rely even more heavily on income from authorship), but in addition his wife, whose dowry had been invested in the mine, suffered a nervous breakdown. In six months she recovered from the paresis in her legs, but her mind was never again completely balanced, and she embittered Pirandello's life with her morbid jealousy, even suspecting him of incest with their daughter. She had to be institutionalized in 1919; she lived until 1959. The author later found a steady companion in the actress Marta Abba. By 1917 his work for the stage became paramount, and his 1921[1] play *Sei personaggi in cerca d'autore* (Six Characters in Search of an Author) made him world-famous. He later directed his own troupe (with Abba as leading lady) and undertook global tours. He was also involved to varying degrees with film versions of his stories and plays.

In 1924, to his own public fanfare, he joined the Fascist party; he became a member of Mussolini's Italian Academy and supported

---

[1] All dates given in the present volume are those of first publication (for stories and novels) or of first performance (for plays).

the regime even in some of its most unsavory adventures (such as the invasion of Ethiopia). This adherence has been explained as the wish of a political *naïf* to associate himself with a movement that would regenerate Italian society, and much emphasis has also been placed on Pirandello's fundamental reclusiveness, on some writings of his that can be construed as anti-Fascist and on certain measures taken against him by the government. But he died in the odor of Fascist sanctity and never rebelled openly. Truly, Pirandello himself was a "Pirandello character."

The Short Stories and the Plan of the Present Volume

The short-story genre has a glorious history in Italy, beginning with the thirteenth-century collection *Il Novellino* and continuing through Boccaccio's *Decameron* in the fourteenth century and those sixteenth-century writers who gave Shakespeare the plots for such plays as *Romeo and Juliet* and *Othello*. After a falling off in the seventeenth and eighteenth centuries, the genre was vigorously revived in the nineteenth. Pirandello's immediate masters were the above-mentioned Capuana and the Sicilian Giovanni Verga, the foremost writer of the late nineteenth-century naturalist school (author of the story and play *Cavalleria rusticana*).

Pirandello wrote short stories from his teens until his death. There are over 230 known. As was the custom, almost all were originally published in newspapers and magazines; from 1896 on, many first appeared in the prestigious literary journal *Il Marzocco*, published in Florence (the "marzocco" is the Florentine heraldic lion); from 1909 on, most were first printed in Italy's leading newspaper, the *Corriere della Sera* (Evening Courier) of Milan. From time to time Pirandello would collect a group of stories into a volume. In 1918 he began regrouping his plays into volumes under the general title *Maschere nude* (Naked Masks), and in 1922 he started to do the same with the stories. The new story groupings were neither chronological nor thematic. Since he called the entire corpus of stories *Novelle per un anno* (Short Stories for a Year), he probably wished to end up with some 365 of them. The fourteen volumes of *Novelle per un anno* that he lived to publish (twenty-four were projected), plus the fifteenth, which appeared posthumously in 1937, contain 211 stories in all. At least 26 other stories already

published elsewhere had not (or not yet) been included in the new collection.

Pirandello's short-story oeuvre was a quarry for his later writings, an ongoing documentation of human types and situations, a gallery of eccentrics who might later reappear in different guises, just as the stories and plots themselves might later be given a substantially new look.

Pirandello was a constant reviser; he rarely ever republished a work of any type without subjecting it to light or heavy changes. In the case of the short stories, the revision could range from the substitution of a couple of words, or insignificant changes in spelling, punctuation and the like, to important additions and deletions or a thorough stylistic reworking.

The eleven stories in the present volume, presented in chronological order of first publication, range in time from the earliest known story published by Pirandello—"Capannetta" (Little Hut) of 1884—to the 1917 story "La signora Frola e il signor Ponza, suo genero" (Mrs. Frola and Mr. Ponza, Her Son-in-Law), the basis of his first major play (of the same year), *Così è (se vi pare)* (Right You Are, If You Think You Are). They include both Sicilian and Roman subject matter, and reflect most of Pirandello's basic themes and concerns. In each case, the text is that of the original periodical publication; the stories chosen were not substantially altered in later revisions. Although a text based on an author's "definitive wishes" or "final testament" has obvious advantages, the present approach has the merit of documenting more accurately Pirandello's growth as a stylist, of presenting the works as they were first given to the world and first gained fame for their author, and—in the case of those stories which were later dramatized—of indicating the *original* basis for the plays.

By 1965 (the date of the only such tabulation), 75 of Pirandello's short stories had been translated into English in various all-Pirandello anthology volumes, and another handful had appeared in English singly, in various journals and other volumes. Some of the earlier translations are quite free, and here and there one finds inaccuracies, sometimes understandable when the Italian is difficult or lends itself to ambiguities, sometimes inexcusable.

The goal of the present translation was to be as complete and literal as possible without sacrificing proper, idiomatic English; to offer an *equivalent* in English for every element in the Italian, although frequently it could not be a word-for-word equivalent; and

not to shirk any difficulties by merely omitting them.[2] Since Pirandello is a very idiomatic writer, touches on many specialized topics and sometimes uses rare or dialectal words not to be found in even the largest dictionaries, it would be presumptuous to claim complete accuracy for the present translation—but the will was there. Occasional footnotes point to particular linguistic problems or other special features in the text.

REMARKS ON THE INDIVIDUAL STORIES SELECTED

"**Capannetta: Bozzetto siciliano**" (Little Hut: Sicilian Sketch) is the earliest known story by Pirandello, published on June 1, 1884 (when he was seventeen and a student in Palermo), in *La Gazzetta del Popolo della Domenica* (People's Sunday Gazette), Turin. Never included by Pirandello in a collected volume, it eluded literary historians until its rediscovery in 1959.

Truly a mere sketch, and heavily indebted to Verga[3] for its picture of rural passions, the story nevertheless prefigures the mature Pirandello, with its lively dialogue, the thematic elements of overbearing father and oppressed woman and child, and its firm rooting in the author's native landscape. Pirandello's literary beginnings as a poet are clearly in evidence.

"**Lumie di Sicilia**" (Citrons from Sicily) was first published in *Il Marzocco*, Florence, in the issues of May 20 and 27, 1900. It was later included in the volume *Quando ero matto . . .* (When I Was Crazy . . .), 1902 (reprinted 1919), and in the tenth volume of *Novelle per un anno*, 1926. Pirandello's one-act play version (same title)

---

[2] One feature of Italian that cannot be reflected sufficiently in an English version is the variation in the second-person mode of address: from the intimate *tu* (with second person singular verb forms), through the mildly respectful *voi* (with second person plural verb forms; no longer in current use), to the fully respectful *lei* and super-respectful *Ella* (with third person singular verb forms). In "Lumie di Sicilia" (Citrons from Sicily) the servant switches from *voi* to *lei* and back depending on his appraisal of Micuccio's status; Micuccio says *voi* to his fiancée's mother, who says *tu* to him. In "Una voce" (A Voice), the Marchese's companion no longer addresses him as *lei* but as *tu* after their engagement, whereas at one point she is addressed with a quite sarcastic *Ella* by the doctor. And so on. Wherever *voi* is a plural, however (that is, more than one *tu*), an attempt has been made to indicate this in the English by means of some such device as "the two of you."

[3] The name Jeli had already been used in Verga's important story "Jeli il pastore" (Jeli the Shepherd), in which, moreover, the hero's wife is named Mara (compare Màlia in the Pirandello story).

was first produced in 1910. The title of the story and play usually appears in English as "Limes from Sicily" or "Sicilian Limes," but the story has also been called "Sicilian Tangerines."

The citrons symbolize the hometown purity that has been lost in the quest for fame and honor. The claustrophobic nature of the plain little room to which Micuccio is confined, with just a distant glimpse of the world of "beautiful people," is also symbolic, and already points to the single-set dramatization. The story version, however, is preferable to the play, in which, for purposes of exposition, the shy Micuccio must reveal the entire background of the plot to the unsympathetic servants. The ending of the story is also more telling than that of the play, which irresistibly calls to mind the nineteenth-century melodramatics of *Camille*.

"Con altri occhi" (With Other Eyes) was first published in *Il Marzocco* on July 28, 1901. It was later included in the volume *Erma bifronte* (Two-Faced Herm), 1906, and in the fifth volume of *Novelle per un anno*, 1923. Singled out in the *Encyclopaedia Britannica* as an exceptional psychological study, it has apparently never been translated before.

This is one of numerous Pirandello stories that deal with marital unhappiness, usually with the wife as a victim. Another theme typical of Pirandello is the realization that one's earlier impressions on a given subject have been entirely wrong. The plot device in which the dénouement is triggered by a woman's discovery of a document in her husband's clothes recurs in the 1910 story "'Leonora, addio!'" ("Leonora, Farewell!").

"Una voce" (A Voice) was first published in the periodical *Regina* on September 20, 1904. It was later included in *Erma bifronte*, 1906, and in the sixth volume of *Novelle per un anno*, 1923. Like the preceding story, it is highly recommended in the *Britannica* and apparently untranslated hitherto.

In certain crucial passages, the turbulent thoughts of the Marchese's fiancée are skillfully rendered in a technique close to interior monologue. The decisions she is called upon to make are of a vital, fundamental nature, like so many others with which Pirandello's characters grapple. It is also possible to interpret the story as one in which the unflinching belief in an unalloyed truth is destructive of happiness. The incessant use of the pluperfect tense up to the time of the engagement and the doctor's third visit helps to establish the climactic atmosphere of what follows.

"La mosca" (The Fly) was first published in *Il Marzocco* on Octo-

ber 2, 1904. It was later included in *Erma bifronte*, 1906, and in the fifth volume of *Novelle per un anno*, 1923.

The doctor's domestic situation is a bitter parody of the author's own when his wife's breakdown and paralysis in 1903 left him in charge of their three small children. The stark beauty and crushing poverty of his native region (all that the peasants can find to chat about is one crop failure after another) are tellingly depicted, as are the hateful envy of the dying man and the tragedy of "Liolà," his life-loving cousin. The 1916 play *Liolà*, although it also concerns a handsome young folk poet and even includes an almond-shelling scene, is based on different material.

"La giara" (The Oil Jar) was first published in the *Corriere della Sera*, Milan, on October 20, 1909. It was later included in the volume *Terzetti* (Sets of Three), 1912, and in the eleventh volume of *Novelle per un anno*, 1928. Pirandello's one-act dramatization was first produced in 1917. A ballet based on the play was performed in Paris in 1924 by Jean Borlin's Ballets Suédois, with music by Alfredo Casella and sets by Giorgio De Chirico. The story has been translated as "The Jar."

This has been called Pirandello's most popular story. The confrontation of the two monomaniacs is delightful, and the wild dance at the end raises the story to almost mythic dimensions.

"Non è una cosa seria" (It's Not to Be Taken Seriously) was first published in the *Corriere della Sera* on January 7, 1910. It was later included in *Terzetti*, 1912, and in the eleventh volume of *Novelle per un anno*, 1928. A previous translation was called "It's Nothing Serious." Certain story elements were reused by Pirandello in his three-act play *Ma non è una cosa seria* (But It's Not to Be Taken Seriously), 1918.

Perazzetti is a first-rate Pirandello eccentric, unable to control himself even though his actions are based on a strong personal philosophy. Pirandello had already used the plot element of a marriage-to-prevent-marriage in his story "La signora Speranza" (Mrs. Speranza; included in the second series of *Beffe della morte e della vita* [Jests of Death and Life], 1903, but not in *Novelle per un anno*), and it is on this earlier story that the above-mentioned play is chiefly based. The only plot elements in the play taken from the 1910 story that is included in the present volume are the wounding of the protagonist in a duel with a prospective brother-in-law and his sending his unwanted wife to live in the country. On the other hand, the 1910 story is the only version containing the significant thematic

elements of the protagonist's helpless laughter, his theory of the "primordial beast" and—most Pirandellian of all—the many roles that different situations compel him to play.

Pirandello evidently liked Perazzetti so much that he used him in another story, the 1914 "Zuccarello distinto melodista" (Zuccarello, the New Kind of Singer), but in that story he merely placed him in another offbeat adventure without resuming the themes of "Non è una cosa seria."

Duels occur in other Pirandello stories as well, usually as grotesque affairs into which the unmartial hero is forced against his will.[4]

"Pensaci, Giacomino!" (Think It Over, Giacomino!) was first published in the *Corriere della Sera* on February 23, 1910. It was later included in *Terzetti*, 1912, and in the eleventh volume of *Novelle per un anno*, 1928. Pirandello's three-act dramatization (same title) was first produced in 1916. The story has been translated with the title "Better Think Twice About It!"

Pirandello's long years as an instructor are reflected in the attitude of Professor Toti and the many other teachers who appear in his stories and plays. The story is told completely in the present tense, so that the dialogue sounds like stage dialogue and the narrative sounds like stage directions. In the 1916 play, the entire first act takes place at the high school and concerns Toti's "wooing" of the janitor's daughter, who is *already* pregnant by Giacomino. The rest of the play follows the story pretty much, the main difference being in the introduction of a slimy jesuitical priest as spiritual adviser of Giacomino's devout sister. Here Pirandello gives all too free rein to his declared atheism and produces a one-sided anticlerical tract.

"La tragedia d'un personaggio" (A Character's Tragedy) was first published in the *Corriere della Sera* on October 19, 1911. It was later included in the volume *La trappola* (The Trap), 1915, and in the fourth volume of *Novelle per un anno*, 1922. It has been translated with the title "The Tragedy of a Character."

Besides being very readable, this story is highly important for its

---

[4] The above discussion of the story reflects what the translator believes to have been Pirandello's intentions. There is ample evidence in the story, however, to suggest viewing Perazzetti as a homosexual, barely aware of his true leanings, whose "wild imagination" is a mental mechanism for avoiding marriage with at least a plausible excuse to society and to himself.

thematic connection with the play *Six Characters* and with the famous manifesto/foreword to that play, one of Pirandello's most explicit statements about his art. Yet another instance of the author's "giving audience" to his characters during announced visiting hours occurs in the 1915 story "Colloquii coi personaggi" (Conversations with My Characters; later included in the volume *Berecche e la guerra* [Berecche and the War], 1919, but not in *Novelle per un anno*), but the nature of those conversations is not really similar to the present story. On the other hand, the 1906 story "Personaggi" (Characters; never included in a collected volume) is extremely closely related to both the 1911 story and the *Six Characters* preface. In the 1902 story "Pallottoline!" (Tiny Spheres!), the main character, an amateur astronomer, forgets his woes by thinking about the Earth's insignificance within the whole universe: a clear analogy to Dr. Fileno's "philosophy of distance" and his reverse use of the telescope.

"La rallegrata" (A Prancing Horse; literally, The Prance) was first published in the *Corriere della Sera* on October 26, 1913. It was later included in *La trappola*, 1915, and in the third volume of *Novelle per un anno*, 1922. It has been translated with the title "Black Horses."

Pirandello's sympathy for the plight of animals (especially dogs and horses) that share human society is evident in a number of stories. But the main subject here is really that of death and burial, a theme that Pirandello developed countless times from every conceivable point of view. (He himself once wished for a simple funeral, with a pauper's hearse drawn by a single horse and no crowd in attendance; his testamentary desire to have his ashes placed humbly in his native home was not fulfilled until long after his death, because the Fascist regime demanded a showy public funeral in Rome.)

The "horsy" vocabulary in this story is quite difficult, and the present translator gratefully acknowledges the borrowing of a few technical terms from the above-mentioned "Black Horses" (in *Better Think Twice About It And Twelve Other Stories*, translated by Arthur and Henrie Mayne, published by John Lane The Bodley Head Ltd, London, 1933)—but even there some of the text is simply omitted! The reader's indulgence is requested for any technical deficiencies that still remain in the present version after exhausting the aid of all available dictionaries.

"La signora Frola e il signor Ponza, suo genero" (Mrs. Frola and Mr. Ponza, Her Son-in-Law) first appeared in the volume of

stories *E domani, lunedì . . .* (And Tomorrow, Monday . . .), published by Treves, Milan, 1917. It was included in the (posthumous) fifteenth volume of *Novelle per un anno,* 1937. It is the source of the three-act play *Così è (se vi pare)* (Right You Are, If You Think You Are), produced the same year that the story was published. The story has been translated with the title "Signora Frola and Her Son-in-Law, Signor Ponza," "Mrs. Frola and Her Son-in-Law, Mr. Ponza" and "A Mother-in-Law."

This is probably the key Pirandello story about the relativity of truth and the impossibility of penetrating other people's minds. Valdana is also used as the name of a provincial town in the 1909 story "L'illustre estinto" (The Illustrious Deceased). In the above-mentioned story "'Leonora, addio!'" there is a woman who is unmistakably kept locked up by an insanely jealous husband.

Even though the play based on this story is one of Pirandello's most important, and was a turning point in his whole career, it is still possible to prefer the original story. Among other things, the play introduces a character who exists merely to speak for the author (like the *raisonneur* role in nineteenth-century French drama) and who literally, and all too mechanically, has the last laugh at the end of each act. The play turns the son-in-law and mother-in-law into more obviously pathetic characters, and converts the puzzled townspeople into pernicious priers. The fruitless questioning of the son-in-law's female companion, a secondary element in the story, becomes the all too carefully prepared climax of the play, in which she appears symbolically veiled, changing the whole tone of the proceedings. Above all, the play lacks the extreme charm of the final two paragraphs of the story, in which the relationship of the two main characters is more lovingly described, and in which it is even possible to detect a delicious conspiracy against the reign of reason and the tyranny of truth.

Eleven Short Stories
Undici Novelle

CAPANNETTA

Bozzetto siciliano

Un'alba come mai fu vista.

Una bimba venne fuori della nera capannetta, coi capelli arruffati sulla fronte e con un fazzoletto rosso-sbiadito in testa.

Mentre andava bottonando la dimessa vesticciola, sbadigliava, ancora abbindolata dal sonno, e guardava: guardava lontano, con gli occhi sbarrati come se nulla vedesse.

In fondo, in fondo, una lunga striscia di rosso infuocato s'intrecciava in modo bizzarro col verde-smeraldo degli alberi, che a lunga distesa lontanamente si perdevano.

Tutto il cielo era seminato di nuvolette d'un giallo croceo, acceso.

La bimba andava sbadatamente, ed ecco . . . diradandosi a poco a poco una piccola collina che a destra s'innalzava le si sciorina davanti allo sguardo l'immensità delle acque del mare.

La bimba parve colpita, commossa dinanzi a quella scena, e stette a guardar le barchette che volavano su l'onde, tinte d'un giallo pallido.

Era tutto silenzio.—Aliava ancora la dolce brezzolina della notte, che faceva rabbrividire il mare, e s'innalzava lento, lento un blando profumo di terra.

Poco dopo la bimba si volse—vagò per quell'incerto chiarore, e giunta sull'alto del greppo, si sedette.

Guardò distratta la valle verdeggiante, che le rideva di sotto, ed aveva cominciato a cantilenare una delicata canzonetta.

Ma, ad un tratto, come colpita da un'idea, smise di cantare, e con quanta voce aveva in gola, gridò:

—Zi' Jeli! Oh zi' Jee . . .

E una voce grossolana rispose dalla valle:

—Ehh . . .

—Salite su . . . ché il padrone vi vuole! . . .

*

2

LITTLE HUT

SICILIAN SKETCH

A dawn like none ever seen.

A little girl came out of the small dark hut, with her hair tousled on her forehead and with a faded red kerchief on her head.

While she buttoned up her plain little dress, she was yawning, still confusedly half-asleep, and she was gazing: gazing into the distance, with her eyes wide open as if she saw nothing.

Far away, far away, a long streak of flaming red was strangely interwoven with the emerald green of the trees, which extended a great distance until disappearing from sight a long way off.

The entire sky was spattered with little clouds of a flaming saffron yellow.

The girl was walking inattentively, and there! . . . as a small hill that rose on the right was gradually lost to her view, the immensity of the waters of the sea was displayed before her eyes.

The girl seemed impressed, moved in the face of that scene, and stopped to look at the small boats that were skimming on the waves, tinged a pale yellow.

All was silence.—The gentle little night breeze was still blowing, creating trembling ripples on the sea, and slowly, slowly a pleasing smell of earth arose.

Shortly afterward the girl turned—wandered in that weak morning light and, when she reached the top of the rocky bank, sat down.

She absentmindedly viewed the green valley that smiled to her from below, and she had begun to hum a charming little song.

But all at once, as if struck by an idea, she stopped singing and, in the loudest tone she could muster, cried:

"'Uncle' Jeli! Oh, 'Uncle' Je . . . "[1]

And a coarse voice answered from the valley:

"Eh . . . "

"Climb up . . . because the boss wants you! . . . "

*

---

[1] "Uncle" and "aunt" were respectful terms of address in rural speech, for people older than the speaker but of the same social class.

3

Frattanto la bimba ritornava verso la capannetta, a capo basso.—Jeli era salito ancora sonnacchioso con la giacca sull'omero sinistro e la pipa in bocca—pipa, che sempre lasciava dormire tra i denti.

Appena entrato salutò papà Camillo, mentre Màlia, la figlia maggiore del castaldo, gli piantò in faccia due occhi come saette, da bucare un macigno.

Jeli ripose allo sguardo.

Era papà Camillo un mozzicone di uomo, grosso come una botte.

Màlia all'incontro aveva il volto d'una *dama* di Paolo Veronese, e negli occhi ci si leggeva chiaramente la beata semplicità del suo cuore.

—Senti, Jeli,—disse Papà Camillo,—prepara delle frutta, ché domani verranno i signori di città.—Buoni, sai!... se no... Come è vero Dio!...

—Oh! sempre la stessa storia,—rispose Jeli,—e sapete voi che queste le son cose da dire... e poi... a me!...

—Intanto,—riprese papà Camillo—e prendendolo pel braccio lo portò fuori della capanna—intanto..., se un'altra volta ti viene il ticchio di... Basta. Tu mi capisci...

Jeli rimase come interdetto.

Papà Camillo scese per la valle.

Non si potea dar di meglio e il giovane saltò alla capannetta.

—Siamo perduti!—fece Màlia.

—Sciocca!—disse Jeli,—se non ci riesco con le buone...

—Oh! Jeli, Jeli che vuoi tu dire?

—Come, non mi comprendi? Fuggiremo.

—Fuggiremo?—disse la fanciulla, sorpresa.

—O...,—soggiunse Jeli—e si mise la falce lucente attorno al collo...

—Mio Dio!—esclamò Màlia, come se un brivido le corresse per tutto il corpo.

—A questa sera, bada, a sette ore!—disse Jeli e sparì.

La fanciulla mandò un grido.

Abbuiava.

L'ora stabilita si avvicinava, e Màlia pallida, pallida, con le labbra come due foglioline di rosa secca, stava seduta dinanzi alla porta.

Guardava il piano verdeggiante che si inondava di buio—e

Meanwhile the girl was returning toward the little hut, her head lowered.—Jeli had climbed up, still sleepy, with his jacket on his left shoulder and his pipe in his mouth—a pipe that he always allowed to sleep between his teeth.

As soon as he had come in, he greeted Papa Camillo, while Màlia, the steward's older daughter, looked him in the face with two eyes like arrows that could pierce a boulder.

Jeli responded to her look.

Papa Camillo was a little stump of a man, fat as a wine cask.

Màlia, on the other hand, had the face of one of Paolo Veronese's noblewomen, and in her eyes the blessed simplicity of her heart could be clearly read.

"Listen, Jeli," said Papa Camillo, "prepare some fruit because tomorrow the master and his family are coming from town.—Good ones, right? . . . otherwise . . . I swear to God! . . . "

"Oh! Always the same story," replied Jeli, "and you should know better than to say things like that . . . and to me of all people! . . . "

"Meanwhile," continued Papa Camillo and, taking him by the arm, led him out of the hut, "meanwhile . . . if you ever again take it into your head to . . . Enough! You understand me . . . "

Jeli seemed thunderstruck.

Papa Camillo went down through the valley.

The situation couldn't be better, and the young man dashed over to the little hut.

"We're lost!" said Màlia.

"Silly!" said Jeli. "If I don't succeed by fair means . . . "

"Oh! Jeli, Jeli, what do you mean?"

"What, you don't understand me? We'll run away."

"Run away?" said the girl, surprised.

"Or else . . . ," Jeli added, and he put his gleaming sickle around his neck . . .

"My God!" exclaimed Màlia, as if a shudder ran all through her body.

"This evening, you hear? At seven o'clock!" said Jeli, and vanished.

The girl uttered a cry.

It was becoming dark.

The arranged time was getting close and Màlia, extremely pale, with lips like two small petals of a dried rose, was sitting in front of the door.

She was looking at the green plain that was being submerged in

quando lontanamente la squilla del villaggio suonò l'Ave, pregò anche lei.

E quel silenzio solenne, parve divina preghiera di Natura! Dopo lungo aspettare Jeli venne. Questa volta avea lasciato la pipa, ed era un poco acceso e molto risoluto.

—Così presto?—disse Màlia tremante.

—Un quarto prima, un quarto dopo, è sempre tempo guadagnato—rispose Jeli.

—Ma . . .

—Santo diavolo! mi pare tempo di finirla con questi *ma* . . . Non sai tu, cuor mio, di che si tratta? . . .

—Lo so bene! lo so tanto bene . . .—s'affrettò a rispondere Màlia, che non poteva adattarsi a quella sconsigliata risoluzione.

Frattanto un fischio lontano avvertì Jeli che la vettura era pronta.

—Su via!—disse;—Maliella mia, coraggio! E la gioja che ci chiama . . .

Màlia mandò un grido—Jeli la prese per il braccio, e di corsa . . .

Come pose il piede nella carretta—A tutta furia!—gridò.

I due giovani si strinsero e si baciarono con libertà per la prima volta.

A nove ore papà Camillo ritornò dalla valle e fischiò potentemente.

Venne la bimba in fretta e prima che fosse giunta:

—Dove è Jeli?—le domandò;—hai tu veduto Jeli?

—Padrone! . . . padrone! . . .—rispose quella con voce ansante, soffocata.

—Che cosa vuoi tu dirmi? Mummietta!—ruggì papà Camillo.

—Jeli . . . è fuggito . . . con Maliella . . .

— . . .

E un suono rauco . . . selvaggio fuggì dalla strozza di papà Camillo.

Corse . . . volò alla capanna: prese lo schioppo e fece fuoco in aria. La fanciulla guardava tramortita.

Era uno spettacolo strano la collera pazza di quell'uomo. Un riso frenetico scattò dalle sue labbra e si perdé in un rantolo strozzato.—Non sapea più quel che si faceva . . . E fuori di sé appiccò il fuoco alla capannetta come per distruggere ogni cosa che gli parlava di sua figlia.—Poi di corsa furiosa, con

darkness—and when, far off, the village bell rang the Angelus, she too prayed.

And that solemn silence was like a divine prayer of Nature!

After a long wait Jeli came. This time he had left behind his pipe, and was a little flushed and very determined.

"So early?" said Màlia, trembling.

"Fifteen minutes sooner, fifteen minutes later, it's all time gained," answered Jeli.

"But . . ."

"Damn it all! I think it's time to put aside all these 'buts' . . . Darling, don't you know what we're undertaking? . . ."

"I do know! I know it very well . . . ," Màlia hurriedly replied, unable to adjust to that rash determination.

Meanwhile a distant whistle informed Jeli that their conveyance was ready.

"Come on!" he said. "Be brave, my little Màlia! It's happiness that's calling for us . . ."

Màlia uttered a cry—Jeli took her by the arm, and off they ran . . .

As he set foot inside the farm wagon, he shouted: "As fast as you can!"

The two young people embraced and kissed freely for the first time.

At nine o'clock Papa Camillo returned from the valley and gave a loud whistle.

The little girl came hurriedly and before she arrived:

"Where is Jeli?" he asked her. "Have you seen Jeli?"

"Boss! . . . Boss! . . . " she replied in a breathless, stifled voice.

"What are you trying to tell me? Helpless simpleton!" roared Papa Camillo.

"Jeli . . . ran away . . . with Màlia . . . "

" . . . "

And a hoarse, . . . wild sound escaped Papa Camillo's throat.

He ran . . . flew to the hut: he took the carbine and fired into the air. The girl was watching, stunned.

That man's mad rage was a strange sight. A frenetic laugh burst from his lips and was lost in a choked rattle.—He no longer knew what he was doing . . . And, beside himself, he set fire to the little hut as if to destroy everything that spoke to him of his daugh-

lo schioppo in mano, via per il viale, dove forse sperava trovare gli amanti.

Per la lugubre sera salivano al cielo sanguigne quelle lingue di fuoco . . .

Fumava la nera capannetta, fumava crepitando, come se col lento scoppiettio volesse salutare la bimba, che pallida, inor-ridita, con gli occhi fissi la guardava.

Pareva che tutti i suoi pensieri seguissero la colonna di fumo, che s'innalzava dalla sua modesta dimora . . .

Fumava la nera capannetta, fumava crepitando, e la bimba stette muta a riposar gli sguardi sulla cenere cupa.

Palermo '83

ter.—Then, gun in hand, he raced furiously off down the path, where he perhaps hoped to find the lovers.

In the mournful evening those tongues of flame rose bloodred into the sky.

The little hut, blackened, was pouring out smoke, pouring smoke and crackling, as if with its slow snapping and popping it wanted to greet the little girl, who, pale, horrified, was watching it with fixed gaze.

All her thoughts seemed to be following the column of smoke that was rising from her humble dwelling . . .

The little hut, blackened, was pouring out smoke, pouring smoke and crackling, and the little girl stood there in silence, resting her gaze on the gloomy ashes.

Palermo '83

LUMIE DI SICILIA

—Teresina sta qui?

Il cameriere, ancora in maniche di camicia, ma già impiccato in un altissimo colletto, coi radi capelli ben lisciati e disposti sul cranio, inarcando le folte ciglia giunte che parevan due baffi spostati, rasi dal labbro e appiccicati lì per non perderli, squadrò da capo ai piedi il giovanotto che gli stava davanti sul pianerottolo della scala: campagnolo all'aspetto, col bavero del pastrano ruvido rialzato fin su gli orecchi e le mani paonazze, gronchie dal freddo, che reggevano un sacchetto sudicio di qua, una vecchia valigetta di là, a contrappeso.

—Chi è Teresina?

Il giovanotto scosse prima la testa per far saltare dalla punta del naso una gocciolina, poi rispose:

—Teresina, la cantante.

—Ah,—sclamò il cameriere con un sorriso d'ironico stupore:—Si chiama così, senz'altro, Teresina? E voi chi siete?

—C'è o non c'è?—domandò il giovanotto, corrugando le ciglia e sorsando pe' l naso.—Ditele che c'è Micuccio e lasciatemi entrare.

—Ma non c'è nessuno,—riprese il cameriere col sorriso rassegato su le labbra.—La signora Sina Marnis è ancora in teatro e . . .

—Zia Marta pure?—lo interruppe Micuccio.

—Ah, lei è parente? Favorisca allora, favorisca . . . Non c'è nessuno. Anche lei a teatro, la Zia. Prima del tocco non ritorneranno. È la serata d'onore di sua . . . come sarebbe di lei, la signora? cugina, forse?

Micuccio restò un istante impacciato.

CITRONS FROM SICILY

"Is Teresina here?"

The servant—still in his shirt sleeves, but with his neck already squeezed into an extremely high collar and with his sparse hair carefully dressed and arranged on his cranium—raised his thick, joined eyebrows, which resembled a displaced mustache that had been shaved off his lips and pasted up there so he wouldn't lose it, and examined from head to foot the young man standing in front of him on the staircase landing: a rustic from the look of him, with the collar of his rough overcoat raised up to his ears and his hands—purple, numbed with cold—holding a dirty little sack on one side and a small old suitcase on the other, as a counterweight.

"Who is Teresina?"

The young man first shook his head to get rid of a little water drop on the tip of his nose, then replied:

"Teresina, the singer."

"Ah!" exclaimed the servant with a smile of ironic amazement: "That's her name, just plain Teresina? And who are you?"[1]

"Is she here or isn't she?" asked the young man, knitting his brows and sniffling. "Tell her that Micuccio is here, and let me in."

"But there's no one here," continued the servant with his smile congealed on his lips. "Madame Sina Marnis is still at the theater and . . ."

"Aunt Marta, too?" Micuccio interrupted him.

"Ah, you're a relative, sir? In that case, step right in, step right in . . . No one's at home. She's at the theater, too, your aunt. They won't be back before one. This is the benefit night[2] of your . . . what is she to you, the lady? Your cousin, perhaps?"

Micuccio stood there embarrassed for a moment.

---

[1] The varying modes of address used by the servant when speaking to Micuccio are very important in this story; see the discussion of "you" in the Introduction, page xiii, footnote 2.

[2] The night, contractually set aside, on which a member of a dramatic or operatic troupe would perform his or her specialties and share in the box-office take.

—Non sono parente, . . . sono Micuccio Bonavino, lei lo sa . . . Vengo apposta dal paese.

A questa risposta il cameriere stimò innanzi tutto conveniente di ritirare il *lei* e riprendere il *voi*: introdusse Micuccio in una cameretta al bujo presso la cucina, dove qualcuno ronfava strepitosamente, e gli disse:

—Sedete qua. Adesso porto un lume.

Micuccio guardò prima dalla parte donde veniva quel ronfo, ma non poté discernere nulla; guardò poi in cucina, dove il cuoco, assistito da un guattero, apparecchiava da cena. L'odor misto delle vivande in preparazione lo vinse: n'ebbe quasi un'ebrietà vertiginosa: era poco men che digiuno dalla mattina; veniva da Reggio di Calabria: una notte e un giorno intero in ferrovia.

Il cameriere recò il lume, e la persona che ronfava nella stanza, dietro una cortina sospesa a una funicella da una parete all'altra, borbottò tra il sonno:

—Chi è?

—Ehi, Dorina, su!—chiamò il cameriere.—Vedi che c'è qui il signor Bonvicino . . .

—Bonavino,—corresse Micuccio che stava a soffiarsi su le dita.

—Bonavino, Bonavino . . . conoscente della signora. Tu dormi della grossa: suonano alla porta e non senti . . . Io ho da apparecchiare, non posso far tutto io, capisci?, badare al cuoco che non sa, alla gente che viene . . .

Un ampio sonoro sbadiglio, protratto nello stiramento delle membra e terminato in un nitrito per un brividore improvviso, accolse la protesta del cameriere, il quale s'allontanò esclamando:

—E va bene!

Micuccio sorrise, e lo seguì con gli occhi attraverso un'altra stanza in penombra fino alla vasta sala in fondo, illuminata, dove sorgeva splendida la mensa, e restò meravigliato a contemplare, finché di nuovo il ronfo non lo fece voltare a guardar la cortina.

Il cameriere, col tovagliolo sotto il braccio, passava e ripas-

"I'm not a relative . . . I'm Micuccio Bonavino, she knows . . . I've come on purpose from our hometown."

Upon receiving this reply, the servant deemed it suitable above all else to take back the polite *lei* form of address and go back to the ordinary *voi*; he led Micuccio into a small unlighted room near the kitchen, where someone was snoring noisily, and said to him:

"Sit here. I'll go and get a lamp."

Micuccio first looked in the direction from which the snoring was coming, but couldn't make out anything; then he looked into the kitchen, where the cook, aided by a scullery boy, was preparing a supper. The mingled aromas of the dishes being prepared overpowered him; their effect on him was like a heady intoxication; he had hardly eaten a thing since that morning; he had traveled from Reggio di Calabria:[3] a night and a full day on the train.

The servant brought the lamp, and the person who was snoring in the room, behind a curtain hung from a cord between two walls, muttered sleepily:

"Who is it?"

"Hey, Dorina, get up!" the servant called. "Look, Mr. Bonvicino is here . . ."

"Bonavino," Micuccio corrected him, as he blew on his fingers.

"Bonavino, Bonavino . . . an acquaintance of the mistress. You really sleep soundly: they ring at the door and you don't hear it . . . I have to set the table; I can't do everything myself, understand—keep an eye on the cook, who doesn't know the ropes; watch for people who come to call . . ."

A big, loud yawn from the maid, prolonged while she stretched and ending in a whinny caused by a sudden shiver, was her reply to the complaint of the manservant, who walked away exclaiming:

"All right!"

Micuccio smiled and watched him depart across another room in semidarkness until he reached the vast, well-lit salon[4] at the far end, where the splendid supper table towered; he kept on gazing in amazement until the snoring made him turn once more and look at the curtain.

The servant, with his napkin under his arm, passed back and

---

[3] In a later version, "from the province of Messina" (perhaps Reggio was thought of as the outset of the journey by *rail*).

[4] Although merely *sala* (room) in the story text, the site of the party is identified as a *salone* and reception room in the play based on the story.

sava borbottando or contro Dorina che seguitava a dormire
or contro il cuoco che doveva esser nuovo, chiamato per l'avvenimento di quella sera, e lo infastidiva chiedendo di continuo spiegazioni. Micuccio, per non infastidirlo anche lui,
stimò prudente di ricacciarsi dentro tutte le domande che gli
veniva di rivolgergli. Avrebbe poi dovuto dirgli o fargli intendere ch'era il fidanzato di Teresina, e non voleva, pur non
sapendone il perché lui stesso, se non forse per questo, che
quel cameriere allora avrebbe dovuto trattar lui Micuccio da
padrone, ed egli, vedendolo così disinvolto ed elegante,
quantunque ancor senza marsina, non riusciva a vincer l'impaccio che già ne provava solo a pensarci. A un certo punto
però, vedendolo ripassare, non seppe tenersi dal domandargli:

—Scusi . . . questa casa di chi è?

—Nostra, finché ci siamo,—gli rispose in fretta il cameriere.

E Micuccio rimase a tentennar la testa.

Perbacco, era vero dunque! La fortuna acciuffata. Affaroni.
Quel cameriere che pareva un gran signore, il cuoco e il guattero, quella Dorina che ronfava di là: tutta servitù a gli ordini
di Teresina . . . Chi l'avrebbe mai detto?

Rivedeva col pensiero la soffitta squallida, laggiù laggiù, a
Messina, dove Teresina abitava con la madre . . . Cinque anni
addietro, in quella soffitta lontana, se non fosse stato per lui,
mamma e figlia sarebbero morte di fame. E lui, lui, aveva
scoperto quel tesoro nella gola di Teresina! Ella cantava sempre, allora, come una passera dei tetti, ignara del suo tesoro:
cantava per dispetto, cantava per non pensare alla miseria, a
cui egli cercava di sovvenire alla meglio, non ostante la guerra
che gli facevano in casa i genitori, la madre specialmente. Ma
poteva egli abbandonar Teresina in quello stato, dopo la
morte del padre di lei? abbandonarla perché non aveva nulla,
mentre lui, bene o male, un posticino ce l'aveva, di sonator di
flauto nel concerto comunale? Bella ragione! e il cuore?

Ah, era stata una vera ispirazione del cielo, un suggerimento
della fortuna, quel por mente alla voce di lei, quando nessuno
ci badava, in quella bellissima giornata d'aprile, presso la finestra dell'abbaino che incorniciava vivo vivo l'azzurro del
cielo. Teresina canticchiava un'appassionata arietta siciliana,
di cui a Micuccio sovvenivano ancora le tenere parole. Era
triste Teresina, quel giorno, per la recente morte del padre e

forth, muttering now about Dorina, who went on sleeping, now about the cook, who was most likely a new man, called in for that evening's event, and who was annoying him by constantly asking for explanations. Micuccio, to avoid annoying him further, deemed it prudent to repress all the questions that he thought of asking him. He really ought to have told him or given him to understand that he was Teresina's fiancé, but he didn't want to, though he himself didn't know why, unless perhaps it was because the servant would then have had to treat him, Micuccio, as his master, and he, seeing him so jaunty and elegant, although still without his tailcoat, couldn't manage to overcome the embarrassment he felt at the very thought of it. At a certain point, however, seeing him pass by again, he couldn't refrain from asking him:

"Excuse me . . . whose house is this?"

"Ours, as long as we're in it," the servant answered hurriedly.

And Micuccio sat there shaking his head.

By heaven, so it was true! Opportunity seized by the forelock. Good business. That servant who resembled a great nobleman, the cook and the scullery boy, that Dorina snoring over there: all servants at Teresina's beck and call . . . Who would ever have thought so?

In his mind he saw once again the dreary garret, way down in Messina, where Teresa used to live with her mother . . . Five years earlier, in that faraway garret, if it hadn't been for him, mother and daughter would have died of hunger. And *he, he* had discovered that treasure in Teresa's throat! She was always singing, then, like a sparrow on the rooftops, unaware of her own treasure: she would sing to annoy, she would sing to keep from thinking of her poverty, which he would try to alleviate as best he could, in spite of the war his parents waged with him at home, his mother especially. But could he abandon Teresina in those circumstances, after her father's death?—abandon her because she had nothing, while he, for better or worse, did have a modest employment, as flute player in the local orchestra? Fine reasoning!—and what about his heart?

Ah, it had been a true inspiration from heaven, a prompting of fortune, when he had paid attention to that voice of hers, when no one was giving it heed, on that very beautiful April day, near the garret window that framed the vivid blue of the sky. Teresina was singing softly an impassioned Sicilian arietta, the tender words of which Micuccio still remembered. Teresina was sad, that day, over the recent death of her father and over his family's stubborn opposi-

per l'ostinata opposizione dei parenti di lui; e anch'egli—ricordava—era triste, tanto che gli erano spuntate le lagrime, sentendola cantare. Pure tant'altre volte l'aveva sentita, quell'arietta; ma cantata a quel modo, mai. N'era rimasto così colpito, che il giorno appresso, senza prevenire né lei né la madre, aveva condotto seco su nella soffitta il direttore del concerto, suo amico. E così erano cominciate le prime lezioni di canto; e per due anni di fila egli aveva speso per lei quasi tutto il suo stipendietto: le aveva preso a nolo un pianoforte, comperate le carte di musica e qualche amichevole compenso aveva pur dato al maestro. Bei giorni lontani! Teresina ardeva tutta nel desiderio di spiccare il volo, di lanciarsi nell'avvenire che il maestro le prometteva luminoso, e, frattanto, che carezze di fuoco a lui per dimostrargli tutta la sua gratitudine, e che sogni di felicità commune!

Zia Marta, invece, scoteva amaramente il capo: ne aveva viste tante in vita sua, povera vecchietta, che ormai non aveva più fiducia nell'avvenire: temeva per la figliola, e non voleva che ella pensasse neppure alla possibilità di togliersi da quella rassegnata miseria; e poi sapeva, sapeva ciò che costava a lui la follia di quel sogno pericoloso.

Ma né lui né Teresina le davano ascolto, e invano ella si ribellò quando un giovane maestro compositore, avendo udito Teresina in un concerto, dichiarò che sarebbe stato un vero delitto non darle migliori maestri e una completa educazione artistica: a Napoli, bisognava mandarla al conservatorio di Napoli, a qualunque costo.

E allora lui, Micuccio, rompendola addirittura coi parenti, aveva venduto un suo poderetto lasciatogli in eredità dallo zio prete, e così Teresina era andata a Napoli a completar gli studii.

Non la aveva più riveduta, da allora; ma aveva le sue lettere dal conservatorio e poi quelle di zia Marta, quando già Teresina s'era lanciata nella vita artistica, contesa dai principali teatri, dopo l'esordio clamoroso al *San Carlo*. A piè di quelle tremule incerte lettere raspate alla meglio sulla carta dalla povera vecchietta c'eran sempre due paroline di lei, di Teresina, che non aveva mai tempo di scrivere: «*Caro Micuccio, confermo quanto ti dice la mamma. Sta' sano e voglimi bene*». Eran rimasti d'accordo che egli le avrebbe lasciato cinque, sei anni di tempo per farsi strada liberamente: eran giovani entrambi e pote-

tion; and he too—he recalled—was sad, so much so that tears had come to his eyes when he heard her sing. And yet he had heard that arietta many other times; but sung that way, never. He had been so struck by it that the following day, without informing her or her mother, he had brought with him his friend, the orchestra conductor, up to the garret. And in that way the first singing lessons had begun; and for two years running he had spent almost all of his small salary on her; he had rented a piano for her, had purchased her sheet music and had also given the teacher some friendly remuneration. Beautiful faraway days! Teresa burned intensely with the desire to take flight, to hurl herself into the future that her teacher promised her would be a brilliant one; and, in the meantime, what impassioned caresses for him to prove to him all her gratitude, and what dreams of happiness together!

Aunt Marta, on the other hand, would shake her head bitterly: she had seen so many ups and downs in her life, poor old lady, that by now she had no more trust left in the future; she feared for her daughter and didn't want her even to think about the possibility of escaping that poverty to which they were resigned; and, besides, she knew, she knew how much the madness of that dangerous dream was costing him.

But neither he nor Teresina would listen to her, and she protested in vain when a young composer, having heard Teresina at a concert, declared that it would be a real crime not to give her better teachers and thorough artistic instruction: in Naples, it was essential to send her to the Naples conservatory, cost what it might.

And then he, Micuccio, breaking off with his parents altogether, had sold a little farm of his that had been bequeathed to him by his uncle the priest, and in that way Teresina had gone to Naples to perfect her studies.

He hadn't seen her again since then; but he had received her letters from the conservatory and afterwards those of Aunt Marta, when Teresina was already launched on her artistic life, eagerly sought by the major theaters after her sensational debut at the San Carlo. At the foot of those shaky and hesitant letters, which the poor old lady scratched onto the paper as best she could, there were always a few words from *her*, from Teresina, who never had time to write: "Dear Micuccio, I go along with everything Mother is telling you. Stay healthy and keep caring for me." They had agreed that he would leave her five or six years' time to pursue her career without impediment: they were both young and could wait.

vano aspettare. E quelle lettere, nei cinque anni già scorsi, egli
le aveva sempre mostrate a chi voleva vederle, per distruggere
le calunnie che i suoi parenti scagliavano contro Teresina e la
madre. Poi s'era ammalato; era stato per morire; e in quell'oc-
casione, a sua insaputa, zia Marta e Teresina avevano inviato
al suo indirizzo una buona somma di danaro: parte se n'era
andata durante la malattia, ma il resto egli lo aveva strappato
a viva forza dalle mani dei suoi parenti e ora, ecco, veniva a
ridarlo a Teresina. Perché, denari—niente! egli non ne voleva. Non perché gli paressero limosina, avendo egli già speso
tanto per lei; ma . . . niente! non lo sapeva dire egli stesso, e
ora più che mai, lì, in quella casa . . .—denari, niente! Come
aveva aspettato tant'anni, poteva ancora aspettare . . . Che se
poi denari Teresina ne aveva d'avanzo, segno che l'avvenire
le si era schiuso, ed era tempo perciò che l'antica promessa
s'adempisse, a dispetto di chi non voleva crederci.

Micuccio sorse in piedi con le ciglia corrugate, come per
raffermarsi in questa conclusione; si soffiò di nuovo su le mani
diacce e pestò i piedi per terra.

—Freddo?—gli disse, passando, il cameriere.—Poco ci
vorrà, adesso. Venite qua in cucina. Starete meglio.

Micuccio non volle seguire il consiglio del cameriere, che
con quell'aria da gran signore lo sconcertava e l'indispettiva.
Si rimise a sedere e a pensare, costernato. Poco dopo una forte
scampanellata lo scosse.

—Dorina, la signora!—strillò il cameriere infilandosi in
fretta e furia la marsina mentre correva ad aprire; ma vedendo che Micuccio stava per seguirlo, s'arrestò bruscamente
per intimargli:

—Voi state qua; prima lasciate che la avverta.

—*Ohi, ohi, ohi* . . .—si lamentò una voce insonnolita dietro
la cortina; e poco dopo apparve un donnone tozzo affagottato
che strascicava una gamba e non riusciva ancora a spicciar
gli occhi, con uno scialle di lana fin sopra il naso, i capelli
ritinti d'oro.

Micuccio stette a mirarla allocchito. Anche lei, sorpresa,
sgranò tanto d'occhi in faccia all'estraneo.

—La signora,—ripeté Micuccio.

Allora Dorina riprese d'un subito coscienza:

—Eccomi, eccomi . . .—disse, togliendosi e buttando dietro
la cortina lo scialle e adoperandosi con tutta la pesante persona
a correr verso l'entrata.

And in the five years that had already elapsed, he had always shown those letters to anyone who wanted to see them, to combat the slanderous remarks his family would hurl at Teresina and her mother. Then he had fallen sick; he had been on the point of dying; and on that occasion, without his knowledge, Aunt Marta and Teresina had sent to his address a large sum of money; part had been spent during his illness, but the rest he had violently torn out of his family's hands and now, precisely, he was coming to return it to Teresina. Because money—no! He didn't want any. Not because it seemed like a handout, seeing that he had already spent so much on her; but . . . no! He himself was unable to say why, and now more than ever, there, in that house . . . money, no! Just as he had waited all those years, he could wait some more . . . Because if Teresina actually had money to spare, it was a sign that the future was now open to her, and therefore it was time for the old promise to be kept, in spite of anyone who refused to believe it.

Micuccio stood up with his brows knitted, as if to reassure himself about that conclusion; once again he blew on his ice-cold hands and stamped on the floor.

"Cold?" the servant said to him passing by. "It won't be long now. Come here into the kitchen. You'll be more comfortable."

Micuccio didn't want to follow the advice of the servant, who confused and irritated him with that lordly air. He sat down again and resumed thinking in dismay. Shortly afterward a loud ring roused him.

"Dorina, the mistress!" screamed the servant, hurriedly slipping on his tailcoat as he ran to open the door; but seeing that Micuccio was about to follow him, he stopped short and issued an order:

"You stay there; let me notify her first."

"Ohi, ohi, ohi . . . ," lamented a sleepy voice behind the curtain; and after a moment there appeared a large, stocky, carelessly dressed woman who trailed one leg on the ground and was still unable to keep her eyes open; she had a woolen shawl pulled up over her nose and her hair was dyed gold.

Micuccio kept looking at her foolishly. She too, in her surprise, opened her eyes wide when confronted by the outsider.

"The mistress," Micuccio repeated.

Then Dorina suddenly returned to consciousness:

"Here I am, here I am . . . ," she said, taking off the shawl and flinging it behind the curtain, and exerting her whole heavy body to run toward the entrance.

L'apparizione di quella strega ritinta, l'intimazione del cameriere diedero a un tratto a Micuccio, avvilito, un angoscioso presentimento. Sentì la voce stridula di zia Marta:

—Di là, in sala! in sala, Dorina!

E il cameriere e Dorina gli passarono davanti reggendo magnifiche ceste di fiori. Sporse il capo a guardare in fondo la sala illuminata e vide tanti signori in marsina, che parlavano confusamente. La vista gli s'annebbiò: era tanto lo stupore, tanta la commozione, che non s'accorse egli stesso che gli occhi gli si erano riempiti di lagrime: li chiuse, e in quel bujo si strinse tutto in sé, quasi per resistere allo strazio che gli cagionava una lunga squillante risata. Teresina rideva così, di là.

Un grido represso gli fece riaprir gli occhi, e si vide dinanzi—irriconoscibile—zia Marta, col cappello in capo, poveretta! oppressa da una ricca splendida mantiglia di velluto.

—Come! Micuccio . . . tu qui?

—Zia Marta . . .—esclamò Micuccio quasi impaurito, restando a contemplarla.

—Come mai!—seguitò la vecchietta sconvolta.—Senza avvertire? Che è stato? Quando sei arrivato? . . . Giusto questa sera . . . Oh Dio, Dio . . .

—Sono venuto per . . .—balbettò Micuccio, non sapendo più che dire.

—Aspetta!—lo interruppe zia Marta.—Come si fa? come si fa? Vedi quanta gente, figlio mio? È la festa di Teresina . . . la sua serata . . . Aspetta, aspetta un po' qua . . .

—Se voi,—si provò a dir Micuccio, a cui l'angoscia stringeva la gola,—se voi credete che me ne debba andare . . .

—No, aspetta un po', ti dico,—s'affrettò a rispondergli la buona vecchietta, tutta imbarazzata.

—Io però,—rispose Micuccio,—non saprei dove andare in questo paese . . . a quest'ora . . .

Zia Marta lo lasciò, facendogli con una mano inguantata segno d'attendere, ed entrò nella sala, nella quale poco dopo a Micuccio pareva si aprisse una voragine; vi s'era fatto d'improvviso silenzio. Poi udì, chiare, distinte, queste parole di Teresina:

—Un momento, signori.

Di nuovo la vista gli s'annebbiò, sotto l'imminenza dell'apparire di lei. Ma Teresina non venne, e la conversazione fu ripresa nella sala. Tornò invece dopo alquanti minuti, che

The apparition of that dyed witch, and the order given by the servant, suddenly gave Micuccio, in his dejection, an anguished presentiment. He heard Aunt Marta's shrill voice:

"Over there, into the salon, into the salon, Dorina!"

And the servant and Dorina passed by him carrying magnificent baskets of flowers. He leaned his head forward so he could observe the illuminated room at the far end, and he saw a great number of gentlemen in tailcoats talking confusedly. His sight grew dim; his amazement and agitation were so great that he himself didn't realize that his eyes had filled with tears; he closed them, and he shut himself up completely in that darkness, as if to resist the torment that a long, ringing laugh was causing him. It was Teresina laughing like that, in the other room.

A muffled cry made him open his eyes again, and he saw before him—unrecognizable—Aunt Marta, with her hat on her head, poor thing! and laden down by a costly and splendid velvet mantilla.

"What! Micuccio . . . you here?"

"Aunt Marta . . . ," exclaimed Micuccio, almost frightened, pausing to examine her closely.

"Whatever for?" continued the old lady, who was upset. "Without letting us know? What happened? When did you get here? . . . Tonight of all nights . . . Oh, God, God . . ."

"I've come to . . . ," Micuccio stammered, not knowing what more to say.

"Wait!" Aunt Marta interrupted him. "What's to be done? What's to be done? See all those people, son? It's Teresina's celebration . . . her night . . . Wait, wait here for a bit . . ."

"If you," Micuccio attempted to say, as anxiety tightened his throat, "if you think I ought to go . . ."

"No, wait a bit, I say," the kind old lady hastened to reply, all embarrassed.

"But," Micuccio responded, "I have no idea where to go in this town . . . at this hour . . ."

Aunt Marta left him, signaling to him with one of her gloved hands to wait, and entered the salon, in which a moment later Micuccio thought an abyss had opened; silence had suddenly fallen there. Then he heard, clear and distinct, these words of Teresina:

"One moment, gentlemen."

Again his sight grew dim with the imminence of her appearance. But Teresina did not come, and the conversation resumed in the salon. Instead, after a few minutes, which seemed an eternity to

a lui parvero eterni, zia Marta senza cappello, senza mantiglia, senza guanti, meno imbarazzata.

—Aspettiamo un po' qui, sei contento?—gli disse.—Io starò con te . . . Adesso si fa cena . . . Noi ce ne staremo qua. Dorina ci apparecchierà questo tavolino, e ceneremo insieme, qui; ci ricorderemo de' bei tempi, eh? . . . Non mi par vero di trovarmi con te, figlietto mio, qui, qui, appartati . . . Lì, capirai, tanti signori . . . Lei, poverina, non può farne a meno . . . La carriera, m'intendi? Eh, come si fa! . . . Li hai veduti i giornali? Cose grandi, figlio mio! Io, come sopra mare, sempre . . . Non mi par vero che me ne possa star qua con te, stasera.

E la buona vecchina, che aveva parlato parlato, istintivamente, per non dar tempo a Micuccio di pensare, alla fine sorrise e si stropicciò le mani, guardandolo intenerita.

Dorina venne ad apparecchiare la tavola in fretta, perché già lì, in sala, il pranzo era cominciato.

Verrà?—domandò cupo, Micuccio, con voce angosciata. —Dico, per vederla almeno.

—Certo che verrà,—gli rispose subito la vecchietta, sforzandosi di vincere l'impaccio.—Appena avrà un momentino di largo: già me l'ha detto.

Si guardarono tutt'e due e si sorrisero, come se finalmente si riconoscessero l'un l'altra. Attraverso l'impaccio e la commozione le loro anime avevan trovato la via per salutarsi con quel sorriso. «Voi siete zia Marta»—dicevan gli occhi di Micuccio.—«E tu, Micuccio, il mio caro e buon figliuolo, sempre lo stesso, poverino!»—dicevan quelli di zia Marta. Ma subito la buona vecchietta abbassò i suoi, perché Micuccio non vi leggesse altro. Si stropicciò di nuovo le mani e disse:

—Mangiamo eh?

—Ho una fame io!—esclamò tutto lieto e raffidato Micuccio.

—La croce, prima: qui posso farmela, davanti a te,—aggiunse la vecchietta con aria birichina, strizzando un occhio, e si segnò.

Il cameriere venne a offrir loro il primo servito. Micuccio stette bene attento a osservare come faceva zia Marta a trarre dal piatto la porzione. Ma quando venne la sua volta, nel levar le mani, pensò che le aveva sporche dal lungo viaggio, arrossì, si confuse, alzò gli occhi a soguardare il cameriere, il quale,

him, Aunt Marta came back, without her hat, without her mantilla, without her gloves, and less embarrassed.

"Let's wait here for a while, would that be all right?" she said to him. "I'll stay with you . . . Now they're having supper . . . We'll remain here. Dorina will set this little table for us, and we'll have supper together, here; we'll reminisce about the good old days, all right? . . . I can't believe it's true that I'm here with you, son, here, here, all by ourselves . . . In that room, you understand, all those gentlemen . . . She, poor girl, can't avoid them . . . Her career, you get my meaning? Ah, what can you do! . . . Have you seen the newspapers? Big doings, son! As for me, I'm all at sea, all the time . . . I can't believe I can really be here with you, tonight."

And the kind old lady, who had gone on talking, instinctively, to keep Micuccio from having time to think, finally smiled and rubbed her hands together, looking at him compassionately.

Dorina came to set the table hastily, because there, in the salon, the meal had already begun.

"Will she come?" Micuccio asked gloomily, with a troubled voice. "I mean, at least to see her."

"Of course she'll come," the old lady immediately replied, making an effort to get out of her awkward situation. "Just as soon as she has a minute free: she's already told me so."

They looked at each other and smiled at each other, as if they had finally recognized each other. Despite the embarrassment and the excitement, their souls had found the way to greet each other with that smile. "You're Aunt Marta," Micuccio's eyes said. "And you're Micuccio, my dear, good son, still the same, poor boy!" said Aunt Marta's. But suddenly the kind old lady lowered her own eyes, so that Micuccio might not read anything else in them. Again she rubbed her hands together and said:

"Let's eat, all right?"

"I'm good and hungry!" exclaimed Micuccio, quite happy and reassured.

"Let's cross ourselves first: here, in front of you, I can do it," added the old lady in a mischievous manner, winking an eye, and she made the sign of the cross.

The manservant came, bringing their first course. Micuccio observed with close attention the way that Aunt Marta transferred her helping from the serving platter. But when his turn came, as he raised his hands, it occurred to him that they were dirty from the long trip; he blushed, he got confused, he raised his eyes to

compitissimo ora, gli fece un lieve inchino col capo e un sorriso, come per invitarlo a servirsi. Fortunatamente zia Marta
venne a trarlo d'impaccio.

—Qua qua, Micuccio, ti servo io.

Se la sarebbe baciata dalla gratitudine! Avuta la porzione,
appena il cameriere si fu allontanato, si segnò anche lui in
fretta.

—Bravo figliuolo!—gli disse zia Marta.

Ed egli si sentì beato, a posto, e si mise a mangiare come
non aveva mangiato mai in vita sua, senza più pensare alle
sue mani, né al cameriere.

Tuttavia, ogni qual volta questi, entrando o uscendo dalla
salla, schiudeva la bussola a vetri e veniva di là come un'ondata
di parole confuse o qualche scoppio di risa, egli si voltava
turbato e poi guardava gli occhi dolenti e affettuosi della vecchina, quasi per leggervi una spiegazione. Ma vi leggeva invece
la preghiera di non chieder nulla per il momento, di rimettere
a più tardi le spiegazioni. E tutt'e due di nuovo si sorridevano
e si rimettevano a mangiare e a parlare del paese lontano,
d'amici e conoscenti, di cui zia Marta gli domandava notizie
senza fine.

—Non bevi?

Micuccio stese la mano per prender la bottiglia; ma, in
quella, la bussola della sala si riaprì; un fruscio di seta, tra
passi frettolosi: uno sbarbaglio, quasi la cameretta si fosse d'un
tratto violentemente illuminata, per accecarlo.

—Teresina . . .

E la voce gli morì su le labbra, dallo stupore. Ah, che regina!

Col le fiamme al volto, gli occhi sgranati, la bocca aperta,
egli restò a contemplarla, istupidito. Come mai ella . . . così!
Nudo il seno, nude le spalle, le braccia nude . . . tutta fulgente
di gemme e di stoffe . . . Non la vedeva, non la vedeva più
come una persona viva e reale innanzi a sé . . . Che gli diceva
ella? . . . Non la voce, né gli occhi, né il riso: nulla, nulla più
riconosceva di lei, in quell'apparizione di sogno.

—Come va? Stai bene ora, Micuccio? Bravo, bravo . . . Sei
stato malato, se non m'inganno . . . Ci rivedremo tra poco.
Tanto, qui hai con te la mamma . . . Siamo intesi . . .

E Teresina scappò via di nuovo in sala, tutta frusciante.

steal a glance at the servant, who, now the height of good manners, nodded slightly to him and smiled, as if inviting him to serve himself. Fortunately Aunt Marta helped him out of his predicament.

"Here, here, Micuccio, I'll serve you."

He could have kissed her out of gratitude! Once he received his helping, as soon as the servant had withdrawn, he too crossed himself hurriedly.

"Good boy!" Aunt Marta said to him.

And he felt carefree, contented, and started eating as he had never eaten in his life, no longer thinking about his hands or the servant.

Nevertheless, each and every time the latter, entering or leaving the salon, opened the glass double door, and a sort of wave of mingled words or some burst of laughter came from that direction, he turned around uneasily and then looked at the old lady's sorrowful, loving eyes, as if to read an explanation there. But what he read there instead was an urgent request to ask no more for the moment, to put off explanations till a later time. And again they both smiled at each other and resumed eating and talking about their far-off hometown, friends and acquaintances, concerning whom Aunt Marta asked him for news endlessly.

"Aren't you drinking?"

Micuccio put out his hand to take the bottle; but, just at that moment, the double door to the ballroom opened again; a rustle of silk, amid hurried steps: a flash, as if the little room had all at once been violently illuminated, in order to blind him.

"Teresina . . ."

And his voice died away on his lips, out of amazement. Ah, what a queen!

With face flushed, eyes bulging and mouth open, he stopped to gaze at her, dumbfounded. How could she ever . . . like that! Her bosom bare, her shoulders bare, her arms bare . . . all ablaze with jewels and rich fabrics . . . He didn't see her, he no longer saw her as a living, real person in front of him . . . What was she saying to him? . . . Not her voice, nor her eyes, nor her laugh: nothing, nothing of hers did he recognize any more in that dream apparition.

"How are things? Are you getting along all right now, Micuccio? Good, good . . . You were sick if I'm not mistaken . . . We'll get together again in a little while. In the meantime, you have Mother with you here . . . Is that a deal? . . ."

And Teresina ran off again into the salon, all a-rustle.

—Non mangi più?—domandò poco dopo zia Marta, timo-
rosa, per rompere l'attonimento muto di Micuccio.

Questi la guardò sbalordito.

—Mangia,—insistette la vecchina, indicandogli il piatto.

Micuccio si portò due dita al colletto affumicato e spiegaz-
zato e se lo stirò, provandosi a trarre un lungo respiro.

—Mangiare?

E agitò più volte le dita presso il mento, come se salutasse,
per significare: non mi va più, non posso. Stette ancora un
pezzo silenzioso, avvilito, assorto nella visione testè avuta, poi
mormorò:

—Come s'è fatta . . .

E vide che zia Marta scoteva amaramente il capo e che aveva
sospeso di mangiare anche lei, come se aspettasse.

—Manco a pensarci . . .—aggiunse poi, quasi tra sé, chiudendo gli occhi.

Vedeva ora, in quel suo bujo, l'abisso che si era aperto tra
loro due. No, non era più lei—quella lì—la sua Teresina. Era
tutto finito . . . da un pezzo, da un pezzo ed egli, sciocco, egli,
stupido, se n'accorgeva solo adesso. Glielo avevano detto in
paese, e lui s'era ostinato a non crederci . . . E ora, che figura
ci faceva a star più oltre lì, in quella casa? Se tutti quei signori,
se quel cameriere stesso avessero saputo che egli, Micuccio
Bonavino, s'era rotte le ossa a venire di così lontano, trentasei
ore di ferrovia, credendosi sul serio ancora il fidanzato di
quella regina, che risate, quei signori e quel cameriere e il
cuoco e il guattero e Dorina! Che risate, se Teresina lo avesse
trascinato al loro cospetto, lì in sala, dicendo: «Guardate,
questo poveretto, sonator di flauto, dice che vuol diventare
mio marito!» Ella, sì, ella glielo aveva promesso: ma come
avrebbe potuto lei stessa allora supporre che un giorno sarebbe divenuta così? Ed era anche vero, sì, che egli le aveva
schiuso quella via e le aveva dato modo d'incamminarvisi; ma
ecco, ella era ormai arrivata tanto, tanto lontano, che egli,
rimasto lì, sempre lo stesso, a sonare il flauto le domeniche
nella piazza del paese, come poteva più raggiungerla? Manco
a pensarci! E che cos'erano poi quei pochi quattrinucci spesi
allora per lei, divenuta adesso una gran signora? Si vergo-
gnava solo a pensare che qualcuno potesse sospettare che egli,
con la sua venuta, volesse accampar qualche diritto per quei
pochi soldi miserabili . . .—Ma gli sovvenne in quel punto di

"You're not eating any more?" Aunt Marta asked timorously after a brief pause, to cut short Micuccio's silent astonishment.

He looked at her in bewilderment.

"Eat," the old lady insisted, showing him his plate.

Micuccio raised two fingers to his smoke-blackened, crumpled collar and tugged at it, trying to draw a deep breath.

"Eat?"

And several times he wiggled his fingers near his chin as if waving goodbye, to indicate: I don't feel like it any more, I can't. For another while he remained silent, dejected, absorbed in the vision he had just seen, then he murmured:

"How she's turned out . . ."

And he saw that Aunt Marta was shaking her head bitterly and that she too had stopped eating, as if in expectation.

"It's not even to be thought of . . . ," he then added, as if to himself, closing his eyes.

Now he saw, in that darkness of his, the gulf that had opened between the two of them. No, she—that woman—was no longer his Teresina. It was all over . . . for some time, for some time, and he, the fool, he, the imbecile, was realizing it only now. They had told him so back home, and he had stubbornly refused to believe it . . . And now, how would he look staying on in that house? If all those gentlemen, if even that servant had known that he, Micuccio Bonavino, had worn himself out coming such a distance, thirty-six hours by train, seriously believing he was still the fiancé of that queen, what laughs they would raise, those gentlemen and that servant and the cook and the scullery boy and Dorina! What laughs, if Teresina had dragged him into their presence, in the salon there, saying: "Look, this pauper, this flute player, says he wants to become my husband!" She, yes, she had promised him this; but how could she herself suppose at that time that one day she would become what she now was? And it was also true, yes, that he had opened that path for her and had given her the means to travel it; but, there! by this time she had come so very far, how could he, who had stayed where he was, always the same, playing the flute on Sundays in the town square, catch up to her any more? It wasn't even to be thought of! And, then, what were those few paltry cents spent on her back then, now that she had become a great lady? He was ashamed merely to think that someone might suspect that he, with his coming, wanted to assert some rights in exchange for those few miserable pennies . . .—But at that moment he remembered

avere in tasca il denaro inviatogli da Teresina durante la malattia. Arrossì: ne provò onta, e si cacciò una mano nella tasca in petto della giacca, dov'era il portafogli.

—Ero venuto, zia Marta,—disse in fretta,—anche per restituirvi questo denaro che mi avete mandato. Vuol esser pagamento? restituzione? Che c'entrava! Vedo che Teresina è divenuta una . . . mi pare una regina! vedo che . . . niente! manco a pensarci più! Ma, questo denaro, no: non mi meritavo questo da lei . . . Che c'entra! È finita, e non se ne parla più . . . ma, denari, niente! Mi dispiace solo che non son tutti . . .

—Che dici, figliuolo mio?—cercò di interromperlo, tremante, afflitta e con le lagrime a gli occhi, zia Marta.

Micuccio le fe' cenno di star zitta.

—Non li ho spesi io: li hanno spesi i miei parenti, durante la malattia, senza ch'io lo sapessi. Ma vanno per quella miseria che spesi io allora . . . vi ricordate? Non ci fa nulla . . . Non ci pensiamo più. Qua c'è il resto. E io me ne vado.

—Ma come! Così d'un colpo?—esclamò zia Marta, cercando di trattenerlo.—Aspetta almeno che lo dica a Teresina. Non hai sentito che voleva rivederti? Vado a dirglielo . . .

—No, è inutile,—le rispose Micuccio, deciso.—Lasciatela star lì con quei signori; lì sta bene, al suo posto. Io, poveretto . . . L'ho veduta; m'è bastato . . . O piuttosto, andate pure . . . andate pure voi di là . . . Sentite come si ride? Io non voglio che si rida di me . . . Me ne vado.

Zia Marta interpretò nel peggior senso quella risoluzione improvvisa di Micuccio: come un atto di sdegno, un moto di gelosia. Le sembrava ormai, poverina, che tutti—vedendo sua figlia—dovessero d'un tratto concepire il più tristo dei sospetti, quello appunto per cui ella piangeva inconsolabile, trascinando senza requie il suo cordoglio segreto fra il tumulto di quella vita di lusso odioso che disonorava la sua vecchiaja vituperosamente.

—Ma io,—le scappò detto,—io ormai non posso più mica farle la guardia, figliuolo mio . . .

—Perché?—domandò Micuccio, leggendole a un tratto negli occhi il sospetto ch'egli non aveva ancora avuto; e si rabbujò in volto.

that he had in his pocket the money sent him by Teresina during his illness. He blushed: he felt a twinge of shame, and he plunged one hand into the breast pocket of his jacket, where his wallet was.

"I've come, Aunt Marta," he said hastily, "also to return to you this money you sent me. Is it meant as a payment? As repayment of a loan? What would that have to do with anything? I see that Teresina has become a . . . she looks like a queen to me! I see that . . . never mind! It's not even to be thought of any longer! But as for this money, no: I didn't deserve such treatment from her . . . Where does that come in? It's all over, and we won't talk about it any more . . . but money, no way! I'm only sorry that it's not all here . . ."

"What are you saying, son?" Aunt Marta tried to interrupt him, trembling, pained and with tears in her eyes.

Micuccio signaled to her to be silent.

"It wasn't I who spent it: my family spent it, during my illness, without my knowledge. But let's say it makes up for that trifle I spent back then . . . you remember? It doesn't matter . . . Let's think no more about it. Here is the difference. And I'm leaving."

"What! Like that, all of a sudden?" exclaimed Aunt Marta, trying to hold him back. "At least wait until I tell Teresina. Didn't you hear that she wanted to see you again? I'm going over to tell her . . ."

"No, it's no use," Micuccio replied, with determination. "Let her stay there with those gentlemen; it suits her there, she belongs there. I, poor fool . . . I got to see her; that was enough for me . . . No, now that I think of it, do go over there . . . you go there, too . . . Do you hear how they're laughing? I don't want the laugh to be on me . . . I'm leaving."

Aunt Marta interpreted that sudden determination of Micuccio's in the worst possible light: as an act of anger, a jealous reaction. By now it seemed to her, the poor woman, as if everybody—seeing her daughter—ought immediately to conceive the meanest of suspicions, that very one which caused her to weep inconsolably as, without a moment's rest, she bore the burden of her secret heartbreak amid the hubbub of that life of detestable luxury which ignominiously dishonored her old age.

"But I," the words escaped her, "by this time there's no way for me to stand guard over her, son . . ."

"Why?" asked Micuccio, suddenly reading in her eyes the suspicion he had not yet formulated; and his face turned dark.

La vecchietta si smarrì nella sua pena e si nascose la faccia con le mani tremule, ma non riuscì a frenar l'impeto delle lagrime irrompenti.

—Sì, sì, vattene, figlio mio, vattene . . .—disse soffocata dai singhiozzi.—Non è più per te, hai ragione . . . Se mi aveste dato ascolto . . .

—Dunque, —proruppe Micuccio chinandosi su lei e strappandole a forza una mano dal volto. Ma fu tanto accorato e miserevole lo sguardo con cui ella gli chiese pietà portandosi un dito su le labbra, che egli si frenò e aggiunse con altro tono, forzandosi a parlar piano:—Ah, lei dunque, lei . . . lei non è più degna di me. Basta, basta, me ne vado lo stesso . . . anzi, tanto più, ora . . . Che sciocco, zia Marta: non l'avevo capito! Non piangete . . . Tanto, che ci fa? Fortuna . . . fortuna . . .

Prese la valigetta e il sacchetto di sotto la tavola e s'avviava per uscire, quando gli venne in mente che lì dentro il sacchetto c'eran le belle lumie ch'egli aveva portate a Teresina dal paese.

—Oh, guardate, zia Marta,—riprese. Sciolse la bocca al sacchetto e, facendo riparo d'un braccio, versò su la tavola quei freschi frutti fragranti.—E se mi mettessi a tirare tutte queste lumie che le avevo portate su la testa di quei galantuomini?

—Per carità,—gemette la vecchina tra le lagrime, facendogli di nuovo cenno supplichevole di tacere.

—No, niente,—soggiunse Micuccio ridendo acre e rimettendosi in tasca il sacchetto vuoto.—Le lascio a voi sola, zia Marta. E dire che ci ho anche pagato il dazio . . . Basta. A voi sola, badate bene . . . A lei dite così: «Buona fortuna!» a nome mio.

Riprese la valigetta e andò via. Ma per la scala, un senso d'angoscioso smarrimento lo vinse: solo, abbandonato, di notte, in una grande città sconosciuta, lontano dal suo paese; deluso, avvilito, scornato. Giunse al portone, vide che pioveva a dirotto. Non ebbe il coraggio d'avventurarsi per quelle vie ignote, sotto quella pioggia. Rientrò pian piano, rifece una rampa di scala, poi sedette sul primo scalino e, appoggiando i gomiti su le ginocchia e la testa tra le mani, si mise a piangere silenziosamente.

Sul finir della cena, Sina Marnis fece un'altra comparsa nella

The old lady became bewildered in her sorrow and hid her face in her trembling hands, but failed to check the onrush of the tears that now gushed forth.

"Yes, yes, go, son, go . . .," she said, strangled by sobs. "She's not for you any more, you're right . . . If the two of you had listened to me . . ."

"And so," Micuccio burst out, bending over her and violently pulling one hand away from her face. But so afflicted and wretched was the look with which she begged him for mercy, as she put a finger to her lips, that he restrained himself and added in a different tone of voice, making an effort to speak softly: "And so she, she . . . she is no longer worthy of me. Enough, enough, I'm leaving just the same . . . in fact, all the more, now . . . What a dumbbell, Aunt Marta: I hadn't understood! Don't cry . . . Anyway, what does it matter? Fate . . . fate . . ."

He took his little suitcase and little sack from under the table and was on his way out when he recalled that there, in the sack, were the beautiful citrons he had brought for Teresina from their hometown.

"Oh, look, Aunt Marta," he continued. He opened the top of the sack and, creating a barrier with one arm, he emptied that fresh, aromatic fruit onto the table. "And what if I started tossing all these citrons I brought for her at the heads of those honorable gentlemen?"

"For mercy's sake," the old lady groaned amid her tears, once more making a beseeching sign to him to be silent.

"No, of course I won't," added Micuccio, smiling sourly and putting the empty sack in his pocket. "I'm leaving them for you alone, Aunt Marta. And to think that I even paid duty on them . . . Enough. For you alone, mind me now. As for her, tell her 'Good luck!' from me."

He picked up the valise again and left. But on the stairs, a sense of anguished bewilderment overpowered him: alone, deserted, at night, in a big city he didn't know, far from his home; disappointed, dejected, put to shame. He made it to the street door, saw that there was a downpour of rain. He didn't have the courage to venture onto those unfamiliar streets in a rain like that. He went back in very quietly, walked back up one flight of stairs, then sat down on the first step and, leaning his elbows on his knees and his head on his hands, began to weep silently.

When the supper was finished, Sina Marnis made another ap-

cameretta; ma trovò sola la mamma che piangeva, mentre di là quei signori schiamazzavano e ridevano.

—È andato via?—domandò sorpresa.

Zia Marta accennò di sì col capo, sensa guardarla. Sina fissò gli occhi nel vuoto, assorta, poi sospirò:

—Poveretto . . .

—Guarda,—le disse la madre, senza frenar più le lagrime col tovagliuolo.—Ti aveva portato le lumie . . .

—Oh, belle!—esclamò Sina rallegrandosi. Strinse un braccio alla vita e ne prese con l'altra mano quanto più poteva portarne.

—No, di là no!—protestò vivamente la madre.

Ma Sina scrollò le spalle nude e corse in sala gridando:

—Lumie di Sicilia! Lumie di Sicilia!

pearance in the little room; but she found her mother alone crying, while back there the gentlemen were clamoring and laughing.

"He left?" she asked in surprise.

Aunt Marta nodded affirmatively, without looking at her. Sina stared into space, lost in thoughts, then sighed:

"Poor guy . . ."

"Look," her mother said to her, no longer stemming her tears with the tablecloth. "He had brought citrons for you . . ."

"Oh, what beauties!" exclaimed Sina, cheering up. She clutched one arm to her waist and with the other hand gathered up as many as she could carry.

"No, not in there!" her mother vigorously protested.

But Sina shrugged her bare shoulders and ran into the salon shouting:

"Citrons from Sicily! Citrons from Sicily!"

CON ALTRI OCCHI

Dall'ampia finestra aperta sul giardinetto pensile della casa l'aria mattinale pura e fresca ilarava la linda cameretta. Un ramo di mandorlo, che pareva tutto fiorito di farfalle, si protendeva verso la finestra; e, misto al roco quatto chioccolìo della vaschetta in mezzo al giardino, si udiva lo scampanìo festivo delle chiese lontane e il garrir delle rondini ebre d'aria e di sole.

Nel ritrarsi dalla finestra sospirando, Anna si accorse che il marito quella mattina s'era dimenticato di guastare il letto, come soleva ogni volta, perché i servi non s'avvedessero che non si era coricato in camera sua. Poggiò i gomiti sul letto non toccato, poi vi si stese con tutto il busto, piegando il bel capo biondo su i guanciali e socchiudendo gli occhi, come per assaporare nella freschezza del lino i sonni che egli soleva dormirvi. Uno stormo di rondini sbalestrate guizzarono strillando innanzi alla finestra.

—Meglio se ti fossi coricato qui . . .—mormorò ella con languore poco dopo, e si rialzò stanca.

Il marito doveva partire quella sera stessa, ed Anna era entrata nella camera di lui a preparargli l'occorrente per il viaggio.

Nell'aprire l'armadio, sentì come uno squittìo nel cassetto interno e subito si ritrasse, impaurita. Tolse da un angolo della camera un bastone dal manico ricurvo e, tenendosi stretta alle gambe la veste, prese il bastone per la punta e si provò ad aprire con esso, così discosta, il cassetto. Ma nel tirare, invece del cassetto, venne fuori agevolmente dal bastone una lucida lama insidiosa. Anna, che non se l'aspettava, n'ebbe vivo ribrezzo e si lasciò cadere di mano il fodero dello stocco.

In quella, un altro squittìo la fece voltare di scatto verso la finestra, in dubbio se anche il primo fosse partito da qualche rondine fuggitiva.

Scostò con un piede l'arma sguainata e trasse in fuori tra i

WITH OTHER EYES

Through the large window that opened onto the house's little hanging garden, the pure, fresh morning air made the pretty little room cheerful. An almond branch, which seemed to be all a-blossom with butterflies, projected toward the window; and, mingled with the hoarse, muffled gurgle of the small basin in the center of the garden, was heard the festive peal of faraway churchbells and the chirping of the swallows intoxicated with the air and the sunshine.

As she stepped away from the window, sighing, Anna noticed that her husband that morning had forgotten to rumple his bed, as he used to do each time, so that the servants couldn't tell that he hadn't slept in his room. She rested her elbows on the untouched bed, then stretched out on it with her whole torso, bending her pretty blonde head over the pillows and half-closing her eyes, as if to savor, in the freshness of the linens, the slumbers he was accustomed to enjoy there. A flock of swallows flashed headlong past the window, shrieking.

"You would have done better to sleep here . . . ," she murmured languidly after a moment, and got up again wearily.

Her husband was to set out that very evening, and Anna had come into his room to prepare for him the things he needed for the trip.

As she opened the wardrobe, she heard what seemed to be a squeak in the inner drawer and quickly drew back, startled. From a corner of the room she picked up a walking stick with a curved handle and, holding her dress tight against her legs, took the stick by the tip and, standing that way at a distance, tried to open the drawer with it. But as she pulled, instead of the drawer coming out, an insidious gleaming blade emerged smoothly from inside the stick. Anna, who hadn't expected this, felt an extreme repulsion and let the scabbard of the swordstick drop from her hand.

At that moment, a second squeak made her turn abruptly toward the window, uncertain whether the first one as well had come from some rapidly passing swallow.

With one foot she pushed aside the unsheathed weapon and

due sportelli aperti il cassetto pieno d'antichi abiti smessi del marito. Per improvvisa curiosità si mise allora a rovistare in esso e, nel riporre una giacca logora e stinta, le avvenne di tastare negli orli sotto il soppanno come un cartoncino, scivolato lì dalla tasca in petto sfondata; volle veder che fosse quella carta smarrita chi sa da quanti anni e dimenticata; e così per caso Anna scoprì il ritratto della prima moglie del marito.

Trasalì dapprima, impallidendo; si passò rapidamente una mano su i capelli scossi da un brivido e, con la vista intorbidata e il cuor sospeso, corse alla finestra, ove rimase attonita a mirare l'immagine sconosciuta, quasi con un senso di sgomento.

La voluminosa acconciatura del capo e la veste d'antica foggia non le fecero notare in prima la bellezza di quel volto; ma appena poté coglierne le fattezze, astraendole dall'abbigliamento che ora, dopo tanti anni, appariva goffo, e fissarne specialmente gli occhi, se ne sentì ferita e, col sangue, un impeto d'odio le balzò dal cuore al cervello: odio quasi di postuma gelosia; l'odio misto di sprezzo che ella aveva provato per colei nell'innamorarsi di Vittore Brivio, dopo undici anni dalla tragedia coniugale che aveva distrutto d'un colpo la prima casa di lui.

Anna aveva odiato quella donna non sapendo intendere come avesse potuto tradir l'uomo ora da lei adorato e, in secondo luogo, perché i suoi parenti si erano opposti al matrimonio suo col Brivio, come se questi fosse stato responsabile dell'infamia e della morte violenta della moglie infedele.—Era lei, sì, era lei senza dubbio! la prima moglie di Vittore: colei che s'era uccisa!

Ne ebbe la conferma dalla dedica scritta sul dorso del ritratto: *Al mio Vittore la sua Almira—11 novembre 1873.*

Anna aveva notizie molto vaghe della morta: sapeva soltanto che Vittore, scoperto il tradimento, la aveva costretta, con l'impassibilità di un giudice, a togliersi la vita.

Ora ella si richiamò con sodisfazione alla mente questa terribile condanna del marito, irritata da quel «mio» e da quel «sua» della dedica, come se colei avesse voluto ostentare la strettezza del legame che reciprocamente aveva unito lei e Vittore, unicamente per farle dispetto.

pulled out, between the two open doors of the wardrobe, the drawer full of her husband's old suits that he no longer wore. Out of sudden curiosity she began to rummage around in it and, as she was putting back a worn-out, faded jacket, she happened to feel, in the hem under the lining, a sort of small paper, which had slipped down there through the torn bottom of the breast pocket; she wanted to see what that paper was which had gone astray and been forgotten there who knows how many years ago; and so by accident Anna discovered the portrait of her husband's first wife.

At first she had a start and turned pale; she quickly ran a hand through her hair, which was shaken by a shudder and, with her vision blurred and her heart stopped, she ran to the window, where she remained in astonishment gazing at the unfamiliar image, almost with a feeling of panic.

The bulky hair style and the old-fashioned dress kept her from noticing at first the beauty of that face; but as soon as she was able to concentrate on the features, separating them from the attire, which now, after so many years, looked ludicrous, and to pay special attention to the eyes, she felt wounded by them and, together with her blood, a flush of hatred leaped from her heart to her brain; a hatred as if caused by posthumous jealousy; that hatred mingled with contempt which she had felt for that other woman when she fell in love with Vittore Brivio, eleven years after the marital tragedy that had at one blow destroyed his first household.

Anna had hated that woman, unable to comprehend how she had been capable of betraying the man whom she now worshiped, and in the second place, because her family had objected to her marriage with Brivio, as if *he* had been responsible for the disgrace and violent death of his unfaithful wife.—It was she, yes, it was she beyond a doubt! Vittore's first wife: the one who had killed herself!

She found the proof in the dedication written on the back of the portrait: "To my Vittore, his Almira—November 11, 1873."

Anna had very vague information about the dead woman: she knew only that Vittore, when the betrayal was discovered, had, with the impassivity of a judge, forced her to take her own life.

Now with satisfaction she recalled that terrible sentence issued by her husband, and was irritated by that "my" and "his" of the dedication, as if the other woman had wished to flaunt the closeness of the mutual ties that had bound her and Vittore, solely to spite her.

A quel primo lampo d'odio guizzato, qual fuoco fatuo, dalla rivalità per lei sola ormai sussistente, seguì nell'anima di Anna la femminile curiosità di esaminare i lineamenti di quel volto, ma quasi trattenuta dalla strana costernazione che si prova alla vista di un oggetto appartenuto a una persona tragicamente morta; costernazione ora più viva, ma a lei non ignota, poiché n'era compenetrato l'amor suo per il marito appartenuto già a quell'altra donna.

Esaminandone il volto, Anna notò subito la dissomiglianza assoluta dal suo, e le sorse a un tempo dal cuore la domanda, come mai il marito che aveva amato quella donna, quella giovinetta, certo bella per lui, si fosse poi potuto innamorare di lei così dissimile.

Sembrava bello, molto più bello del suo anche a lei quel volto che, dal ritratto, appariva bruno. Ecco: e quelle labbra si erano congiunte nel bacio alle labbra di lui; ma perché mai a gli angoli della bocca quella piega dolorosa? e perché così mesto lo sguardo di quegli occhi intensi? Tutto il volto spirava un profondo cordoglio; e Anna fu colpita ed ebbe quasi dispetto della bontà umile e vera che quei lineamenti esprimevano, e quindi un moto di repulsione e di ribrezzo, sembrandole a un tratto di scorgere nello sguardo di quegli occhi la medesima espressione degli occhi suoi allorché, pensando al marito, ella si guardava nello specchio, la mattina, dopo essersi acconciata.

Ebbe appena il tempo di cacciarsi in tasca il ritratto: il marito si presentò, sbuffando, sulla soglia della camera.

—Che hai fatto? Al solito? Ogni volta che entri in questa camera per rassettare mi scombini tutto . . .

Poi, vedendo lo stocco sguainato per terra:

—Hai tirato di scherma con gli abiti dell'armadio?

E rise di quel suo riso che partiva soltanto dalla gola, quasi qualcuno gliel'avesse vellicata; e, ridendo così, guardò la moglie, come se domandasse a lei il perché del suo proprio riso. Guardando, batteva di continuo le palpebre celerissimamente su gli occhietti acuti, neri, irrequieti.

Vittore Brivio trattava la moglie come una bambina non d'altro capace che di quell'amore ingenuo, esclusivo e quasi puerile, di cui si sentiva circondato spesso con fastidio e al quale egli si era prefisso di prestar solo attenzione a tempo

That first flare-up of hatred, ignited, like a will-o'-the-wisp, by a rivalry which by now existed only for her, was succeeded in Anna's mind by feminine curiosity: she desired to examine the features of that face, although she was partially restrained by the odd sorrow one feels at the sight of an object that belonged to a person who died tragically—a sorrow that was sharper now, but not unfamiliar to her, because it permeated her love for her husband, who had formerly belonged to that other woman.

Examining her face, Anna immediately noticed how entirely dissimilar it was to hers, and at the same time there arose in her heart the question of how the husband who had loved that woman, that girl, whom he must have found beautiful, could ever have later fallen in love with *her*, who was so different.

It seemed beautiful, even to her it seemed much more beautiful than hers—that face which, from the portrait, looked swarthy. There!—those lips had joined in a kiss with his lips; but why that sorrowful crease at the corners of the mouth? And why was the gaze in those intense eyes so sad? The entire face spoke of deep suffering; and Anna was moved and almost vexed by the humble and genuine kindness expressed by those features, and after that she felt a twinge of repulsion and disgust, when all at once she believed she had observed in the gaze of those eyes the same expression her own eyes had, whenever, thinking of her husband, she looked at herself in the mirror, in the morning, after arranging her hair.

She had barely enough time to thrust the portrait into her pocket: her husband appeared, fuming, on the threshold to the room.

"What have you been doing? The usual thing? Every time you come into this room to straighten up, you rearrange everything . . . "

Then, seeing the unsheathed swordstick on the floor:

"Have you been fencing with the suits in the wardrobe?"

And he laughed that laugh of his which came only from the throat, as if someone had tickled him there; and, laughing in that fashion, he looked at his wife, as if asking *her* why he himself was laughing. As he looked, his eyelids constantly blinked with extreme rapidity against his sharp, black, restless little eyes.

Vittore Brivio treated his wife like a child capable of nothing but that ingenuous, exclusive and almost childish love with which he felt himself surrounded, frequently to his annoyance, and to which he had determined to pay attention only on due occasion, and even

debito, mostrando anche allora una condiscendenza quasi soffusa di lieve ironia, come se volesse dire: «Ebbene, via! per
un po' diventerò anch'io bambino con te: bisogna fare anche
questo, ma non perdiamo troppo tempo!».

Anna si era lasciata cadere ai piedi la vecchia giacca in cui
aveva trovato il ritratto. Egli la raccattò infilzandola con la
punta dello stocco, poi chiamò dalla finestra nel giardino il
servotto che fungeva anche da cocchiere e che in quel momento attaccava al biroccio il cavallo. Appena il ragazzo si
presentò in maniche di camicia nel giardino innanzi alla finestra, il Brivio gli buttò in faccia sgarbatamente la giacca
infilzata, accompagnando la limosina con un: «Tieni, è per
te!».

—Così avrai meno da spazzolare—aggiunse, rivolto alla
moglie,—e da rassettare, speriamo!

E di nuovo emise, lappoleggiando, quel suo riso stentoreo.

Altre volte il marito si era allontanato dalla città e non per
pochi giorni soltanto, partendo anche di notte come quella
volta; ma Anna, ancora sotto l'impressione vivissima della scoperta del ritratto in quel giorno stesso, provò una strana paura
di restar sola, e pianse nel dargli l'addio.

Vittore Brivio, tutto frettoloso nel timore di non fare a
tempo e preoccupato evidentemente dei suoi affari, accolse
con mal garbo quel pianto insolito della moglie.

—Come! Perché? Via, via, bambinate!

E andò via di furia, senza neppur salutarla.

Anna sussultò al rumor della porta ch'egli si chiuse dietro
con impeto; rimase col lume in mano nella saletta e sentì rag-
gelarsi le lagrime negli occhi. Poi si scosse e si ritirò in fretta
nella sua camera, per andar subito a letto.

Nella camera già in ordine ardeva il lampadino da notte.

—Va' pure a dormire—disse Anna alla cameriera che la
attendeva.—Fo da me. Buona notte.

Spense il lume, ma invece di posarlo, come soleva, su la
mensola, lo posò sul tavolino da notte, presentendo—pur contro la propria volontà—che forse ne avrebbe avuto bisogno
più tardi. Cominciò a svestirsi in fretta, tenendo gli occhi fissi

at those times displaying an indulgence partially mixed with light irony, as if he meant to say: "All right, have it your way! For a while I too will become a child along with you: this, too, must be done, but let's not waste too much time!"

Anna had let the old jacket in which she had found the portrait drop to her feet. He picked it up, piercing it with the point of the swordstick; then, through the garden window he called the young servant who also doubled as a coachman and was at that moment harnessing the horse to the cabriolet. As soon as the boy showed up, in his shirt sleeves, in the garden in front of the window, Brivio rudely threw the dangling jacket in his face, accompanying the handout with a: "Take it, it's yours."

"This way, you'll have less to brush," he added, turning toward his wife, "and to straighten up, I hope!"

And again, blinking, he uttered that stentorean[1] laugh of his.

On other occasions her husband had traveled out of the city, and not merely for a few days, also leaving at night like this time; but Anna, still extremely shaken by the discovery of the portrait on that very day, felt a strange fear of being left alone and wept when she said goodbye to him.

Vittore Brivio, in a great rush from fear of being late and evidently preoccupied with his business, reacted ill-manneredly to those uncustomary tears of his wife.

"What! Why? Come on now, come on now, that's so childish!"

And he left in hot haste, without even saying goodbye.

Anna jumped at the sound of the door that he closed behind him with force; she remained in the little room with the lamp in her hand and felt her tears growing cold in her eyes. Then she roused herself and hurriedly withdrew to her room, intending to go to bed at once.

In the room, which was already prepared, the little night light was burning.

"Go to bed," Anna said to the maid who was waiting for her. "I'll take care of things myself. Good night."

She extinguished the lamp, but instead of putting it on the shelf, as she usually did, she put it on the night table, with the feeling—actually against her will—that she might need it later. She started to undress hastily, gazing fixedly at the floor in front of her. When

---

[1] From a later revision, it would appear that Pirandello meant to say, not that the laugh was loud but that it was *stentato* (forced and unnatural).

a terra, innanzi a sé. Quando la veste le cadde attorno ai piedi, pensò che il ritratto era là e con viva stizza si sentì guardata e commiserata da quegli occhi dolenti, che tanto la avevano colpita. Si chinò risolutamente a raccogliere dal tappeto la veste e la posò senza ripiegarla su la poltrona a piè del letto, come se la tasca che nascondeva il ritratto e il viluppo della stoffa dovessero e potessero impedirle di ricostruirsi l'immagine di quella morta.

Appena coricata, chiuse gli occhi e s'impose di seguir col pensiero il marito per la via che conduceva alla stazione ferroviaria. Se l'impose per astiosa ribellione al sentimento che tutto quel giorno la aveva tenuta vigile a osservare, a studiare il marito. Sapeva donde quel sentimento le era venuto e voleva espungerlo da sè.

Nello sforzo della volontà, che le produceva una viva sovreccitazione nervosa, si rappresentò con straordinaria chiaroveggenza la via lunga, deserta nella notte, rischiarata dai fanali projettanti il loro lume tremulo sul lastrico che pareva ne palpitasse: a piè d'ogni fanale, un cerchio d'ombra; le botteghe, tutte chiuse; ed ecco la vettura che conduceva Vittore: come se ella la avesse aspettata al varco, si mise a seguirla fino alla stazione: vide il treno lugubre, sotto la tettoia a vetri; una gran confusione di gente in quell'interno vasto, fumido, mal rischiarato, cupamente sonoro: ecco, il treno partiva; e, come se veramente ella lo vedesse allontanare, sparir nelle tenebre, rientrò d'un subito in sé, aprì gli occhi nella camera silenziosa e provò un senso angoscioso di vuoto, come se qualcosa le mancasse dentro. Sentì allora confusamente, in un baleno, smarrendosi, che da tre anni forse, dal momento in cui era partita dalla casa paterna, ella era in quel vuoto, di cui ora soltanto assumeva coscienza. Non se n'era accorta prima, perché ella lo aveva riempito solo di sè stessa, dell'amor suo, quel vuoto; se ne accorgeva ora, perchè in tutto quel giorno aveva tenuto quasi sospeso l'amor suo, per vedere, per osservare.

—Non mi ha neppure salutata!—pensò; e si mise a piangere di nuovo, quasi che questo pensiero fosse determinatamente la cagione del pianto.

Sorse a seder sul letto: ma subito arrestò la mano tesa, nel levarsi, per prendere dalla veste il fazzoletto. Via, era ormai

her dress fell around her feet, it occurred to her that the portrait was there, and with acute vexation she felt herself being looked at and pitied by those sorrowful eyes, which had made such an impression on her. With determination she stooped down to pick up the dress from the carpet and, without folding it, she placed it on the armchair at the foot of the bed, as if the pocket that hid the portrait and the tangle of the fabric should and could prevent her from reconstructing the image of that dead woman.

As soon as she lay down, she closed her eyes and forced herself to follow her husband mentally along the road leading to the railroad station. She forced this upon herself as a spiteful rebellion against the feeling that had kept her alert all day long observing and studying her husband. She knew where that feeling had come from and she wanted to get rid of it.

In this effort of her will, which caused her an acute nervous agitation, she pictured to herself with an extraordinary second sight the long road, deserted at night, illuminated by the streetlamps projecting their wavering light onto the pavement, which seemed to palpitate because of it; at the foot of every lamp, a circle of shadow; the shops, all closed; and there was the carriage in which Vittore was riding: as if she had been lying in wait for it, she started following it all the way to the station: she saw the gloomy train beneath the glass shed; a great many people milling about in that vast, smoky, poorly lit, mournfully echoing interior: now the train was pulling out; and, as if she were really watching it move away and disappear into the darkness, she suddenly came back to herself, opened her eyes in the silent room and felt an anguished feeling of emptiness, as if something were missing inside her. She then felt confusedly, in a flash, becoming bewildered, that for three years perhaps, from the moment in which she had left her parents' home, she had been in that void of which she was only now becoming conscious. She had been unaware of it before, because she had filled that void with herself alone, with her love; she was becoming aware of it now, because all day long she had, as it were, suspended her love in order to look and to observe.

"He didn't even say goodbye to me," she thought; and she started to cry again, as if that thought were the definite reason for her tears.

She sat up in bed: but she suddenly held back the hand she had stretched out, while sitting up, to get her handkerchief from her dress. No, it was no longer any use to forbid herself to take another

inutile vietarsi di rivedere, di riosservare quel ritratto! Lo prese. Riaccese il lume.

Come se la era raffigurata diversamente quella donna! Contemplandone ora la vera effigie, provava rimorso dei sentimenti che la immaginaria le aveva suggeriti. Si era raffigurata una donna, piuttosto grassa e rubiconda, con gli occhi lampeggianti e ridenti, inclinata al riso, a gli spassi volgari . . . E invece, ora, eccola: una giovinetta che dalle pure fattezze spirava un'anima profonda e addolorata; dagli occhi, quasi un silenzio assorbente; diversa sì, da lei, ma non nel senso sguajato di prima: al contrario; anzi quella bocca pareva non avesse dovuto mai sorridere, mentre la sua tante volte e lietamente aveva riso, e certo, se bruno quel volto (come dal ritratto appariva), di un'aria men ridente del suo, biondo e roseo.

Perché, perché così triste?

Un pensiero odioso le balenò in mente, e subito con violenta repulsione ella staccò gli occhi dall'immagine di quella donna, scorgendovi d'improvviso un'insidia non solo alla sua pace, all'amor suo, che pure in quel giorno aveva ricevuto più d'una ferita, ma anche alla sua orgogliosa dignità di donna onesta che non s'era mai permesso neppure il più lontano pensiero contro il marito.

Colei aveva avuto un amante! E per lui forse ella era sì triste, per quell'amore adultero, e non per il marito!

Buttò il ritratto sul comodino e spense di nuovo il lume, sperando di addormentarsi, questa volta, senza pensar più a quella donna, con la quale ella non poteva aver nulla di comune. Ma, chiudendo le palpebre, rivide subito, suo malgrado, gli occhi della morta, e invano cercò di scacciare quella vista.

—Non per lui, non per lui!—mormorò allora con smaniosa ostinazione, come se, ingiuriandola, sperasse di liberarsene.

E si sforzò di richiamare alla memoria quanto sapeva intorno a quell'altro, all'amante, costringendo quasi lo sguardo e la tristezza di quegli occhi a rivolgersi non più a lei, ma all'antico amante, di cui ella conosceva soltanto il nome: Arturo Valli. Sapeva che costui aveva sposato qualche anno dopo quella tragedia, quasi a provare ch'era innocente della colpa che voleva addebitargli Vittore, di cui aveva respinto energicamente la sfida, protestando che non si sarebbe mai battuto con un pazzo assassino. Dopo questo rifiuto, Vittore aveva

look at that portrait, to reexamine it! She took it. She put the light back on.

How differently she had pictured that woman! Now, contemplating her real likeness, she felt remorse for the feelings that the imaginary woman had aroused in her. She had pictured a woman rather fat and ruddy, with flashing, smiling eyes, always ready to laugh, enjoying common amusements . . . And instead, now, there she was: a young woman whose cleancut features expressed a profound, sorrowful soul; whose eyes expressed a sort of all-absorbing silence; yes, different from herself, but not in that earlier vulgar sense: just the opposite; no, that mouth looked as if it had never smiled, whereas her own had laughed so often and so gaily; and surely, if that face was swarthy (as it seemed to be from the portrait), it had a less smiling air than her own blonde and rosy face.

Why, why so sad?

A hateful thought flashed across her mind, and all at once with violent repulsion she tore her eyes away from that woman's picture, suddenly discovering in it a snare threatening not only to her peace of mind, to her love, which, as it was, had received more than one wound that day, but also to her proud dignity as an honest woman who had never allowed herself even the remotest thought hostile to her husband.

That woman had had a lover! And perhaps it was because of him she was so sad, because of that adulterous love, and not because of her husband!

She tossed the portrait onto the bedside table and put out the light again, hoping to fall asleep this time without thinking any more about that woman, with whom she could have nothing in common. But, closing her eyes, she suddenly saw, in spite of herself, the dead woman's eyes, and sought in vain to dispel that sight.

"Not because of him, not because of him!" she then murmured with frenzied persistence, as if by insulting her she hoped to be rid of her.

And she made an effort to recall everything she knew about that other man, the lover, as if compelling the gaze and the sadness of those eyes to look no longer at her but at the former lover, whom she knew only by name: Arturo Valli. She knew that he had married a few years later as if to prove his innocence of the blame that Vittore wanted to ascribe to him, that he had vigorously declined Vittore's challenge to a duel, protesting that he would never fight with a mad killer. After this refusal, Vittore had threatened to kill

minacciato di ucciderlo ovunque lo avesse incontrato, foss'anche in chiesa; e allora egli era andato via con la moglie dal paese, nel quale era poi tornato, appena Vittore, riammogliatosi, se n'era partito.

Ma dalla tristezza di questi avvenimenti da lei rievocati, dalla viltà del Valli e, dopo tant'anni, dall'obblio completo del marito, il quale, come se nulla fosse stato, si era potuto rimettere nella vita e riammogliare, dalla gioja che ella stessa aveva provato nel divenir moglie di Vittore, da quei tre anni ch'ella aveva passati insieme con lui senza mai un pensiero per quell'altra, inaspettatamente un motivo di compassione per costei s'impose ad Anna, spontaneo; ne rivide viva la immagine e le parve che con quegli occhi, intensi di tanta pena, colei le dicesse:

«Io sola però ne son morta! Voi tutti vivete!»

Si vide, si sentì sola nella casa: ebbe paura. Viveva, sì, lei; ma da tre anni, dal giorno delle nozze, non aveva più riveduto, neanche una volta, i suoi genitori, la sorella. Lei che li adorava, figliuola docile, sorella confidente, aveva potuto ribellarsi alla loro volontà per amore del marito; per lui, respinto dai suoi, si era mortalmente ammalata, sarebbe morta senza dubbio, se i medici non avessero piegato il padre ad accontentarla. E il padre aveva ceduto, non consentendo però, anzi giurando che ella per lui, per la casa, dopo quelle nozze, non sarebbe più esistita. Oltre alla differenza di età, ai diciotto anni che il marito aveva più di lei, ostacolo più grave per il padre era stata la posizione finanziaria del Brivio soggetta a rapidi cambiamenti per le imprese rischiose a cui egli, uomo intraprendentissimo e di straordinaria attività, soleva lanciarsi con temeraria fiducia in se stesso e nella fortuna.

In tre anni di matrimonio Anna, circondata di agi, aveva potuto ritenere ingiuste o dettate da prevenzione contraria le considerazioni della prudenza paterna, quanto alle sostanze del marito, nel quale del resto ella, ignara, riponeva la medesima fiducia che egli in se stesso; quanto poi alla differenza d'età, finora nessun argomento manifesto di delusione per lei o di meraviglia per gli altri, poiché dagli anni il Brivio non risentiva il menomo danno nella persona piccola vivacissima

him wherever he came across him, even in church; and then he had left the town with his wife, returning later as soon as Vittore, remarried, had departed.

But from the sadness of those events which she now brought back to mind, from Valli's cowardice and, after so many years, from the way the first wife had been completely consigned to oblivion by her husband, who had been able to resume his life and remarry as if nothing had happened, from the joy that she herself had felt upon becoming Vittore's wife, from those three years she had spent together with him with never a thought about that other woman, unexpectedly a cause of pity for her spontaneously forced itself upon Anna; she saw her image again vividly and it seemed to her that with those eyes, intense from so much suffering, that woman was saying to her:

"But I'm the only one that died as a result! All of you are still living!"

She saw, she felt, that she was alone in the house: she got frightened. Yes, *she* was living; but for three years, since her wedding day, she hadn't seen her parents or sister, not even once. She who adored them, a dutiful daughter, a trusting sister, had had the courage to oppose their wishes out of love for her husband; for his sake, when he was rejected by his own family, she had fallen seriously ill, and would no doubt have died if the doctors hadn't induced her father to accede to her desire. And her father had yielded, but without giving his consent; in fact, he swore that after that wedding she would no longer exist for him or for that household. Besides the difference in age, the husband being eighteen years older than the wife, a more serious obstacle for the father had been Brivio's financial position, which was subject to rapid ups and downs because of the risky undertakings on which this most enterprising and extraordinarily active man was accustomed to embark with foolhardy confidence in himself and his luck.

In three years of marriage Anna, surrounded by comforts, had been able to consider as unjust, or dictated by hostile prejudice, her father's prudent misgivings as to the financial means of her husband, in whom, moreover, in her ignorance, she placed as much confidence as he had in himself; then, as for the difference in their ages, up to then there had been no manifest cause of disappointment for her or surprise for others, because Brivio's advanced years produced in him not the slightest impairment to his small, highly

nervosa e tanto meno poi nell'anima dotata d'infaticabile energia, d'irrequieta alacrità.

Di ben altro Anna, ora per la prima volta, guardando (senza neppur sospettarlo) nella sua vita con gli occhi di quella morta effigiata lì nel ritratto sul comodino, trovava da lagnarsi del marito. Sì, era vero: della noncuranza quasi sdegnosa di lui ella si era altre volte sentita ferire; ma non mai come quel giorno; e ora per la prima volta ella si sentiva così angosciosamente sola, divisa dai suoi parenti, i quali le pareva in quel momento la avessero abbandonata lì, quasi che, sposando il Brivio, avesse già qualcosa di comune con quella morta e non fosse più degna d'altra compagnia. E il marito che avrebbe dovuto consolarla, il marito stesso pareva non volesse darle alcun merito del sacrificio ch'ella gli aveva fatto del suo amore filiale e fraterno, come se a lei non fosse costato nulla, come se a quel sacrificio egli avesse avuto diritto, e per ciò nessun dovere avesse ora di compensarnela. Diritto, sì, ma perché ella se ne era così perdutamente innamorata allora; dunque il dovere per lui adesso di compensarla. E invece . . .

«*Sempre così!*» parve ad Anna di sentirsi sospirare dalle labbra dolenti della morta.

Riaccese il lume e di nuovo, contemplando l'immagine, fu colpita dall'espressione di quegli occhi. Anche lei dunque, davvero, aveva sofferto per lui? anche lei, anche lei, accorgendosi di non essere amata, aveva sentito quel vuoto angoscioso?

—Sì? sì?—domandò Anna soffocata dal pianto, all'immagine.

E le parve allora che quegli occhi buoni, intensi di passione e di cordoglio, la commiserassero a lor volta, la compiangessero di quell'abbandono, del sacrificio non rimeritato, dell'amore che le restava chiuso in seno quasi tesoro in uno scrigno, di cui egli avesse le chiavi, ma per non servirsene mai, come l'avaro.

animated and robust body and even less to his mind, which was endowed with tireless energy and restless eagerness.

It was something totally different that Anna, now for the first time, looking into her life (without even realizing it) with the eyes of that dead woman depicted there in the portrait on the bedside table, found to complain of in her husband. Yes, it was true: she had felt hurt at other times by his almost disdainful indifference; but never so much as on that day; and now for the first time she felt so frighteningly alone, separated from her family, who at that moment seemed to her to have abandoned her there, as if, upon marrying Brivio, she already had something in common with that dead woman and was no longer worthy of anyone else's company. And her husband, who ought to have consoled her, it seemed that even her husband was unwilling to give her any credit for the sacrifice of her daughterly and sisterly love that she had offered him, just as if it had cost her nothing, as if he had had a right to that sacrifice and therefore had no obligation now to make it up to her. Yes, he had a right, but it was because she had fallen so totally in love with him at that time; therefore he now had an obligation to repay her. And instead . . .

"It's always been like that!" Anna thought she heard the sorrowful lips of the dead woman sigh to her.

She lit the lamp again and once more, contemplating the picture, she was struck by the expression of those eyes. So then, it was true, she too had suffered on his account? She too, she too, realizing she wasn't loved, had felt that frightening emptiness?

"Yes? Yes?" Anna, choking with tears, asked the picture.

And it then seemed to her that those kindly eyes, intense with passion and heartbreak, were pitying her in their turn, were condoling with her over that abandonment, that unrequited sacrifice, that love which remained locked up in her breast like a treasure in a casket to which he had the keys but would never use them, like a miser.

UNA VOCE

Pochi giorni prima che morisse, la marchesa Borghi, più per uno scrupolo di coscienza che per altro, aveva voluto consultare anche il dottor Giunio Falci, per il proprio figlio Silvio, cieco da circa un anno. Lo aveva fatto visitare dai più illustri oculisti d'Italia e dell'estero e tutti le avevano detto che era afflitto d'un glaucoma, irrimediabile.

Il dottor Giunio Falci aveva vinto da poco, per concorso, il posto di direttore della clinica oftalmica; ma sia per la sua aria stanca, e sempre astratta, sia per la figura sgraziata, per quel suo modo di camminare tutto rilassato e dinoccolato, con la grossa testa precocemente calva, scoperta, buttata indietro, il gran naso gracile a vento, come una vela nella faccetta ossuta, magra, dalla breve barba rada, ispida, già un po' grigia, spartita sul mento, riusciva così poco simpatico alla gente, che molti arrivavano financo a negargli ogni valore scientifico. Egli lo sapeva e pareva ne godesse. Diventava di giorno in giorno più astratto e non si scoteva più dal suo stanco attonimento se non per rivolgere domande curiose, penetranti, che aggelavano e sconcertavano. S'era a poco a poco formato un concetto della vita così nudo di tutte quelle intime e quasi necessarie ipocrisie, di quelle spontanee, inevitabili illusioni che ciascuno, senza volerlo, si compone e si crea, per un bisogno istintivo, quasi di pudor sociale, che la sua compagnia era divenuta ormai insopportabile.

Invitato dalla marchesa Borghi, egli era andato una mattina nella nuova via ariosa, solitaria, tutta di villini, in fondo ai Prati di Castello, di là da Ponte Margherita; aveva esaminato a lungo, attentamente, gli occhi del giovane, senza prestare ascolto, almeno in apparenza, a tutto ciò che la marchesa intanto gli diceva intorno alla malattia, ai giudizii degli altri medici, alle varie cure tentate. Glaucoma? No. Non aveva creduto di riscontrare in quegli occhi i segni caratteristici di questa malattia, il colore azzurrognolo o verdiccio dell'opacità, ecc. ecc.; gli era parso piuttosto che si trattasse di una rara e strana manifestazione di quel male che comunemente suol chiamarsi

A VOICE

A few days before she died, the Marchesa Borghi, more from a qualm of conscience than for any other reason, had decided to consult even Dr. Giunio Falci regarding her son Silvio, who had been blind for about a year. She had had him examined at home by the most famous oculists in Italy and abroad, and all of them had told her that he was suffering from incurable glaucoma.

Dr. Giunio Falci had recently gained the position of director of the eye clinic by competitive examination; but, whether it was due to his weary and always absentminded manner, or whether it was due to his ungraceful appearance—that completely lax and listless way he had of walking, with his big, prematurely bald, uncovered head thrown back, his long, thin nose in the air, like a sail on his bony, emaciated little face with its short, sparse, rough beard, already somewhat gray, parted on his chin—he was liked so little by people in general that many even went so far as to deny him any medical skill. He was aware of this and seemed to enjoy the situation. He became more absentminded daily and no longer shook himself out of his weary stupefaction except to pose curious, penetrating questions that chilled and disconcerted the listener. He had gradually formed a concept of life so devoid of all those friendly and almost necessary hypocrisies, those spontaneous, inevitable illusions composed and created by each of us without our volition, through an instinctive need—for social decency, one might say—that his company had now become intolerable.

At the invitation of the Marchesa Borghi, he had gone one morning to the airy, solitary new street, lined with villas, at the far end of Castle Meadows, across Margherita Bridge; he had made a long, careful examination of the young man's eyes, without paying attention—at least seemingly—to all that the Marchesa was telling him in the meantime about the ailment, the diagnoses of the other doctors and the various cures that had been tried. Glaucoma? No. He did not think he had found in those eyes the characteristic signs of that complaint, the bluish or greenish color of the opacity, etc., etc.; instead, he had decided that what he had before him was a rare and strange manifestation of that disease commonly known as cata-

cateratta. Ma non aveva voluto manifestare così in prima alla madre il suo dubbio, per non farle nascere d'improvviso foss'anche una tenue speranza, di cui, del resto, non si sentiva ben sicuro neanche lui. Dissimulando il vivissimo interesse che quel caso strano gli destava, le aveva invece manifestato il desiderio di tornare a visitar l'infermo fra qualche giorno.

Ed era infatti ritornato; ma, insolitamente, per quella via nuova, in fondo ai Prati di Castello dove sorgeva il villino della marchesa Borghi, sempre deserta, aveva trovato una frotta di curiosi davanti al cancello aperto del villino. La marchesa Borghi era morta d'improvviso, durante la notte.

Che fare? Tornarsene indietro? Aveva pensato che, se nella prima visita egli avesse manifestato il dubbio che il male di quel giovane non fosse, a suo modo di vedere, un vero e proprio glaucoma, forse quella povera madre non sarebbe morta con la disperazione di lasciare il figlio irrimediabilmente cieco. Ebbene, se non gli era più dato di consolare con questa speranza la madre, non avrebbe potuto almeno cercare di recar con essa un gran conforto al povero superstite, così tremendamente colpito da quella nuova, improvvisa sciagura?

Ed era salito al villino.

Dopo una lunga attesa, fra il trambusto che vi regnava, gli si era presentata una giovine vestita di nero, bionda, dall'aria rigida, anzi severa: la dama di compagnia della defunta marchesa. Il dottor Falci le aveva esposto il perché di quella sua visita, che sarebbe stata altrimenti importuna. A un certo punto, con una lieve meraviglia che tradiva la diffidenza, ella gli aveva domandato:

—Ma vanno dunque soggetti anche i giovani alla cateratta?

Il Falci la aveva guardata un tratto negli occhi, poi, con un sorriso ironico, percettibile più nello sguardo che su le labbra, le aveva risposto:

—E perché no? Moralmente, sempre, signorina: quando s'innamorano. Ma anche fisicamente, pur troppo.

Ella aveva allora troncato il discorso, dicendo che, nelle condizioni in cui il marchese si trovava in quel momento, non era assolutamente possibile parlargli di nulla; ma che, quando si fosse un po' quietato, ella gli avrebbe detto di quella visita e certo egli lo avrebbe fatto chiamare.

Eran trascorsi più di tre mesi: il dottor Giunio Falci non era stato chiamato.

Veramente, durante la prima visita la marchesa defunta

ract. But he had not wished to reveal his doubt to the mother all at once, in order to keep her from suddenly cherishing even the slenderest hope; besides, he himself did not feel entirely sure of the matter. Instead, disguising the very keen interest awakened in him by that strange case, he had declared his wish to call on the patient again in a few days.

And he had in fact returned; but, oddly, on that new, always deserted street at the far end of Castle Meadows where the Marchesa Borghi's villa was located, he had found a crowd of curious onlookers in front of the open gate of the villa. The Marchesa Borghi had died suddenly during the night.

What should he do? Turn back? Then it had occurred to him that, if on his first call he had expressed his opinion that, from his point of view, the young man's ailment was not really glaucoma, perhaps that poor mother would not have died with the grief of leaving behind a son who was incurably blind. Well, if he was no longer able to console the mother with this hope, couldn't he at least try to convey it to the unhappy survivor, thus affording him a great consolation now that he was so terribly stricken by this new, unexpected misfortune?

And he had proceeded up to the villa.

After a long wait amid the prevailing confusion, he had been greeted by a young woman dressed in black. Blonde, and with a stiff, in fact severe manner, she was the hired companion of the late Marchesa. Dr. Falci had explained to her the reason for his call, which would otherwise have been out of place. At a certain point, with a slight tinge of astonishment that indicated a lack of trust, she had asked him:

"But, in that case, are even young people subject to cataract?"

Falci had looked her in the eye for a moment, then, with an ironic smile more noticeable in his eyes than on his lips, he had replied:

"And why not? Spiritually always, Miss: when they fall in love. But physically also, unfortunately."

She had then cut the conversation short, saying that, under the circumstances in which the Marchese was situated at that moment, it was absolutely impossible to speak to him about anything; but that, when he had calmed down a little, she would tell him about this call and he would surely send for him.

More than three months had gone by: Dr. Giunio Falci had not been sent for.

To tell the truth, on the occasion of his first call the doctor had

aveva ricevuto una pessima impressione del dottore. La signorina Lydia Venturi, rimasta come governante e lettrice del giovine marchese, lo ricordava bene. Ma non sarebbe stata diversa quella impressione, se il Falci fin da principio avesse fatto sperare alla marchesa non improbabile la guarigione del figlio? Questa domanda la signorina Lydia non volle rivolgere a se stessa e, per conto suo, stimò da ciarlatano e peggio la seconda visita del medico, quel venire proprio nel giorno in cui la marchesa era morta a manifestare un dubbio, ad accendere una speranza di quella sorta.

Il giovine marchese pareva ormai rassegnato alla sciagura. Mortagli così d'un tratto la madre, oltre al buio della sua cecità, si era sentito addensare nell'anima un altro buio, ben più terribile, di fronte al quale, è vero, tutti gli uomini sono ciechi. Ma da questo buio, chi abbia gli occhi sani può almeno distrarsi con la vista delle cose intorno: egli no: cieco per la vita, cieco ora anche per la morte. E in quest'altro buio, più nudo, più freddo, più tenebroso, sua madre era scomparsa, silenziosamente, lasciandolo solo, in un vuoto orrendo.

A un tratto—non sapeva bene da chi—una voce d'una dolcezza infinita era venuta a lui, come una luce soavissima in quel suo doppio buio. E a questa voce tutta l'anima sua, sperduta in quel vuoto orrendo, s'era aggrappata.

Non era altro che una voce per lui la signorina Lydia. Ma era pur colei che più di tutti, negli ultimi mesi, era stata vicina a sua madre. E sua madre—egli lo ricordava—parlandogliene, s'era tanto lodata di lei. Egli dunque la sapeva buona, attenta, di squisite maniere, colta, intelligente, e tale ora la sperimentava nelle cure che aveva per lui, nei conforti che gli dava.

Lydia, fin dai primi giorni, aveva sospettato che la marchesa Borghi, prendendola al suo servizio, non avrebbe veduto male, nel suo egoismo materno, che il figlio infelice si fosse in qualche modo consolato con lei: se n'era acerbamente offesa e aveva costretto la sua naturale alterezza a irrigidirsi in un contegno addirittura severo. Ma, dopo la sciagura, quand'egli, tra il pianto disperato, le aveva preso una mano e vi aveva appoggiato il bel volto pallido, gemendo: «Non mi lasci! . . . non mi lasci!», s'era sentita vincere dalla compassione, dalla tenerezza, e s'era dedicata tutta a lui.

made a very bad impression on the late Marchesa. Miss Lydia Venturi, who had stayed on as the young Marchese's housekeeper and reader, remembered this clearly. But wouldn't that impression have been different if Falci had right from the start given the Marchesa hopes that her son's recovery was not unlikely? This was a question that Miss Lydia was unwilling to ask herself, and as far as she herself was concerned, she considered the doctor's second call as quackery or worse—coming on the very day the Marchesa had died to declare his dissenting opinion and kindle a hope of that sort.

By this time the young Marchese seemed resigned to his misfortune. His mother having died so suddenly, he had felt another darkness gathering in his soul in addition to that of his blindness: another, much more terrible darkness, in the face of which, it is true, all men are blind. But people with good eyes can at least find distraction from that other darkness by looking at the things around them: he could not. Blind in life, he was now blind in death as well. And into this other darkness, more bare, more cold, more shadowy, his mother had disappeared, silently, leaving him behind alone, in a frightening void.

All at once—he couldn't tell clearly from whom—an infinitely sweet voice had come to him, like a soft, soft light in that double darkness of his. And his entire soul, lost in that frightening void, had seized hold of that voice.

Miss Lydia was no more than a voice to him. Yet it was she who, in the last months, had been closer to his mother than anybody else. And his mother—he recalled this—when speaking to him about her, had expressed great satisfaction with her. Therefore he knew that she was kind, attentive, possessed of perfect good manners, well educated, intelligent; and now, from the attentions she paid him, from the consolations she gave him, he found that she really had all those merits.

From the first day of her employment, Lydia had suspected that the Marchesa Borghi, when hiring her, would not have objected, in her maternal egotism, if her unhappy son had in some way consoled himself in her company: Lydia had been seriously insulted and had forced her natural pride to stiffen into a deportment that was positively severe. But after the misfortune, when, amid his desperate weeping, he had taken hold of her hand, and had leaned his handsome, pale face on it, moaning, "Don't leave me! . . . don't leave me!," she had felt herself overcome by compassion, by tenderness, and had devoted herself to him entirely.

Presto, con la timida ma ostinata e accorante curiosità dei ciechi, egli s'era messo a torturarla. Voleva «vederla» nel suo buio; voleva che la voce di lei diventasse imagine entro di sé. Furono dapprima domande vaghe, brevi. Egli volle dirle come se la imaginava, sentendola leggere e parlare.

—Bionda, è vero?

—Sì . . .

Bionda era; ma i capelli, alquanto ruvidi e non molti e contrastavano stranamente col colore un po' torbido della pelle. Come dirglielo? E perché?

—E gli occhi, cerulei?

—Sì . . .

—Cerulei; ma cupi, dolenti, troppo affossati sotto la fronte grave, triste, prominente. Come dirglielo? E perché?

Bella non era, di volto; ma di corpo elegantissima, svelta e formosa a un tempo. Belle, veramente belle, aveva le mani e la voce.

La voce, segnatamente. D'una ineffabile soavità, in contrasto con l'aria cupa, altera e dolente del volto.

Ella sapeva com'egli, per la malia di questa voce e attraverso alle timide risposte che riceveva alle sue domande insistenti, incalzanti, la vedeva; e si sforzava dinanzi allo specchio di somigliare a quell'imagine fittizia di lei, si sforzava di vedersi com'egli nel suo buio la vedeva. E la sua voce, ormai, per lei stessa non usciva più dalle sue proprie labbra, ma da quelle ch'egli le imaginava; e, se rideva, aveva subito l'impressione di non aver riso lei, ma d'aver piuttosto imitato un sorriso non suo, il sorriso di quell'altra se stessa che viveva in lui.

Tutto ciò le cagionava come un sordo tormento, la sconvolgeva: le pareva di non esser più lei, di mancare man mano a se medesima, per la pietà che quel giovane le ispirava. Pietà soltanto? No: era anche amore, adesso. Non sapeva più ritrarre la mano dalla mano di lui, scostare il volto dal volto di lui, se egli la attirava troppo a sé.

—No: così, no . . . , così, no . . .

Si dové presto, ormai, venire a una determinazione, che alla signorina Lydia costò una lunga e dura lotta con se stessa. Il giovane marchese non aveva parenti, né prossimi, né lontani, era padrone di sé e dunque di fare quel che gli pareva e pia-

Soon, with the timid but obstinate and heartbreaking curiosity of the blind, he had begun to torture her. He wanted to "see" her in his darkness; he wanted her voice to become an image within him.

At first he posed vague, brief questions. He wanted to tell her how he pictured her when hearing her read and speak.

"You're blonde, aren't you?"

"Yes . . . "

She *was* blonde; but her hair was somewhat coarse and thin, and it contrasted strangely with the slightly lusterless color of her skin. How could she tell him that? And why should she?

"And your eyes, blue?"

"Yes . . . "

Blue they were; but melancholy, sorrowful, too deeply recessed beneath her serious, sad, prominent brow. How could she tell him that? And why should she?

Her face was not beautiful, but her body was extremely elegant, svelte and shapely at the same time. Her hands and her voice were beautiful, truly beautiful.

Her voice, especially. Of an unutterable sweetness, in contrast to the melancholy, haughty and sorrowful expression of her face.

She knew how he saw her from the charm of that voice and from the timid replies she received to his insistent, relentless questions; and in front of her mirror she made every effort to resemble that fictitious image he had of her, every effort to see herself the way he saw her in his darkness. And by this time, even for her, her voice no longer issued from her own lips, but from those he imagined she had; and if she laughed, she suddenly had the impression of not having laughed herself, but rather of having imitated a smile that was not hers, the smile of that other self who lived within his mind.

All of this caused her a kind of muted torment, it perturbed her: she felt that she was no longer herself, that she was gradually doing an injustice to her own self because of the pity the young man aroused in her. Only pity? No: it was also love now. She was no longer able to snatch her hand away from his hand, to turn her face away from his face, if he drew her too closely to him.

"No! like this, no . . . , like this, no . . . "

By this time it was necessary to arrive quickly at a decision which cost Miss Lydia a long, hard struggle with herself. The young Marchese had no relatives, close or distant, he was his own master and thus able to do anything he wished or chose. But wouldn't people

ceva. Ma non avrebbe detto la gente che ella approfittava della sciagura di lui per farsi sposare, per diventar marchesa e ricca? Oh sì, certamente, questo e altro avrebbe detto. Ma, tuttavia, come poteva ella rimanere più oltre in quella casa, se non a questo patto? E non sarebbe stata una crudeltà abbandonare quel cieco, privarlo delle sue cure amorose, per paura dell'altrui malignità? Era, senza dubbio, per lei una gran fortuna; ma sentiva, in coscienza, di meritarsela, perché ella lo amava; anzi, per lei la maggior fortuna era questa, di poterlo amare apertamente, di potersi dir sua, tutta e sempre sua, di potersi consacrare a lui unicamente, anima e corpo. Egli non si vedeva: non vedeva altro entro di sè che la propria infelicità; ma era pur bello, tanto! e delicato come una fanciulla; e lei, guardandolo, beandosene, senza che egli se n'accorgesse, poteva pensare: «Ecco, sei tutto mio, perché non ti vedi e non ti sai; perché l'anima tua è come prigioniera della tua sventura e ha bisogno di me per vedere, per sentire». Ma non bisognava prima, condiscendendo alla voglia di lui, confessargli ch'ella non era com'egli se la immaginava? Non sarebbe stato il tacere un inganno, da parte sua? Sì, un inganno. Ma egli era pur cieco, e per lui dunque poteva bastare un cuore, come quello di lei, devoto e ardente, e l'illusione della bellezza. Brutta, del resto, ella non era. E poi una bella, veramente bella, forse, chi sa! avrebbe potuto ingannarlo ben altrimenti, approfittando della sciagura di lui, se veramente egli, più che d'un bel volto, che non avrebbe potuto mai vedere, aveva bisogno d'un cuore innamorato.

Dopo alcuni giorni d'angosciosa perplessità, le nozze furono stabilite. Si sarebbero effettuate senz'alcuna pompa, presto, appena spirato il sesto mese di lutto per la madre.

Ella aveva dunque innanzi a sé circa un mese e mezzo di tempo per preparar l'occorrente alla meglio. Furono giorni d'intensa felicità: le ore volavano fra le lietissime, affrettate cure del nido e le carezze, da cui ella si scioglieva un po' ebbra, con dolce violenza, per salvare da quella libertà che la convivenza dava al loro amore, qualche gioia, la più forte, per il giorno delle nozze.

Ci mancava ormai poco più d'una settimana, quando a Lydia fu annunziata improvvisamente una visita del dottor Giunio Falci.

say that she was taking advantage of his misfortune in order to get married, to become a Marchesa and rich? Oh, yes, they would surely say that and much more. But, all the same, how could she stay on in that house except on those terms? And wouldn't it be an act of cruelty to abandon that blind man, to deprive him of her loving attentions, through fear of other people's malice? No doubt, it was great good luck for her; but in her conscience she felt that she deserved it because she loved him; in fact, the greatest good luck for her was to be able to love him openly, to be able to say she was his, entirely and eternally his, to be able to devote herself to him exclusively, body and soul. He couldn't see himself: he saw nothing within himself but his own unhappiness; nevertheless, he was hand-some—very much so—and as delicate as a little girl; and she, look-ing at him, delighting in him, without his being aware of it, could think: "There, you're all mine because you don't see yourself and you don't know yourself; because your soul is like a prisoner of your misery and needs me to see, to feel." But wasn't it first necessary, complying with his wishes, to confess to him that she was not like his mental image of her? Wouldn't keeping silent be a deception on her part? Yes, a deception. And yet he was blind, and so he could be satisfied with a heart like hers, devoted and ardent, and with the illusion of beauty. Besides, she was not ugly. And then, a woman who was beautiful, really beautiful, might be able—who knows?–to deceive him in a much worse way, taking advantage of his misfortune, if he really had need of a loving heart rather than a pretty face, which he could never see.

After several days of anguished uncertainty, the wedding was arranged. It would be celebrated unostentatiously and quickly, just as soon as the sixth month of mourning for his mother had passed.

Therefore she had about a month and a half's time ahead of her to make the necessary preparations as best she could. They were days of tremendous happiness: the hours flew by, divided between her joyful, busy furnishing of their home together and his caresses, from which she would free herself in a mild state of delirium, with gentle force. She wished to preserve that one, most intense, plea-sure from the license which their sharing one roof gave to their love, and to save it for their wedding day.

Now there remained little more than a week, when Lydia unex-pectedly received the announcement of a visit from Dr. Giunio Falci.

Di primo impeto, fu per rispondere:

—Non sono in casa!

Ma il cieco, che aveva udito parlar sottovoce, domandò:

—Chi è?

—Il dottor Falci,—ripetè il servo.

—Sai?—disse Lydia,—quel medico che la tua povera mamma fece chiamare pochi giorni prima della disgrazia.

—Ah, sì!—esclamò il Borghi, sovvenendosi.—Mi osservò a lungo . . . a lungo, ricordo bene, e disse che voleva ritornare, per . . .

—Aspetta,—lo interruppe subito Lydia, agitatissima. —Vado a sentire.

Il dottor Giunio Falci stava in piedi in mezzo al salotto, con la grossa testa calva rovesciata indietro, gli occhi socchiusi, e si stirava distrattamente con una mano la barbetta ispida sul mento.

—S'accomodi, dottore,—disse la signorina Lydia, ch'era entrata senza ch'egli se n'accorgesse.

Il Falci si scosse, s'inchinò e prese a dire:

—Mi scuserà, se . . .

Ma ella, turbata, eccitata, volle premettere:

—Lei finora veramente non era stato chiamato, perché . . .

—La mia visita è stata impronta,—disse il Falci, col lieve sorriso sarcastico su le labbra.—Ma lei mi perdonerà, signorina.

—No . . . perchè? anzi . . .—fece Lydia, arrossendo.

—Lei non sa,—riprese il Falci,—l'interesse che a un pover'uomo che si occupa di scienza possono destare certi casi di malattia . . . Ma io voglio dirle tutta la verità, signorina: mi ero dimenticato di questo caso, quantunque a parer mio molto raro e strano, del marchese Borghi. Ieri, però, chiacchierando del più e del meno con alcuni amici, ho saputo del prossimo matrimonio con lei, signorina; è vero?

Lydia impallidì e affermò, alteramente, col capo.

—Permetta ch'io me ne feliciti,—soggiunse il Falci.—Ma guardi, allora, tutt'a un tratto, mi son ricordato. Mi son ricordato della diagnosi di glaucoma fatta da tanti illustri miei colleghi, se non m'inganno. Diagnosi spiegabilissima, in principio, non creda. Io son sicuro, infatti, che se la signora marchesa avesse fatto visitare il figliuolo da questi miei colleghi quando

Her first impulse was to answer:

"I'm not home!"

But the blind man, who had heard people talking in low tones, asked:

"Who is it?"

"Dr. Falci," the servant repeated.

"You know," said Lydia, "that doctor your late mother called for a few days before the sad occurrence."

"Oh, yes!" Borghi exclaimed, recalling it to mind. "He gave me a long examination . . . a long one, I remember it clearly, and he said he wanted to come back, in order to . . . "

"Wait," Lydia suddenly interrupted him, in a state of great agitation. "I'll see what he wants."

Dr. Giunio Falci was standing in the center of the reception room, with his large bald head thrown back and his eyes half-closed, and with one hand he was absentmindedly smoothing out the rough little beard on his chin.

"Have a seat, Doctor," said Miss Lydia, who had come in without his noticing.

Falci roused himself, bowed and began saying:

"You will excuse me if . . . "

But she, upset, excited, insisted on saying first:

"You really weren't sent for up to now because . . . "

"My last call was out of place," said Falci, with a light, sarcastic smile on his lips. "But you will forgive me, Miss."

"No . . . Why? Not at all . . . ," said Lydia, blushing.

"You don't know," Falci continued, "how great an interest a poor man concerned with science can take in certain medical cases . . . But I want to tell you the whole truth, Miss: I had forgotten this case of the Marchese Borghi's, even though in my opinion it was very unusual and strange. But yesterday, while chatting about this and that with some friends, I learned about his forthcoming marriage to you, Miss. Is it true?"

Lydia turned pale and nodded affirmatively, in a haughty manner.

"Allow me to congratulate you," Falci added. "But, you see, at that moment, all at once, I remembered. I remembered the diagnosis of glaucoma made by a number of famous colleagues of mine, if I'm not mistaken. A diagnosis that is very easy to explain, in general, I assure you. In fact, I'm certain that if the Marchesa had had those colleagues of mine examine her son at the time I called

l'ho visitato io, anch'essi avrebbero detto facilmente che di glaucoma vero e proprio non era più il caso di parlare. Basta. Mi sono ricordato anche della mia seconda visita disgraziatissima, e ho pensato che lei, signorina, dapprima nello scompiglio cagionato dall'improvvisa morte della marchesa, poi nella gioia di questo avvenimento, si era di certo dimenticata, è vero? dimenticata . . .

—No!—negò con durezza Lydia a questo punto, ribellandosi alla tortura che il lungo discorso avvelenato del dottore le infliggeva.

—Ah, no?—fece il Falci.

—No,—ripeté ella con accigliata fermezza.—Io ho ricordato piuttosto la poca, per non dir nessuna fiducia, scusi, che ebbe la marchesa, anche dopo la sua visita, su la guarigione del figlio.

—Ma io non dissi alla marchesa,—ribatté pronto il Falci,—che la malattia del figlio, a mio modo di vedere . . .

—È vero, lei lo disse a me,—troncò Lydia di nuovo.—Ma anch'io, come la marchesa . . .

—Poca, anzi, nessuna fiducia, è vero? Non importa,—interruppe a sua volta il Falci.—Ma lei non riferì, intanto, al signor marchese la mia venuta e la ragione . . .

—Sul momento, no.

—E poi?

—Neppure. Perché . . .

Il dottor Falci alzò una mano:

—Comprendo. Nato l'amore . . . Ma lei, signorina, mi perdoni: si dice, è vero, che l'amore è cieco; lei però lo desidera proprio cieco fino a questo punto, l'amore del signor marchese? Cieco anche materialmente?

Lydia sentì che contro la sicura freddezza mordace di quell'uomo non bastava il contegno altero, in cui man mano, per difendere la sua dignità da un sospetto odioso, s'irrigidiva vieppiù. Tuttavia si sforzò di contenersi ancora e domandò con apparente calma:

—Lei insiste nel ritenere che il marchese possa, con l'ajuto di lei, riacquistar la vista?

—Piano, signorina,—rispose il Falci, alzando un'altra volta la mano.—Io non sono onnipossente. Ho esaminato una volta sola gli occhi del signor marchese, e m'è parso di dovere escludere assolutamente che si tratti di glaucoma. Ecco: questo, che può essere un dubbio, che può essere una speranza, mi pare che dovrebbe bastarle, se veramente, com'io credo, le sta a cuore il bene del suo fidanzato.

on him, even they would have said readily that it was no longer proper to speak of a genuine glaucoma. But let that be. I also remembered my second, extremely unfortunate, call, and I thought that you, Miss, at first in the confusion caused by the unexpected death of the Marchesa, and later in the happiness of this new event, had surely forgotten—am I correct?–forgotten . . . "

"No!" said Lydia at that point, contradicting him sharply, in protest against the torture that the doctor's long, poisonous speech was inflicting on her.

"Ah, no?" said Falci.

"No," she repeated, with glowering firmness. "Rather, I remembered how little confidence—actually none at all, forgive me!—the Marchesa had about her son's cure even after your call."

"But I didn't tell the Marchesa," Falci rebutted at once, "that her son's ailment from my point of view . . . "

"It's true, you told that to me," Lydia cut in again. "But I also, like the Marchesa . . . "

"Little confidence—actually none at all, right? It doesn't matter," Falci interrupted in his turn. "But in the meantime you did not inform the Marchese of my coming and the reason for it . . . "

"Not all at once, no."

"And later on?"

"Not then, either. Because . . . "

Dr. Falci raised one hand:

"I understand. After love was born . . . But pardon me, Miss: it's true they say that love is blind; but do you really wish the Marchese's love to be as blind as all that? Blind physically as well?"

Lydia realized that, to combat this man's self-assured, biting coldness, she couldn't make do with the haughty deportment in which she was gradually wrapping herself more and more tightly in order to defend her dignity from an odious suspicion. Nevertheless, she made an effort to contain herself further, and asked with apparent calm:

"You insist on maintaining that the Marchese, with your help, can regain his sight?"

"Don't be hasty, Miss," Falci answered, raising his hand again. "I am not all-powerful. I examined the Marchese's eyes only once, and I thought it proper to rule out glaucoma as a diagnosis absolutely. Now: I think that this conclusion, which may be merely a doubt, or which may be a source of hope, ought to be enough for you if, as I believe, you really have your fiancé's welfare at heart."

—E se il dubbio,—s'affrettò a replicare Lydia, con aria di sfida,—dopo la sua visita non potesse più sussistere, se la speranza restasse delusa? Non avrà lei inutilmente, crudelmente, ora, turbata un'anima che si è già rassegnata?

—No, signorina,—ripose con dura e seria calma il Falci.—Tanto vero, ch'io ho stimato mio dovere, di medico, venire senza invito. Perché qua, lo sappia, io credo di trovarmi non solo di fronte a un caso di malattia, ma anche di fronte a un caso di coscienza.

—Lei sospetta . . .—si provò a interromperlo Lydia; ma il Falci non le diede tempo di proseguire.

—Lei stessa,—seguitò,—ha detto or ora di aver taciuto al marchese la mia venuta, con una scusa ch'io non posso accettare, non perché m'offenda, ma perché la fiducia o la sfiducia verso me non doveva esser sua, ma del marchese, se mai. Guardi, signorina: sarà anche puntiglio da parte mia, non nego; le dico anzi che io non prenderò nulla dal marchese, se egli verrà nella mia clinica, dove avrà tutte le cure e l'ajuto che la scienza può prestargli, disinteressatamente. Dopo questa dichiarazione, sarà troppo chiederle che Ella annunzii al signor marchese la mia visita?

Lydia si levò in piedi.

—Aspetti,—disse allora il Falci, levandosi anche lui e riprendendo la sua aria consueta.—La avverto ch'io non dirò affatto al marchese d'essere venuto quella volta. Dirò anzi, se vuole, che lei, premurosamente, mi ha fatto chiamare, prima delle nozze.

Lydia lo guardò fieramente negli occhi.

—Lei dirà la verità. Anzi la dirò io.

—Di non aver creduto in me?

—Precisamente.

Il Falci si strinse ne le spalle, sorrise.

—Potrebbe nuocerle. E io non vorrei. Se lei anzi volesse rimandar la visita a dopo le nozze, guardi, io sarei anche disposto a ritornare.

—No,—fece, più col gesto che con la voce, Lydia, soffocata dall'orgasmo, avvampata in volto dall'onta che quell'apparente generosità del medico le cagionava; e con la mano gli fe' cenno di passare.

Silvio Borghi attendeva impaziente nella sua camera.

—Ecco qua il dottor Falci, Silvio;—disse Lydia, entrando, tutta vibrante.—Abbiamo chiarito di là un equivoco. Tu ri-

"And what if the doubt," Lydia hurriedly replied, in a challenging manner, "could no longer be sustained after your examination, what if the hopes were dashed? Wouldn't you now have uselessly, cruelly perturbed a soul that has already resigned itself to its lot?"

"No, Miss," Falci answered with hard, serious calm. "So little so, that I esteemed it my duty as a physician to come uninvited. Because in this instance, I'd like you to know, I believe I am involved not merely in a medical case but also in a case of conscience."

"You suspect . . . ," Lydia tried to interrupt him, but Falci gave her no time to continue.

"You yourself," he proceeded, "said just now that you failed to inform the Marchese of my call, using an excuse I cannot accept, not because it is insulting to me, but because the confidence or lack of confidence in me ought to come not from you, but from the Marchese, if from anyone. Look, Miss: it may also be obstinacy on my part, I don't deny it; but I tell you that I won't take any payment from the Marchese if he comes to my clinic, where he will have every care and aid that science can offer him, disinterestedly. After this declaration, would it be too much to ask you to announce my call to the Marchese?"

Lydia stood up.

"Wait," Falci then said, getting up also and resuming his customary manner. "I want you to know that I will not say a word to the Marchese about having come that time. In fact, if you like, I'll say that, out of thoughtfulness, you sent for me, before the wedding."

Lydia looked him in the eye undauntedly.

"You shall tell him the truth. No, *I'll* tell him."

"That you didn't believe me."

"Exactly."

Falci shrugged his shoulders, smiled.

"It might do you harm. And I wouldn't want that. But if you wanted to postpone my call until after the wedding—look, I would be equally willing to come back."

"No," said Lydia, speaking more with her gesture than with her voice. Stifled by her agitation, her face flushed with shame caused by that apparent generosity of the doctor, she signaled with her hand for him to come with her.

Silvio Borghi was waiting impatiently in his room.

"Here is Dr. Falci, Silvio," said Lydia, entering, trembling all over. "Downstairs we cleared up a misunderstanding. You remember,

cordi che il dottore, nella sua prima visita, disse che voleva
ritornare, è vero?

—Sì,—ripose il Borghi.—Ricordo benissimo, dottore!

—Non sai ancora,—riprese Lydia,—ch'egli di fatti ritornò,
nella stessa mattina in cui avvenne la disgrazia di tua madre.
E parlò con me e mi disse ch'egli riteneva che il tuo male
non fosse propriamente quello che tant'altri medici avevano
dichiarato e che perciò non fosse, secondo lui, del tutto improbabile la tua guarigione. Io non te ne dissi nulla.

—Perché la signorina, badi,—s'affrettò a soggiungere il
dottor Falci,—trattandosi d'un dubbio espresso da me, in quel
momento, in termini molto vaghi, lo considerò piuttosto come
un conforto ch'io volessi apprestare, e non vi diede molto peso.

—Questo è ciò che ho detto io, non quel che pensa lei,—rispose Lydia, fieramente.—Il dottor Falci, Silvio, ha sospettato
ciò che, del resto, è vero, ch'io cioè non ti dissi nulla della sua
seconda visita; ed è voluto venir lui spontaneamente, prima
delle nozze, per prestarti le sue cure, senz'alcun compenso.
Ora puoi credere con lui, Silvio, ch'io volessi lasciarti cieco,
per farmi sposare da te.

—Che dici, Lydia?—esclamò il cieco, sussultando.

—Ma sì,—riprese ella subito, con uno strano riso. —E può
esser vero anche questo, perché, difatti, a questo solo patto io
potrei diventare la tua . . .

—Che dici?—ripeté il Borghi, interrompendola.

—Te ne accorgerai, Silvio, se il dottor Falci riuscirà a ridarti
la vista. Io vi lascio.

—Lydia! Lydia!—chiamò il Borghi.

Ma ella era già uscita, tirando l'uscio a sé con violenza. Andò
a buttarsi sul letto, morse rabbiosamente il guanciale e ruppe
dapprima in singhiozzi irrefrenabili. Ceduta la prima furia
del pianto, rimase attonita e come raccapricciata di fronte alla
propria coscienza. Le parve che tutto ciò che il medico le aveva
detto, con quel suo fare freddo e mordace, da molto tempo
lei lo avesse detto a se stessa, o meglio, che qualcuno in lei lo
avesse detto; e lei aveva finto di non udire. Sì, sempre, sempre
si era ricordata del dottor Falci, e ogni qual volta l'imagine di
lui le si era affacciata alla mente, come il fantasma d'un rimorso, ella la aveva respinta con una ingiuria: «Ciarlatano!».
Perché,—come negarlo più, ormai?—ella voleva, voleva pro-

don't you, that on his first call the Doctor said he wanted to come back?"

"Yes," answered Borghi. "I remember very well, Doctor."

"What you don't know yet," continued Lydia, "is that he did in fact come back, on the very morning when your mother's sad death occurred. And he spoke with me and told me that he believed your ailment was not really what so many other doctors had declared it to be, and that, in his opinion, therefore, it was not at all unlikely that you could be cured. I told you nothing about it."

"Because, you see, your fiancée," Dr. Falci hastened to add, "seeing that it was a doubt that I expressed in very vague terms at that moment, considered it, more than anything else, as a consolation I wished to offer, and didn't attach much importance to it."

"That is what I said, not what you think," Lydia replied intrepidly. "Dr. Falci, Silvio, suspected what is actually the truth, that I told you nothing about his second call; and he was kind enough to come entirely on his own, before the wedding, to offer you his treatment without any remuneration. Now, Silvio, you are free to think, as he does, that I wanted you to stay blind to get you to marry me."

"What are you saying, Lydia?" the blind man exclaimed with a start.

"Oh, yes," she continued at once, with a strange laugh. "And even that may be true, because, in fact, that's the only way I could become your . . . "

"What are you saying?" Borghi repeated, interrupting her.

"You'll see for yourself, Silvio, if Dr. Falci succeeds in restoring your sight. I'll leave you now."

"Lydia! Lydia!" Borghi called.

But she had already gone out, slamming the door behind her violently. She went and threw herself on her bed, bit the pillow in her rage and at first broke out into uncontrollable sobbing. When the first fury of her tears had abated, she remained dumbfounded and as if horrified in the face of her own conscience. It seemed to her that everything the doctor had said to her, in that cold and biting way of his, she had already said to herself for some time; or, rather, someone inside her had said it; and she had pretended not to hear. Yes, all along, all along she had remembered Dr. Falci, and every time his image had surfaced in her mind, like the ghost of a remorse, she had suppressed it with an insult: "Charlatan!" Because—how could she go on denying it now?–she wished, truly

prio che il suo Silvio rimanesse cieco. La cecità di lui era la
condizione imprescindibile del suo amore. Che se egli, domani, avesse riacquistato la vista, bello com'era, giovine, ricco,
signore, perché avrebbe sposato lei? Per gratitudine? Per
pietà? Ah, non per altro! E dunque, no, no! Seppure egli
avesse voluto, lei, no; come avrebbe potuto accettare, lei che
lo amava e non lo voleva per altro? lei, che nella sventura di
lui vedeva la ragione del suo amore e quasi la scusa, di fronte
alla malignità altrui? E si può dunque transigere così, inavver-
titamente, con la propria coscienza, fino a commettere un delitto? fino a fondar la propria felicità su la sciagura di un altro?
Ella, sì, veramente, non aveva allora creduto che colui, quel
suo nemico, potesse fare il miracolo di ridar la vista al suo
Silvio; non lo credeva neanche adesso; ma perché aveva taciuto? proprio perché non aveva creduto di prestar fiducia a
quel medico, o non piuttosto perché il dubbio che il medico
aveva espresso e che sarebbe stato per Silvio come una luce
di speranza, sarebbe stato invece per lei la morte, la morte del
suo amore, se poi si fosse affermato? Pur ora ella poteva credere che il suo amore sarebbe bastato a compensar quel cieco
della vista perduta; credere che, se pure egli, per un miracolo,
avesse ora riacquistato la vista, né questo bene sommo, né tutti
i piaceri che avrebbe potuto pagarsi con la sua ricchezza, né
l'amore d'alcun'altra donna, avrebbero potuto compensarlo
della perdita dell'amore di lei. Ma queste erano ragioni per
sé, non per lui. Se ella fosse andata a dirgli: «Silvio, tu devi
scegliere fra il bene della vista e il mio amore», «E perché tu
vuoi lasciarmi cieco?» avrebbe egli certamente risposto. Ma
perché così soltanto, cioè a patto della sciagura di lui, era possibile la sua felicità.
   Si levò in piedi improvvisamente, come per un subito richiamo. Durava ancora la visita, di là? Che diceva il medico?
Che pensava egli? Ebbe la tentazione di andare in punta di
piedi a origliare dietro quell'uscio ch'ella stessa aveva chiuso;
ma si trattenne. Ecco: dietro l'uscio era rimasta; ella stessa,
con le sue mani, se l'era chiuso, per sempre. Ma poteva forse
accettare le velenose profferte di colui? Egli era arrivato finanche a proporle di rimandar la visita a dopo le nozze.—Se
ella avesse accettato . . .—No! No! Si strinse tutta in sé, dal
ribrezzo, dalla nausea. Che mercato infame sarebbe stato! il
più laido degli inganni! E poi? Disprezzo, e non più amore . . .

wished her Silvio to remain blind. His blindness was the indispensable condition for his love. For, if he should regain his sight tomorrow, handsome as he was, young, rich, a nobleman, why would he marry her? Out of gratitude? Out of pity? Ah, for no other reason! And, in that case, no, no! And even if *he* were willing, *she* wouldn't be; how could she accept that?—she who loved him and wanted him for no other reason; she who saw in his misfortune the reason for her love and almost the excuse for it in the face of other people's malice. Can one, then, make compromises with one's own conscience that way, without realizing it, to the point of committing a crime, to the point of founding one's own happiness on someone else's suffering? To be perfectly honest, at that time she had not believed that he, her enemy, could perform the miracle of restoring her Silvio's sight; she didn't believe it even now; but why had she remained silent? Was it really because she had not thought it proper to lend credence to that doctor, or wasn't it rather because the doubt the doctor had expressed, which would have been like a ray of hope for Silvio, would have meant death instead for her, the death of her love, if it later proved to be true? Even now she could believe that her love would have been sufficient to compensate that blind man for the loss of his sight; she could believe that, even if by some miracle he now regained his sight, neither that supreme blessing, nor all the pleasures he could buy himself with his wealth, nor the love of some other woman, could compensate him for the loss of *her* love. But these were reasons for herself, not for him. If she had gone to him and said, "Silvio, you have to choose between the joy of seeing and my love," he surely would have replied, "And why do you want to leave me blind?" Because only this way, that is, on the condition of his misfortune, was her happiness possible.

All at once she stood up, as if in answer to a sudden call. Was the examination still going on in that other room? What was the doctor saying? What was *he* thinking? She was tempted to tiptoe over and eavesdrop behind that door she herself had closed; but she restrained herself. There you had it: she was left behind the door; she herself, with her own hands, had closed it on herself, forever. But could she really accept that man's poisonous offers? He had gone so far as to propose postponing his call until after the wedding.—If she had accepted . . . No! No! She felt herself tighten up with disgust, with nausea. What a hateful deal that would have been! The most loathsome of deceptions! And later on? Contempt in place of love . . .

Sentì schiudere l'uscio; ebbe un sussulto; corse istintivamente al corridojo per cui il Falci doveva passare.

—Ho rimediato, signorina, alla sua soverchia fran-
chezza,—diss'egli freddamente.—Io mi sono raffermato
nella mia diagnosi. Il marchese verrà domattina nella mia clinica. Vada, vada intanto da lui che la aspetta. A rivederla.

Ella rimase come annientata, vuota; lo seguì con gli occhi
fino all'uscio, in fondo al corridojo; poi udì la voce di Silvio
che la chiamava, di là. Si sentì tutta rimescolata, una vertigine;
fu per cadere; si recò le mani al volto, per frenar le lagrime;
accorse.

Egli la attendeva, seduto, con le braccia aperte; la strinse,
forte, forte, forte a sé, gridando con brevi frasi spezzate la sua
felicità e che per lei soltanto voleva riacquistar la vista, per
veder la sua cara, la sua bella, la sua dolce sposa; per lei!

—Piangi? Perché? Ma piango anch'io, vedi? Ah che gioja!
Ti vedrò . . . Io vedrò! io vedrò!

Era ogni parola per lei una morte; tanto che egli, pur nella
gioja, intese che il pianto di lei non era come il suo e prese
allora a dirle che certo, oh! ma certo neanche lui, in un giorno
come quello, avrebbe creduto alle parole del medico, e
dunque, via, basta ora! Che andava più pensando? Era giorno
di festa, quello! Via tutte le afflizioni! via tutti i pensieri, tranne
uno, questo: che la sua felicità sarebbe stata intera, ormai,
perché egli avrebbe veduto la sua sposa. Ora ella avrebbe
avuto più agio, più tempo di preparare il nido; e doveva esser
bello, come un sogno, questo nido, che'egli avrebbe veduto
per prima cosa. Sì, prometteva che sarebbe uscito con gli occhi
bendati dalla clinica, e che li avrebbe aperti lì, per la prima
volta, lì, nel suo nido.

—Parlami! parlami! Non lasciar parlare me solo!

—Ti stanchi?

—No . . . Chiedimi di nuovo: «Ti stanchi?» con questa tua
voce. Lasciamela baciare, qui, su le tue labbra, questa tua
voce . . .

—Sì . . .

—E parla, ora; dimmi come me lo preparerai, il nido.

—Come?

—Sì, io non t'ho domandato nulla, finora. Ma no, non voglio saper nulla, neanche adesso. Farai tu. Sarà per me uno
stupore, un incanto . . . Ma io non vedrò nulla, dapprima: te
sola! te sola!

She heard the door open; she shuddered; instinctively she ran to the corridor through which Falci had to pass.

"I made up for your excessive frankness, Miss," he said coldly. "I have confirmed my diagnosis. The Marchese will come to my clinic tomorrow morning. Meanwhile, go to him, go, he's waiting for you. Goodbye."

She stood there annihilated, drained; she watched him go all the way to the door at the far end of the corridor; then she heard Silvio's voice calling her from his room. She felt all confused, dizzy; she was on the point of falling; she put her hands to her face to hold back her tears; she hastened toward him.

He was sitting and awaiting her with open arms; he hugged her to himself with tremendous strength, shouting his happiness in short, choppy phrases, saying that it was for her alone that he wanted to regain his sight, to see her face, to see his beautiful, sweet bride; for her!

"You're crying? Why? But I'm crying, too, see? Oh, what joy! I'll see you . . . I'll see! I'll see!"

Every word was death to her; so much so that, happy as he was, he realized that her tears were not the same as his, and he then started to tell her that surely—oh, but surely—not even he, on a day like that one, would have believed what the doctor said, and so, forget it, enough now! What was she still thinking about? Today was a holiday! Away with all sorrows! Away with all thoughts, except one: that his happiness would now be complete because he would see his bride. Now she would have more leisure, more time to furnish their home together; and it had to be beautiful as a dream, that home, which would be the first thing he saw. Yes, he promised that he would leave the clinic with his eyes bandaged, and that he would open them there, for the first time, in his home.

"Speak to me! Speak to me! Don't let me go on speaking alone!"

"Are you getting tired?"

"No . . . Ask me again, 'Are you getting tired?' with that voice of yours. Let me kiss it, here, on your lips, that voice of yours . . . "

"Yes . . . "

"And speak, now; tell me how you'll furnish it for me, our home."

"How?"

"Yes, I haven't asked you anything yet up to now. But no, I don't want to know anything, not even now. You will take care of it. For me it will be a marvel, an enchantment . . . But I will see nothing at first: only you! only you!"

Ella, risolutamente, soffocò il pianto disperato, s'ilarò tutta in volto, e lì, inginocchiata innanzi a lui, con lui curvo su di lei, abbracciato, cominciò a parlargli del suo amore, quasi all'orecchio, con quella sua voce più che mai dolce e malïosa. Ma quand'egli, ebbro, la strinse e minacciò di non lasciarla più, in quel momento, ella si sciolse, si rizzò, fiera, come d'una vittoria di fronte a se stessa. Ecco: avrebbe potuto, anche ora, legarlo a sé indissolubilmente. Ma no! Perché ella lo amava.

Tutto quel giorno, fino a tarda notte, lo inebriò della sua voce, sicura, perché egli era ancora nel buio, là, suo; nel buio, in cui già fiammeggiava la speranza, bella come l'imagine ch'egli s'era finto di lei.

La mattina seguente volle accompagnarlo in vettura fino alla clinica e nel lasciarlo, gli disse che si sarebbe messa subito, subito all'opera, come una rondine frettolosa.

—Vedrai!

Attese due giorni, in un'ansia terribile, l'esito dell'operazione. Quando lo seppe felice, attese ancora un po', nella casa vuota; gliela preparò amorosamente, mandando a dire a lui che, esultante, la voleva lì, anche per un minuto, che avesse pazienza ancora per qualche giorno; non accorreva per non agitarlo; il medico non permetteva . . .

—Sì?—Ebbene, allora sarebbe venuta . . .

Raccolse le sue robe, e il giorno prima che egli lasciasse la casa di salute, se ne partì ignorata, per rimanere almeno nella memoria di lui una voce, ch'egli forse, uscito ora dal suo buio, avrebbe cercata su molte labbra, invano.

She resolutely stifled her anguished weeping, made her face completely cheerful, and there kneeling in front of him, with him bending over her, in her embrace, she began speaking to him of her love, practically in his ear, with that voice of hers, sweeter and more bewitching than ever. But when he, in rapture, held her tight and threatened never to let her go again, at that moment she freed herself and stood straight up, as if proud of a victory over herself. There! Even now, she would have been able to tie him to her indissolubly. But no! Because she loved him.

All that day, till late at night, she intoxicated him with that voice of hers, self-assured because he was still there, in his darkness; in the darkness in which hope was already flaring up, as beautiful as the image he had formed of her.

The next morning she insisted on accompanying him in the carriage up to the clinic and, as she left him there, she told him she would get right to work, right away, like an industrious swallow building her nest.

"You'll see!"

For two days, in terrible anxiety, she awaited the result of the operation. When she heard it was successful, she waited a little longer, in the empty house; she furnished it for him lovingly. In his exultation he wanted to see her, if only for a moment, but she sent a message asking him to be patient for a few more days; if she wasn't hurrying over, it was to avoid exciting him; it was against the doctor's orders . . .

"Really? Well, in that case she would have come . . . "

She gathered up her possessions, and the day before he left the clinic, she departed without anyone knowing, in order to remain, at least in his memory, a voice, which perhaps, now that he had emerged from his darkness, he would seek on many lips, in vain.

LA MOSCA

Trafelati, ansanti—quando furono sotto il borgo, che siede con le fitte casupole cretose su l'altipiano d'argille azzurre—s'arrampicarono per far più presto, su per il lubrico scoscendimento, ajutandosi con le mani, poiché i grossi scarponi imbullettati—Dio sacrato!—scivolavano.

Le donne, affollate e vocianti innanzi a la fontanella, con le lor brocche di terracotta fra le braccia, si voltarono e tacquero, costernate, vedendo venir su quei due, affocati, paonazzi, tutti in sudore, arrangolati. O non erano i fratelli Tortorici, quei due? Sì, Neli e Saro Tortorici. Poveretti! Poveretti! Non si riconoscevano più, in quello stato. Che era loro accaduto? Perchè quella fuga disperata?

Neli, il minore dei fratelli, non potendone più, s'era fermato per tirar fiato e rispondere a quelle donne; ma Saro se lo trascinò via, per un braccio.

—Giurlannu Zarù, nostro cugino!—disse allora Neli, voltandosi, e alzò una mano in atto di benedire.

Le donne proruppero in esclamazioni di compianto e d'orrore, e una domandò, forte:

—Chi è stato?

—Nessuno, Dio!—gridò Neli da lontano.

Voltarono, corsero alla piazzetta, ov'era la casa del medico condotto.

Il signor dottore, Sidoro Lopiccolo, scamiciato, spettorato, con una barbaccia di almeno dieci giorni su le guance flosce, squallido, con gli occhi gonfi, acquosi, ammaccati, s'aggirava per le stanze, strascicando le ciabatte, reggendo su le braccia una povera bambina malata, pelle e ossa, ingiallita, di circa nove anni. La moglie, in un fondo di letto, da undici mesi inutile; sei figliuoli per casa, oltre a quella che teneva in braccio, ch'era la maggiore, laceri, sudici, inselvaggiti; tutta la casa, sossopra, una rovina: cocci di piatti, bucce, l'immondizia a mucchi per terra; seggiole rotte, poltrone sfondate, letti non più rifatti chi sa da quanto tempo, con le coperte a brandelli,

74

THE FLY

Out of breath, panting—when they were below the village, which sits with its densely packed chalky little houses on the blue-clay plateau—to save time they climbed up the slippery slope, making use of their hands, because their large, coarse hobnailed shoes were sliding, damn it!

The women, closely gathered and talking loudly in front of the little fountain, with their terra-cotta pitchers under their arms, turned around and fell silent in alarm when they saw those two men coming, overheated, purple in the face, drenched with sweat, worn out. Say, weren't those two the Tortorici brothers? Yes, Neli and Saro Tortorici. Poor things! Poor things! They were unrecognizable in that state. What had happened to them? Why that desperate haste?

Neli, the younger of the brothers, totally exhausted, had stopped to catch his breath and answer the women's questions; but Saro dragged him away with him by one arm.

"Giurlannu Zarù, our cousin!" Neli then said, turning around, and raised one hand in a gesture of benediction.

The women broke out into exclamations of sympathy and horror, and one loudly asked:

"Who did it?"

"Nobody, God!" Neli shouted from the distance.

They turned a corner and ran to the little village square, where the house of the municipal doctor stood.

The physician in question, Sidoro Lopiccolo, in his shirt sleeves, with his chest exposed, with a rough beard of at least ten days' growth on his flabby cheeks, unkempt, with swollen, watery, sunken eyes, was moving about through the rooms, dragging his slippers, and carrying in his arms a poor little sick girl—nothing but skin and bones, with a sallow complexion—about nine years old. His wife, bedridden for eleven months, unable to help; six little children in the house—besides the one he was holding in his arms, who was the eldest—all in tatters, dirty, running wild; the whole house upside down, a ruin; broken dishes, rinds, the garbage piled on the floor; broken chairs, bottomless armchairs, beds that hadn't

75

perché i ragazzi amavano di far la guerra su i letti, a cuscinate, bellini! Solo intatto, in una stanza ch'era stata salottino, un ritratto fotografico ingrandito, appeso alla parete: il ritratto di lui, del signor dottore, Sidoro Lopiccolo, quand'era giovincello, laureato da poco: lindo, attillato, fresco e sorridente.

Davanti a questo ritratto egli si recava ora, ciabattando; gli mostrava i denti gialli, in un ghigno orrendo; squassava la testa; gli presentava la figliuola inferma:

—Sisinello, Sisinè!

Così, *Sisinello*, lo chiamava, per vezzeggiarlo, sua madre, allora; sua madre che si riprometteva grandi cose da lui, ch'era il beniamino, la colonna d'oro, lo stendardo della casa.

—Sisinello, Sisinè!

Accolse come un mastino idrofobo quei due contadini.

—Che volete?

Parlò Saro Tortorici, affannato, con la berretta in mano:

—Signor dottore, c'è un poverello, nostro cugino, che sta morendo . . .

—Beato lui! Sonate a festa le campane!—gridò il dottore.

—Nossignore . . . Sta morendo, tutt'insieme, non si sa di che—riprese quegli.—Nelle terre di Montelusa, in una stalla.

Il dottore si tirò un passo indietro ed esplose, inferocito:

—A Montelusa?

C'erano, dal paese, sette miglia buone di strada. E che strada!

—Sissignore, presto presto, per carità!—pregò il Tortorici.—È tutto nero, come il fegato! gonfio, che fa paura. Per carità!

—Ma come, a piedi?—urlò il dottore.—Dieci miglia a piedi? Voi siete pazzi! La mula! Voglio la mula. L'avete portata?

—Corro subito a prenderla,—s'affrettò a rispondere il Tortorici.—Me la faccio prestare.

—E io allora,—disse Neli, il minore,—nel frattempo, scappo a farmi la barba.

Il dottore si voltò a guardarlo, come se lo volesse mangiar con gli occhi.

—È domenica, signorino,—si scusò Neli, sorridendo, smarrito.—Sono fidanzato, io.

been made for who knows how long, with the blankets in shreds, because the boys enjoyed playing war on the beds with the pillows as weapons, the little dears! The only thing still intact, in a room that had once been the little parlor, was an enlarged photographic portrait hung on the wall: the portrait of him, Dr. Sidoro Lopiccolo, when he was a young man, recently graduated: handsome, well dressed, fresh-looking and smiling.

To this portrait he now made his way, with flopping slippers; he bared his yellow teeth at it, in a frightening leer; he shook his head; he showed it his sick daughter:

"Sisinello, Sisinè!"

Sisinello, that's what his mother used to call him as a pet name back then; his mother, who expected great things of him, the favorite son, the golden pillar, the banner of the household.

"Sisinello, Sisinè!"

He greeted the two farmhands like a rabid mastiff:

"What do you want?"

It was Saro Tortorici who spoke, short of breath, with his cap in his hand:

"Doctor, there's a poor man, our cousin, who's dying . . . "

"Good for him! Ring the church bells to celebrate!" the doctor shouted.

"No, sir . . . He's dying just like that, nobody knows what from," the other man continued. "On the Montelusa property, in a stable."

The doctor took a step backward and exploded in fury:

"At Montelusa?"

From the village it was a good seven miles along the road. And what a road!

"Yes, sir, hurry, hurry, for mercy's sake!" Tortorici begged. "He's black, like a liver! So swollen up, it's frightening. Please!"

"But how, on foot?" the doctor howled. "Ten miles on foot? You're crazy! A mule! I want a mule. Did you bring one?"

"I'll run right over and get one," Tortorici hastened to reply. "I'll borrow one."

"In that case," said Neli, the younger brother, "I'll dash over in the meantime and get a shave."

The doctor turned around and looked at him as if he wanted to eat him up alive.

"It's Sunday, sir," Neli apologized, smiling in confusion. "I'm engaged."

—Ah, fidanzato sei?—sghignò allora il medico, fuori di
sé.—E pigliati questa, dunque!

Gli rivesciò, così dicendo, fra le braccia la figliuola malata;
poi prese a uno a uno gli altri piccini che gli si erano affollati
attorno e glieli spinse di furia tra le gambe:

—E quest'altro! e quest'altro! e quest'altro! e quest'altro!
Bestia! bestia! bestia!

Gli voltò le spalle, fece per andarsene, ma tornò indietro,
si riprese la malatuccia e gridò ai due:

—Andate via! La mula! Vengo subito.

Neli Tortorici tornò a sorridere, scendendo la scala, dietro
al fratello. Aveva vent'anni, lui; la fidanzata, Luzza, sedici:
una rosa. Sette figliuoli? Ma pochi! Dodici, ne voleva. E a man-
tenerli, si sarebbe ajutato con quel pajo di braccia sole, ma
buone, che Dio gli aveva dato. Allegramente, sempre. Lavorare e cantare, tutto a regola d'arte: zappa e canto. Non per
nulla lo chiamavano Liolà, il poeta.

Egli sorrideva finanche all'aria che respirava, perchè si sentiva amato da tutti, per la sua bontà servizievole, per il suo
buon'umore costante, per la sua bellezza florida. Il sole non
era ancora riuscito a cuocergli la pelle, a inaridirgli il bel
biondo dorato dei capelli riccioluti, che tante donne gli avrebbero invidiato, tante donne che arrossivano, turbate, se egli
le guardava in un certo modo, con quegli occhi ceruli, vivi
vivi.

Più che del caso del cugino Zarù, egli, quel giorno, era afflitto in fondo del broncio che gli avrebbe tenuto la sua Luzza,
che da sei giorni sospirava quella domenica per stare un po'
con lui. Ma poteva egli, in coscienza, esimersi da quella carità
di cristiano? Povero Giurlannu! Era fidanzato anche lui! Che
guajo, così all'improvviso! Abbacchiava le mandorle, laggiù,
nella tenuta del Lopes, a Montelusa. La mattina avanti, sabato,
il tempo s'era messo all'acqua; ma non pareva ci fosse pericolo
di pioggia imminente. Verso mezzogiorno, però, il Lopes dice:

—In un'ora Dio lavora; non vorrei che le mandorle mi ri-
manessero per terra, sotto la pioggia.—E aveva comandato
alle donne che stavano a raccogliere, di andar su, nel magaz-
zino, a smallare. —Voi,—dice, rivolto agli uomini che abbacchiavano, e c'erano pure loro, Neli e Saro Tortorici,—Voi, se
volete, andate anche su, con le donne, a smallare.—Giurlannu

"Ah, you're engaged?" the doctor then sneered, beside himself. "If that's the case, take this one!"

So saying, he dumped his sick daughter into his arms; then, one by one, he took the other little ones who had crowded around him and furiously shoved them between his knees:

"And this one! And this one! And this one! And this one! Fool! Fool! Fool!"

He turned his back on him, started to leave, but came back again, took back the sick girl and shouted at the two:

"Go away! Get the mule! I'll be right with you."

Neli Tortorici resumed smiling as he went down the stairs behind his brother. He was twenty; his fiancée, Luzza, sixteen: a rose. Seven children? That's not many! He wanted twelve. And to support them he would rely on nothing but that pair of arms, good ones, that God had given him. Cheerfully, as always. Working and singing, all in a professional way: his mattock and his song. It wasn't for nothing they called him Liolà, the poet. He smiled even at the air he breathed, because he felt loved by everyone, because of his help-fulness and good nature, because of his unfailing good humor, because of his youthful good looks. The sun had not yet managed to tan his skin, to wither the beautiful golden blonde of his curly hair, which plenty of women would have envied him, all those women who blushed in their agitation if he looked at them in a certain way with those extremely vivid blue eyes.

That day, he was fundamentally less afflicted by the case of his cousin Zarù than by the sulky treatment he would receive from his Luzza, who for six days had been yearning for that Sunday to spend a little time with him. But could he in all conscience shirk that duty of Christian charity? Poor Giurlannu! He was engaged, too! What a disaster, all of a sudden like that! He was knocking down the almonds out there, on the Lopes farm at Montelusa. The morning before, Saturday, the weather had begun to threaten rain; but there seemed to be no imminent danger of its falling. Toward noon, however, Lopes said: "Things happen fast;[1] I wouldn't want my almonds to lie on the ground, exposed to the rain." And he had ordered the women who were gathering them to go up to the store-house and shell them. "You," he said, addressing the men who were knocking down the nuts, among them Neli and Saro Tortorici, "you, if you want, go up, too, with the women to shell them." Giur-

---

[1] Literally, "God does his work in a single hour."

Zarù:—Pronto,—dice,—ma la giornata mi corre col mio salario, di venticinque soldi?—No, mezza giornata,—dice il Lopes,—te la conto col tuo salario; il resto, a mezza lira, come le donne.—Soperchieria! Perché, mancava forse per gli uomini di lavorare e di guadagnarsi la giornata intera? Non pioveva; né piovve difatti per tutta la giornata, né la notte.—Mezza lira, come le donne?—dice Giurlannu Zarù.—Io porto calzoni. Mi paghi la mezza giornata a venticinque soldi, e vado via.

Non se n'andò: rimase ad aspettare fino a sera i cugini, che s'erano contentati di smallare, a mezza lira, con le donne. A un certo punto, però, stanco di stare in ozio, a guardare, s'era recato in una stalla lì vicino per buttarsi a dormire, raccomandando alla ciurma di svegliarlo quando sarebbe venuta l'ora d'andar via.

S'abbacchiava da un giorno e mezzo, e le mandorle raccolte erano poche. Le donne proposero di smallarle tutte quella sera stessa, lavorando fino a tardi e rimanendo a dormir lì il resto della notte, per risalire al paese la mattina dopo, levandosi a bujo. Così fecero. Il Lopes portò fave cotte e due fiaschi di vino. A mezzanotte, finito di smallare, si buttarono tutti, uomini e donne, a dormire al sereno su l'aja, dove la paglia rimasta era bagnata dall'umido, come se veramente fosse piovuto.

—Liolà, canta!

E lui, Neli, s'era messo a cantare, all'improvviso. La luna entrava e usciva di tra un fitto intrico di nuvolette bianche e nere; e la luna era il volto di Luzza che sorrideva e s'oscurava alle vicende or tristi or liete dell'amore.

Giurlannu Zarù era rimasto ne la stalla. Prima dell'alba, Saro si era recato a svegliarlo e lo aveva trovato lì, gonfio e nero, con un febbrone da cavallo.

Questo raccontò Neli Tortorici, là, dal barbiere, il quale, a un certo punto, distraendosi, lo inicciò col rasojo. Una feritina, presso il mento, che non pareva nemmeno, via! Neli non ebbe neanche il tempo di risentirsene, perché alla porta del barbiere s'era affacciata Luzza con la madre e Mita Lumìa, la povera fidanzata di Giurlannu Zarù, che gridava e piangeva, disperata.

Ci volle del bello e del buono per fare intendere a quella poveretta che non poteva andare fino a Montelusa, a vedere il fidanzato: lo avrebbe veduto prima di sera, appena lo avreb-

lannu Zarù said: "Fine, but will I still get my full day's wages, twenty-five *soldi*?" "No, half-pay," said Lopes; "I'll count it in when I pay you; for the rest of the day, the rate is half a *lira,* like the women." What an outrage! Why? Maybe there wasn't enough work for the men to do and earn a full day's pay? It wasn't raining; in fact, it didn't rain all that day, or that night. "Half a *lira,* like the women? said Giurlannu Zarù. "I wear pants. Pay me for the half day at the rate of twenty-five *soldi,* and I'll leave."

He didn't leave; he stayed there waiting until evening for his cousins, who consented to shell almonds, at the rate of half a *lira,* along with the women. At a certain point, however, tired of standing around idle and looking on, he had gone into a nearby stable to catch a nap, asking the work crew to wake him up when it was time to go.

They had been knocking down almonds for a day and a half, but not many had been gathered. The women suggested shelling all of them that very evening, working late and staying there to sleep for the rest of the night, then making their way back up to the village the next morning, getting up while it was still dark. And that's what they did. Lopes brought them boiled beans and two bottles of wine. At midnight, when the shelling was over, all of them, men and women, went out to sleep in the open air on the threshing floor, where the straw that had been left there was wet with dew, as if it really had rained.

"Liolà, sing!"

And he, Neli, had begun singing, all at once. The moon passed in and out of a dense tangle of little white and black clouds; and the moon was Luzza's face, smiling and darkening in accordance with the vicissitudes—now sad, now happy—of love.

Giurlannu Zarù had remained in the stable. Before dawn, Saro had gone to awaken him and had found him there, swollen and black, with a raging fever.

That is the story Neli Tortorici told there, at the barber's; at a certain point the barber, his attention wandering, nicked him with the razor. A tiny cut, near his chin, that wasn't even visible—forget it! Neli didn't even have time to feel it, because Luzza had appeared at the barber's door with her mother and Mita Lumìa, Giurlannu Zarù's poor fiancée, who was yelling and weeping in despair.

It took a lot of talking to make the poor girl understand that she couldn't go all the way to Montelusa to see her fiancé: she would see him before evening, as soon as they brought him up as best

bero portato su, alla meglio. Sopravvenne Saro, sbraitando che il medico era già a cavallo e non voleva più aspettare. Neli si tirò Luzza in disparte e la pregò che avesse pazienza: sarebbe ritornato prima di sera e le avrebbe detto tante belle cose.

Belle cose, di fatti, sono anche queste, per due fidanzati che se le dicono stringendosi le mani e guardandosi negli occhi.

Stradaccia scellerata! Certi precipizii, che al dottor Lopiccolo facevano veder la morte con gli occhi, non ostante che Saro di qua, Neli di là reggessero la mula per la cavezza.

Dall'alto si scorgeva tutta la vasta campagna, a pianure e convalli; coltivata a biade, a oliveti, a mandorleti; gialla ora di stoppie e qua e là chiazzata di nero dai fuochi della debbiatura; in fondo, si scorgeva il mare, d'un aspro azzurro. Gelsi, carrubi, cipressi, olivi serbavano il loro vario verde, perenne; le corone dei mandorli s'erano già diradate. Tutt'intorno, nell'ampio giro dell'orizzonte, c'era come un velo di vento. Ma la calura era estenuante; il sole spaccava le pietre. Arrivava or sì or no, di là dalle siepi polverose di fichidindia, qualche strillo di calandra o la risata d'una gazza, che faceva drizzar le orecchie alla mula del dottore.

—Mula mala! mula mala!—si lamentava egli allora.

Per tener gli occhi fissi a quelle orecchie, non avvertiva neppure al sole che aveva davanti, e lasciava l'ombrellaccio aperto appoggiato su l'omero.

—Vossignoria non abbia paura, ci siamo qua noi,—lo esortavano i fratelli Tortorici.

Paura, veramente, il dottore non avrebbe dovuto averne. Ma egli diceva che temeva pei figliuoli. Doveva guardarsi la pelle per quei sette disgraziati, sì o no?

Per distrarlo, i Tortorici si misero a parlargli della mal'annata: scarso il frumento, scarso l'orzo, scarse le fave; pe' mandorli, si sapeva: non raffermano sempre: carichi un anno e l'altro no; e delle ulive non parlavano: la nebbia le aveva distrutte, sul nascere; nè c'era da rifarsi con la vendemmia, ché tutti i vigneti della contrada eran presi dal male.

—Bella consolazione!—andava dicendo a ogni tanto il dottore, dimenando la testa.

they could. They were joined by Saro, shouting loudly that the doctor was already mounted and didn't want to wait any longer. Neli drew Luzza aside and begged her to be patient: he would return before evening and would "tell her all sorts of nice things."

In fact, even sad things like this are nice, for an engaged couple who say them to each other while holding hands and looking into each other's eyes.

What a godforsaken road! There were some cliffs that made Dr. Lopiccolo see death before his eyes, even though Saro on one side and Neli on the other were leading the mule by the halter.

From the heights one could make out the entire vast countryside, all plains and dales; planted with grain, olive groves and almond groves; already yellow with fields of stubble and flecked with black here and there by land-clearing fires; in the background one could make out the sea, of a harsh blue. The mulberry, carob, cypress and olive trees still retained their various shades of perennial green; the tops of the almond trees had already thinned out. All around, in the extensive circle of the horizon, there was a sort of veil of wind. But the heat was overpowering; the sun split the stones. From time to time, from beyond the dusty hedges of prickly pear, there was heard the call of a lark or the chatter of a magpie, making the doctor's mule prick up its ears.

"Bad mule! Bad mule!" he would then lament.

In order to keep his gaze fixed on those ears, he didn't even pay attention to the sunshine striking him from the front, and he left his wretched open parasol leaning on his shoulder.

"Don't be afraid, sir, *we're* here," the Tortorici brothers encouraged him.

To tell the truth, the doctor ought not to have been afraid. But he said that he feared for his children. Didn't he have to save his skin for the sake of those seven unfortunates?

To distract him, the Tortoricis started telling him about the bad crops: not much wheat, not much barley, not many beans. As for the almond trees, it's well known—they don't always form good nuts: one year they're chock-full, the next year not. They wouldn't even mention the olives: the fog had destroyed them as they were developing. Nor could the farmers make up their losses with the grape harvest, because all the vineyards in the region were stricken by blight.

"Fine way to cheer me up!" the doctor would say every once in a while, shaking his head.

In capo a due ore di cammino, tutti i discorsi furono esauriti. Ciascuno si concentrò in sè. La via correva per un lungo tratto piana, e lì, su lo strato alto di polvere bianchiccia conversavano ora i quattro zoccoli della mula e gli scarponi imbullettati de' due contadini. Liolà, a un certo punto, si diede a cantilenare svogliato, a mezza voce; smise presto. Non s'incontrava per la strada anima viva, essendo tutti i contadini, la domenica, in paese, chi per la messa, chi per le spese, chi per sollievo. Forse laggiù a Montelusa, non era rimasto alcuno accanto a Giurlannu Zarù, che moriva solo, seppure era vivo ancora, poveraccio.

Solo, difatti, lo trovarono, nella stalluccia intanfata, steso su un murello: livido, enorme, irriconoscibile e ancora vivo! Rantolava.

Dalla finestra ferrata, presso la mangiatoja, entrava il sole a percuotergli la faccia, che non pareva più umana: il naso, nel gonfiore, sparito; le labbra, orribilmente tumefatte. E il rantolo usciva da quelle labbra, esasperato, come un ringhio. Tra i capelli fitti, ricci, neri da moro, una festuca di paglia splendeva nel sole.

I tre si fermarono un tratto a guatarlo, sgomenti e come trattenuti dall'orrore di quella vista. La mula scalpitò, sbruffando, su l'acciottolato de la stalla. Allora Saro Tortorici s'accostò al moribondo e lo chiamò amorosamente:

—Giurlà, Giurlà, c'è il dottore.

Neli andò a legar la mula alla mangiatoja, presso alla quale, sul muro, era come l'ombra di un'altra bestia, l'orma dell'asino che abitava in quella stalla e vi s'era stampato a forza di stropicciarsi.

Giurlannu Zarù, a un nuovo richiamo, smise di rantolare; si provò ad aprir gli occhi, insanguati, anneriti, pieni di paura; aprì la bocca orrenda e gemette, com'arso dentro:

—Muojo!

—No, no,—s'affrettò a dirgli Saro, angosciato.—C'è qua il medico. L'abbiamo condotto noi; lo vedi?

—Portatemi al paese!—pregò il Zarù.—Oh mamma mia!

—Sì, ecco, c'è qua la mula!—rispose subito Saro.

—Ma anche in braccio, Giurlà, ti ci porto io!—disse Neli, accorrendo e chinandosi su lui.—Non t'avvilire!

After two hours on the road, all topics of conversation were exhausted. Each man was shut up within himself. The road was flat for a long stretch and there, on the deep layer of whitish dust, the conversation was now carried on between the four hooves of the mule and the big hobnailed shoes of the two farmhands. Liolà, at a certain point, began to sing listlessly in low tones; he soon stopped. Not a living soul was to be found on the road, because all the countryfolk were in the village on Sundays, some in church, some shopping, some for amusement. Perhaps out there, at Montelusa, nobody had remained beside Giurlannu Zarù, who was dying all alone; that is, if he was still alive, poor guy.

In fact, they did find him alone, in the little musty stable, stretched out on a low wall: livid, swollen up, unrecognizable, but still alive!

He was breathing stertorously.

Through the barred window, near the manger, the sun came in and struck his face, which no longer seemed human: his nose had been swallowed up in the swelling; his lips were horribly puffed up. And from those lips issued the heavy breathing, intensified, like a snarl. In his thick, curly hair, dark as a Moor's, a wisp of straw glistened in the sunlight.

The three men stopped for a while to stare at him, frightened and seemingly immobilized by the horror of that sight. The mule, sputtering, pawed the cobbled floor of the stable. Then Saro Tortorici went over to the dying man and called to him affectionately:

"Giurlà, Giurlà, the doctor is here."

Neli went to tie the mule to the manger, near which, on the wall, was the seeming shadow of another animal, the trace of the donkey that resided in that stable and had impressed his outline on it by dint of rubbing up against it.

Giurlannu Zarù, on being called again, stopped his heavy breathing; he tried to open his eyes, which were bloodshot, circled with black and full of fear; he opened his horrendous mouth and groaned, as if burning inside.

"I'm dying!"

"No, no," Saro quickly said to him in anguish. "The doctor is here. We brought him. See him?"

"Take me to the village!" Zarù begged. "Oh, Mother!"

"Yes, look, we've got the mule here!" Saro at once replied.

"But I'll even carry you there in my arms, Giurlà," said Neli, running up and bending over him. "Don't lose courage!"

Giurlannu Zarù si volse alla voce di Neli, lo guardò un tratto con quegli occhi che mettevano spavento, poi mosse un braccio e lo prese per la cintola.

—Tu, bello? Tu?

—Io, sì, coraggio! Piangi? Non piangere, Giurlà, non piangere . . . È nulla!

E gli posò una mano sul petto sussultante dai singhiozzi che non potevano uscirgli dalla gola. Soffocato, il Zarù scosse il capo rabbiosamente, poi alzò una mano, prese Neli per la nuca e l'attirò a sé:

—Insieme, noi, dovevamo sposare . . .

—E insieme sposeremo, non dubitare!—disse Neli, levandogli la mano, che gli s'era avvinghiata alla nuca.

Intanto il medico osservava il moribondo. Era chiaro: un caso di carbonchio.

—Dite un po', vi ricordate di qualche insetto che v'abbia morso?

—No, fece col capo il Zarù.

—Insetto?—domandò Saro.

Il medico spiegò, come poteva a quei due ignoranti, il male. Qualche bestia doveva esser morta, in quei dintorni, di carbonchio. Su la carogna, buttata via in qualche burrone, chi sa quanti insetti s'erano posati; qualcuno d'essi aveva potuto inoculare il male al Zarù.

Questi, mentre il medico parlava, aveva voltato la faccia verso il muro. Nessuno lo sapeva, e la morte intanto era lì, ancora; così piccola, che si sarebbe appena potuta scorgere, se qualcuno ci avesse fatto caso. Era una mosca, lì sul muro, che pareva immobile; ma, a guardarla bene, or cacciava fuori la piccola proboscide e pompava, or si nettava celermente le due esili zampine anteriori, stropicciandole fra loro, come soddisfatta. Il Zarù la scorse e la fissò con gli occhi.

Una mosca . . .

Poteva essere stata quella o un'altra . . . Chi sa? Perché, ora, sentendo parlare il medico, gli pareva di ricordarsi. Sì, il giorno avanti, quando s'era buttato lì, a dormire, aspettando che i cugini finissero di smallar le mandorle del Lopes, una mosca gli aveva dato tanto fastidio . . . Poteva esser questa? Le vide spiccare il volo e la seguì con gli occhi. Ecco, era andata a posarsi su la guancia di Neli. Dalla guancia, lieve lieve, essa ora scorreva, in due tratti, sul mento, fino alla scalfittura del rasojo, e s'attaccava lì, vorace.

Giurlannu Zarù turned toward Neli's voice, looked at him for a while with those fear-provoking eyes, then moved one arm and took hold of his belt.

"You, Handsome? You?"

"Yes, me; be brave! You're crying? Don't cry, Giurlà, don't cry . . . It's nothing!"

And he placed a hand on his chest, which was shaken by the sobs that were stuck in his throat. Choking, Zarù shook his head furiously, then raised one hand, took Neli by the nape of his neck and drew him toward himself:

"We were supposed to get married at the same time . . . "

"And we *will* get married at the same time, have no doubts!" said Neli, removing his hand, which had clasped his neck tightly.

Meanwhile the doctor was observing the dying man. It was clear: a case of anthrax.

"Tell me, do you recall being bitten by any insect?"

"No," Zarù indicated by shaking his head.

"Insect?" asked Saro.

The doctor explained the disease to those two uneducated men as best he could. Some animal must have died of anthrax in that vicinity. Insects—who knows how many?—had lighted on the carcass, which had been thrown away into some ravine; one of them could have transmitted the disease to Zarù.

While the doctor was speaking, Zarù had turned his face to the wall. No one knew it, but all the same death was still there; so small that it could hardly have been descried if anyone had intentionally looked for it. It was a fly, there on the wall, seemingly immobile; but, if you looked closely, now it was projecting its little mouth-tube and pumping, now it was rapidly cleaning its two thin front feet, rubbing them together, as if in contentment. Zarù caught sight of it and stared at it.

A fly . . .

It might have been that one or another one . . . Who knows? Because now, hearing the doctor talk, he thought he remembered. Yes, the day before, when he had lain down there to sleep, waiting for his cousins to finish shelling Lopes' almonds, a fly had bothered him terribly . . . Could it be this one? He saw it take flight and followed its movements with his eyes. There! it had landed on Neli's cheek. From his cheek, softly, softly, it was now moving, in a broken line, to his chin, right up to the razor scratch, and there it dug in, voraciously.

Giurlannu Zarù stette a mirarla un pezzo, intento, assorto. Poi, tra l'affanno catarroso, domandò con una voce da caverna:

—Una mosca, può essere?

—Una mosca? E perché no?—rispose il medico.

Giurlannu Zarù non disse altro: si rimise a mirare quella mosca che Neli, quasi imbalordito dalle parole del medico, non cacciava via. Egli, il Zarù, non badava al discorso del medico, ma godeva che questi, parlando, assorbisse così l'attenzione del cugino da farlo stare immobile come una statua, da non fargli avvertire il fastidio di quella mosca. Oh fosse la stessa! Allora, sì, davvero, avrebbero sposato insieme! Una cupa invidia, una sorda gelosia feroce lo avevano preso di quel giovine cugino, così florido, per cui piena di promesse rimaneva la vita, che a lui, ecco, veniva improvvisamente a mancare . . .

A un tratto Neli, come se si sentisse punto, alzò una mano, si cacciò la mosca e con le dita cominciò a pizzicarsi il mento, sul taglietto, volgendosi al Zarù che lo guardava e aveva aperto le labbra orrende, come a un sorriso mostruoso. Si guardarono un po' così. Poi il Zarù disse, quasi senza volerlo:

—La mosca . . .

Neli non comprese e inchinò l'orecchio:

—Che dici?

—La mosca . . .—ripeté quegli.

—Quale? dove?—chiese Neli, costernato, guardando il medico.

—Lì, dove ti gratti. Lo so sicuro!—disse il Zarù.

Neli mostrò al dottore la feritina sul mento:

—Che ci ho? Mi prude . . .

Il medico lo guardò, accigliato; poi, come se volesse osservarlo meglio, lo condusse fuori de la stalla. Saro li seguì.

Che avvenne poi? Giurlannu Zarù attese, attese a lungo, con un'ansia che gl'irritava dentro tutte le viscere. Udiva parlare, là fuori, confusamente. A un tratto, Saro rientrò di furia ne la stalla, prese la mula e, senza neanche volgersi a guardarlo, uscì, gemendo:

—Ah, Neluccio mio! ah, Neluccio mio!

Dunque, era vero? Ed ecco, lo abbandonavano lì, come un

Giurlannu Zarù kept looking at it for a while intently, with concentration. Then, through his catarrhal panting, he asked in a cavernous voice:

"Could it be a fly?"

"A fly? Why not?" the doctor replied.

Giurlannu Zarù said nothing more: he resumed staring at that fly, which Neli, as if dazed by the doctor's words, failed to shoo away. He, Zarù, was paying no attention to the doctor's speech, but was pleased that, with his talking, he was engrossing his cousin's attention to such an extent that Neli remained as motionless as a statue and paid no heed to the annoyance that fly was causing him. Oh, if it were only the same one! Yes, then they really would get married at the same time! He had been seized by a sullen envy, an unspoken ferocious jealousy of that young cousin, so strong and healthy, for whom life remained full of promise—life, which suddenly was running out for *him* . . .

All at once Neli, as if he had felt himself bitten, raised one hand, drove away the fly and with his fingers began to pinch his chin, where the little cut was, turning toward Zarù, who was looking at him and had opened his horrendous lips, as if in a monstrous smile. They looked at each other in that way for a while. Then Zarù said, as if not meaning to:

"The fly . . . "

Neli didn't understand and bent down his head to listen.

"What are you saying?"

"The fly . . . ," he repeated.

"Which one? Where?" asked Neli, in alarm, looking at the doctor.

"There, where you're scratching. I'm sure of it!" said Zarù.

Neli showed the doctor the tiny wound in his chin.

"What's wrong with me? It itches . . . "

The doctor looked at him, frowning; then, as if he wanted to examine him more closely, he led him out of the stables. Saro followed them.

What happened next? Giurlannu Zarù waited, waited a long time, with an anxiety that irritated all his insides. He heard a confused sound of talking outside. All of a sudden, Saro came back into the stable furiously, took the mule and, without even turning around to look at him, went out, moaning:

"Ah, my Neluccio! Ah, my Neluccio!"

Was it true, then? And look, were they abandoning him there,

cane? . . . Provò a rizzarsi su un gomito, chiamò due volte:
—Saro . . . Saro . . .

Silenzio. Nessuno. Non si resse più sul gomito, ricadde a giacere e si mise per un pezzo come a grufare, per non sentire il silenzio della campagna, che lo atterriva. A un tratto, gli nacque il dubbio che avesse sognato, che avesse fatto quel sogno cattivo, nella febbre; ma, nel rivoltarsi verso il muro, vide la mosca, lì di nuovo. Or cacciava fuori la piccola proboscide e pompava, or si nettava celermente le due esili zampine anteriori, stropicciandole fra loro, come soddisfatta.

like a dog? . . . He tried to raise himself on one elbow and called out twice:

"Saro . . . Saro . . . "

Silence. Nobody. He couldn't support himself any longer on his elbow, he fell back into a recumbent position and for a while he seemed to be rooting and grubbing around, in order not to hear the silence of the countryside, which terrified him. Suddenly he began to wonder whether he had dreamed the whole thing, whether he had had that bad dream in his feverish state; but, when he turned to the wall, he saw the fly there again. Now it was projecting its little mouth-tube and pumping, now it was rapidly cleaning its two thin front feet, rubbing them together, as if in contentment.

LA GIARA

Piena anche per gli olivi, quell'annata. Piante massaie, cariche l'anno avanti, avevano raffermato tutte, a dispetto della nebbia che le aveva oppresse sul fiorire.

Lo Zirafa, che ne aveva un bel giro nel suo podere delle Quote a Primosole, prevedendo che le cinque giare vecchie di coccio smaltato, che aveva in cantina, non sarebbero bastate a contener tutto l'olio della nuova raccolta, ne aveva ordinata a tempo una sesta più capace a Santo Stefano di Camastra, dove si fabbricavano: alta a petto d'uomo, bella panciuta e maestosa, che fosse delle altre cinque la badessa.

Neanche a dirlo, aveva litigato anche col fornaciajo di là per questa giara. E con chi non litigava, don Lollò Zirafa? Per ogni nonnulla, anche per una pietruzza caduta dal murello di cinta, anche per una festuca di paglia, litigava. E a furia di carta bollata e d'onorari agli avvocati, citando questo e quello e pagando sempre le spese per tutti, s'era mezzo rovinato.

Dicevano che il suo consulente legale, stanco di vederselo comparir dinanzi su la mula due o tre volte la settimana, per levarselo di torno, gli aveva regalato un libricino prezioso, piccolo piccolo, come quelli da messa: il codice, perché si scapasse a cercar da sé il fondamento giuridico alle liti che voleva intentare.

Prima, tutti coloro con cui aveva da dire, per prenderlo in giro gli gridavano:—Sellate la mula!—. Ora, invece, gli dicevano:—Consultate il calepino!

E don Lollò rispondeva:

—Sicuro, e vi fulmino, figli d'un cane!

Quella giara nuova, pagata quattr'onze ballanti e sonanti, in attesa del posto da trovarle in cantina, fu allogata lì per lì nel palmento. Una giara così non s'era mai veduta: capiva a dir poco duecento litri. Allogata in quell'antro umido, intanfato di

THE OIL JAR

A bumper crop of olives, too, that year. Productive trees, laden down the year before, had all borne firm fruit, in spite of the fog that had stifled them when in blossom.

Zirafa, who had a fair number of them on his farm Le Quote at Primosole, foreseeing that the five old glazed ceramic oil jars he had in his cellar wouldn't be enough to hold all the oil from the new harvest, had ordered a sixth, larger one in advance from Santo Stefano di Camastra, where they were made: as tall as a man's chest, beautiful, big-bellied and majestic, it would be the "abbess" of the five others.

Needless to say, he had litigated even with the kiln operator there over this jar. And with whom did Don[1] Lollò Zirafa fail to litigate? Over any trifle, even over a crumb of stone that had fallen from the perimeter wall, even over a wisp of straw, he would go to court. And by dint of all those legal documents and lawyers' fees, summonsing this man and that and always paying the costs for everyone, he had half ruined himself.

They said that his legal adviser, tired of seeing him showing up on his mule two or three times a week, in order to get rid of him had made him a present of a tiny, tiny little gem of a book, like a missal—the law code—so that he could rack his brains searching out for himself the legal basis for the lawsuits he wished to institute.

Before that, all those he had quarrels with, to make fun of him, used to shout at him: "Saddle the mule!" Now, instead, they said to him: "Consult the handbook!"

And Don Lollò would answer:

"I sure will, and I'll annihilate you, sons of bitches!"

That new jar—for which he had paid four good *onze*[2] in hard cash—while awaiting the right spot to be found for it in the cellar, was temporarily stored in the grape-pressing shed. A jar like that had never been seen: it could hold at least two hundred liters.

---

[1] A term of respect for a landowner, nobleman or other prominent member of society in Sicily.

[2] *Onza*, or *oncia*, an old Sicilian monetary unit.

mosto e di quell'odore acre e crudo che cova ne' luoghi senz'aria e senza luce, faceva pena. Qualche grosso dispiacere doveva prendersi per essa, glielo dicevano tutti. Ma don Lollò, all'avvertimento, dava una spallata.

Da due giorni era cominciata l'abbacchiatura delle olive, ed egli era su tutte le furie, perché non sapeva dove spartirsi prima, essendo venuti con le mule cariche anche quelli del concime da depositare a mucchi qua e là per la favata della nuova stagione. Da un canto, avrebbe voluto assistere allo scarico di quella continua processione di bestie; dall'altro, non voleva lasciar gli uomini che abbacchiavano; e bestemmiava come un turco e minacciava di fulminar questi e quelli, se un'oliva, che fosse un'oliva, gli sarebbe mancata, come se le avesse prima contate tutte ad una ad una su gli alberi; o se non fosse ogni mucchio di concime della stessa misura degli altri. Col cappellaccio bianco, in maniche di camicia, spettorato, affocato in volto e tutto sgocciolante di sudore, correva di qua e di là, girando gli occhi lupigni e stropicciandosi con rabbia le guance rase, su cui la barba prepotente rinasceva quasi sotto la raschiatura del rasoio.

Ora, alla fine della terza giornata, tre dei contadini che avevano abbacchiato, entrato nel palmento per deporvi le scale e le canne, restarono come tre ceppi alla vista de la bella giara nuova, spaccata quasi in due. Un gran lembo davanti s'era staccato, tutto d'un pezzo, come se qualcuno—«zà!»—l'avesse tagliato netto con la mannaja, prendendo tutta l'ampiezza della pancia, fin giù.

—Muojo! muojo! muojo!—sclamò, quasi senza voce, uno dei tre, battendosi una mano sul petto.

—E chi è stato?—domandò l'altro.

E il terzo:

—Mamma mia! Chi lo sente ora don Lollò? Chi gliele dice? In coscienza, la giara nuova! ah, che peccato!

Il primo, più spaurito di tutti, propose di raccostar subito la porta e andar via zitti zitti, lasciando fuori, appoggiate al muro, le scale e le canne. Ma il secondo s'oppose energicamente:

—Siete pazzi? Con don Lollò? Sarebbe capace di credere che gliel'abbiamo rotta noi. Fermi qua tutti!

Uscì innanzi al palmento e, facendosi portavoce delle mani, chiamò:

Stored in that dark cave, reeking of must and that acrid, raw smell that lurks in places without air or light, it was pitiful to behold. Some serious misfortune had to be suffered on its account, everyone told him. But Don Lollò, at that warning, would shrug his shoulders.

Two days earlier they had begun to knock down the olives, and he was in a vile temper, because he didn't know where to turn first, since the people with the fertilizer to be deposited in heaps here and there for the new season's bean crop had also arrived with their laden mules. On the one hand, he would have liked to be present while that steady parade of animals was being unloaded; on the other hand, he didn't want to leave the men who were knocking down the olives; and he went around cursing like a Turk and threatening to annihilate this man and that, if a single well-grown olive should be missing, just as if he had already counted them all, one by one, on the trees; or if each pile of manure wasn't as high as all the rest. With his homely white hat, in his shirt sleeves, his chest bare, his face all red, dripping all over with sweat, he kept running back and forth, rolling his wolflike eyes and furiously rubbing his shaven cheeks, on which the heavy beard grew back again almost at the very moment it was shaved off.

Now, at the end of the third day, three of the farmhands who had been knocking down the olives, coming into the wine-press shed to put away the ladders and the poles, stood stock still at the sight of the beautiful new jar, split almost in two. A large strip in front had been detached, all in one piece, as if someone —"whack!"—had cut it clean through with his hatchet, across the widest part of its belly, all the way down.

"I'm dying! I'm dying! I'm dying!" exclaimed one of the three, almost tonelessly, beating his chest with one hand.

"Who did it?" asked the second.

And the third:

"Oh, mother! Who is going to face Don Lollò now? Who's going to tell him? Honestly, the new jar! Oh, what a shame!"

The first man, the most frightened of them all, suggested that they immediately close the shutters of the door again and go away as quietly as possible, leaving the ladders and poles outside leaning up against the wall. But the second man vigorously objected:

"Are you crazy? With Don Lollò? He's liable to believe that *we* broke it. We stay right here!"

He went out in front of the shed and, using his hands to amplify his voice, called:

—Don Lollò! Ah, don Lollòoo!

Era sotto la costa laggiù con gli scaricatori del concime e gesticolava al solito furiosamente, dandosi di tratto in tratto con ambo le mani una rincalcata al cappellaccio bianco. Arrivava talvolta, a forza di quelle rincalcate, a non poterselo più strappare dalla nuca e dalla fronte. Già nel cielo si spegnevano gli ultimi fuochi del crepuscolo, e tra la pace che scendeva su la campagna con le ombre della sera e la dolce frescura, avventavano i gesti di quell'uomo sempre infuriato.

—Don Lollò! Ah, don Lollòoo!

Quando venne su e vide lo scempio, parve che volesse impazzire; si scagliò prima contro quei tre; ne afferrò uno per la gola e lo impiccò al muro, gridando:

—Sangue della Madonna, me la pagherete!

Afferrato a sua volta dagli altri due, stravolti nelle facce terrigne, arsicce, bestiali, rivolse contro se stesso la rabbia furibonda, sbatacchiò a terra il cappellaccio, si percosse a lungo il capo e le guance, pestando i piedi e sbraitando a modo di quelli che piangono un parente morto:

—La giara nuova! Quattr'onze di giara! Non incignata ancora!

Voleva sapere chi gliel'avesse rotta! S'era rotta da sé? Qualcuno per forza doveva averla rotta, per infamità o per invidia! Ma quando? ma come? Non si vedeva segno di violenza! Che fosse arrivata rotta dalla fabbrica? Ma che! Sonava come una campana!

Appena i contadini videro che la prima furia gli era ceduta, cominciarono a esortarlo a calmarsi. La giara si poteva sanare. Non era poi rotta malamente. Un pezzo solo. Un bravo conciabrocche la avrebbe rimessa su, nuova. C'era giusto Zi' Dima Licasi, che aveva scoperto un mastice miracoloso, di cui serbava gelosamente il segreto: un mastice, che neanche il martello ci poteva, quando aveva fatto presa. Ecco: se don Lollò voleva, domani, alla punta dell'alba, Zi' Dima Licasi sarebbe venuto lì e in quattro e quattr'otto, la giara, meglio di prima.

Don Lollò diceva di no, a quelle esortazioni: ch'era tutto inutile; che non c'era più rimedio; ma alla fine si lasciò persuadere, e il giorno appresso, all'alba, puntuale, si presentò a Primosole Zi' Dima Licasi con la cesta degli attrezzi dietro le spalle.

"Don Lollò! Oh, Don Lollòoo!"

The Don was down the hillside over there with the men who were unloading the fertilizer, and was gesticulating furiously in his accustomed manner, from time to time pulling his ugly white hat down over his eyes with both hands. Every once in a while, he pulled it down so hard that he could no longer wrench it off his neck and forehead. In the sky the last flames of the sunset were already going out, and amid the peace that descended onto the countryside with the shades of evening and the pleasant coolness, the gestures of that permanently enraged man stood out conspicuously.

"Don Lollò! Oh, Don Lollòoo!"

When he arrived and saw the havoc, it seemed he would go mad; first he hurled himself at those three men: he seized one of them by the throat and pinned him to the wall, shouting:

"Blood of the Madonna, you'll pay for this!"

Seized in his turn by the other two, their earth-colored, parched, brutish faces distorted by excitement, he turned his violent rage against himself, flung his ugly hat to the ground, and beat his head and cheeks for a long time, stamping his feet and bawling in the fashion of people mourning a dead relative:

"The new jar! Four *onze's* worth of jar! Not even used once!"

He wanted to know who had broken it! Did it break by itself? Someone must have broken it, out of meanness or out of envy! But when? How? There were no visible signs of violence! Could it have arrived broken from the potter's shop? No! It rang like a bell!

As soon as the farmhands saw that his first fury had abated, they started urging him to calm down. The jar could be repaired. You see, it wasn't damaged badly. Just a single piece was broken. A competent tinker could fix it, make it as good as new. And Uncle Dima Licasi was the very man; he had discovered a miraculous resin cement, the secret formula for which he guarded jealously: a cement that couldn't even be broken by a hammer, once it had taken hold. There. If Don Lollò was willing, tomorrow, at the crack of dawn, Uncle Dima Licasi would come and, before you knew it, the jar would be better than before.

Don Lollò said no to those exhortations: it was all useless; there was no longer any way to put things right; but finally he allowed himself to be persuaded, and the next day, at dawn, punctually, Uncle Dima Licasi showed up at Primosole with his tool chest on his back.

Era un vecchiotto sbilenco, dalle giunture storpie e nodose, come un ceppo antico d'olivo saraceno. Per cavargli una parola di bocca ci voleva l'uncino. Era mutria, quella taciturnità, era tristezza che aveva radice in quel suo corpo deforme, era anche sconfidenza che gli altri potessero capire e apprezzar giustamente il suo merito d'inventore non ancor patentato. Voleva che parlassero i fatti, Zi' Dima Licasi. Doveva poi guardarsi davanti e dietro, perché non gli rubassero il segreto della confezione di quel mastice miracoloso.

—Fatemelo vedere,—gli disse per prima cosa don Lollò, dopo averlo squadrato a lungo, con diffidenza.

Zi' Dima negò col capo, pieno di dignità.

—All'opera si vede.

—Ma verrà bene?

Zi' Dima posò a terra la cesta, ne cavò un fazzoletto di cotone logoro, stinto tutto avvoltolato; lo svolse; ne trasse fuori religiosamente un pajo d'occhiali col sellino e le stanghe rotti e legati con lo spago; se li inforcò, e si mise a esaminare attentamente la giara tratta fuori, all'aperto, sull'aja. Disse:

—Verrà bene.

—Col mastice solo però,—pose innanzi per patto lo Zirafa,—non mi fido. Ci voglio anche i punti.

—E allora me ne vado,—rispose senz'altro Zi' Dima, rimettendosi la cesta dietro le spalle.

Don Lollò lo acchiappò per un braccio.

—Dove? Messere e porco, così trattate? Ma guarda un po' che arie da Carlomagno! Scannato miserabile, brutto conciabrocche sei, pezzo d'asino, e devi stare agli ordini! Ci devo metter olio, io, là dentro, e l'olio trasuda, bestione! Un miglio di spaccatura, col mastice solo? Ci voglio i punti. Mastice e punti. Comando io.

Zi' Dima chiuse gli occhi, strinse le labbra e scosse il capo. Tutti così! Gli era negato il piacere di fare un lavoro pulito, filato coscienziosamente a regola d'arte, e di dare una prova della virtù del suo mastice.

—Se la giara—disse—non suona di nuovo come una campana . . .

—Niente, niente!—lo interruppe don Lollò.—I punti! Pago mastice e punti. Quanto vi debbo dare?

He was a crooked old man, with knotty arthritic joints, like an old stump of Saracen[3] olive tree. To wrench a word out of his mouth you needed a hook. It was haughtiness, that taciturnity, it was sadness rooted in that misshapen body of his; it was also a lack of belief that others could understand and rightly appreciate his deserts as an inventor who had not yet received any patent. He wanted the facts to speak for themselves, did Uncle Dima Licasi. And thus he had to be constantly on his guard so that his secret formula for making that miraculous cement wasn't stolen.

"Show it to me," Don Lollò said to him, first off, after looking him up and down for some time in distrust.

Uncle Dima shook his head in refusal, full of dignity.

"You'll see when it's done."

"But will it work?"

Uncle Dima put his tool chest on the ground and took out of it a tattered and faded cotton handkerchief, all rolled up; he unfolded it; he religiously drew out of it a pair of eyeglasses with the bridge and side pieces broken and tied with string; he put them on and began to examine attentively the jar, which had been brought out into the open air, on the threshing floor. He said:

"It will work."

"But with the cement alone," Zirafa laid down as a condition, "I wouldn't feel safe. I want rivets as well."

"In that case I'm leaving," Uncle Dima replied tersely, putting his tool chest behind his back again.

Don Lollò caught him by one arm.

"Where are you off to? Sir Pig, is that how you deal with people? Look, he puts on airs as if he were Charlemagne! A down-and-out, miserable, ugly tinker, that's what you are, you donkey, and you ought to follow orders! I've got to put oil in there, and oil oozes out, you dumb animal! A crack a mile long, with nothing but cement? I want rivets. Cement and rivets. I'm the one giving the orders."

Uncle Dima shut his eyes, pressed his lips together and shook his head. They were all the same! He was denied the pleasure of doing a clean job, in a conscientious, artisanlike manner, and thus furnishing a proof of the powers of his cement.

"If the jar," he said, "doesn't ring again like a bell . . . "

"No, no!" Don Lollò interrupted him. "Rivets! I'm paying for cement and rivets. How much are you asking?"

---

[3] That is, planted by the former Arab occupants of Sicily.

—Se col mastice solo . . .

—Càzzica, che testa!—esclamò lo Zirafa.—Come parlo? V'ho detto che ci voglio i punti. C'intenderemo a lavoro finito: non ho tempo da perdere con voi.

E se n'andò a badare a' suoi uomini.

Zi' Dima si mise all'opera gonfio d'ira e di dispetto. E l'ira e il dispetto gli crebbero a ogni foro che praticava col trapano nella giara e nel lembo staccato per farvi passare il fil di ferro della cucitura. Accompagnava il frullo de la saettella con grugniti a mano a mano più frequenti e più forti; e il viso gli diventava più verde dalla bile e gli occhi vieppiù aguzzi e accesi di stizza. Finita quella prima operazione, scagliò con rabbia il trapano nella cesta; applicò il lembo staccato alla giara per provar se i fori erano a ugual distanza e in corrispondenza tra loro, poi con le tanaglie fece del fil di ferro tanti pezzetti quant'erano i punti che doveva dare, e chiamò per ajuto uno dei contadini che abbacchiavano.

—Coraggio, Zi' Dima!—gli disse quello, vedendogli la faccia alterata.

Zi' Dima alzò la mano a un gesto rabbioso. Aprì la scatola di latta che conteneva il mastice, e lo levò al cielo, scotendolo, come per offrirlo a Dio, poichè gli uomini non volevano riconoscerne la virtù: poi col dito cominciò a spalmarlo tutt'in giro al lembo staccato e lungo la spaccatura; prese le tanaglie e i pezzetti di fil di ferro preparati avanti, e si cacciò dentro la pancia aperta della giara.

—Di dentro?—gli domandò il contadino, a cui aveva dato a reggere il lembo.

Non rispose. Col gesto gli ordinò d'applicar quel lembo alla giara, come aveva fatto lui poc'anzi, e rimase dentro. Prima di mettersi a dare i punti:

—Tira!—disse dall'interno della giara al contadino, con voce di pianto.—Tira con tutta la tua forza! Vedi se si stacca più! Mannaggia a chi non ci crede! E picchia, picchia! Senti come suona, anche con me qua dentro? Va' a dirlo al tuo bel padrone.

—Chi è sopra comanda, Zi' Dima,—sospirò il contadino,—e chi è sotto si danna! Date i punti, date i punti.

E Zi' Dima si mise a far passare ogni pezzetto di fil di ferro attraverso i due fori accanto, l'uno di qua e l'altro di là della

"If it's with the cement only . . . "

"Damn it, what a thick head!" exclaimed Zirafa. "What have I been saying? I told you I want rivets in it. We'll settle up when the job is done: I have no time to waste with you."

And he went off to keep an eye on his men.

Uncle Dima started working, swollen with anger and vexation. And his anger and vexation grew with every drill hole he made in the jar and in the detached piece for the iron wire of the riveting to pass through. He accompanied the whirring of the bit with grunts that became gradually more frequent and louder; and his face became greener with bile and his eyes more and more sharp and inflamed with rage. When that first operation was over, he furiously hurled the drill into the tool chest; he fitted the detached piece to the jar to make sure that the holes were equidistant and matching, then with his pincers he snipped the iron wire into as many small lengths as there were rivets to insert, and he called as an assistant one of the farmhands who were knocking down olives.

"Cheer up, Uncle Dima," that man said to him, seeing his face all upset.

Uncle Dima raised one hand in a furious gesture. He opened the tin box that contained the cement, and raised it to the sky, shaking it, as if to offer it to God, inasmuch as mankind refused to acknowledge its efficacy: then with a finger he began to spread it all around the edges of the detached piece and along the crack; he took the pincers and the previously prepared small lengths of iron wire, and thrust himself into the open belly of the jar.

"From inside?" asked the farmhand, to whom he had given the detached piece to support.

He didn't reply. With a gesture he ordered him to fit that piece to the jar, as he himself had done shortly before, and stayed inside. Before beginning to insert the rivets:

"Pull!" he said to the farmhand from inside the jar, in a tearful voice. "Pull with all your might! See if it comes off again! The devil take anyone who doesn't believe it! And bang on it, bang on it! Hear how it sounds, even with me inside here? Go and tell that to your fine master."

"The man on top gives the orders, Uncle Dima," the farmhand sighed, "and the man on the bottom is damned! Put in the rivets, put in the rivets."

And Uncle Dima began passing every piece of iron wire through the two adjacent holes, one on either side of the mend; and with

saldatura; e con le tanaglie ne attorceva i due capi. Ci volle circa un'ora a passarli tutti. I sudori, giù a fontana, lì dentro la giara. Lavorando, si lagnava pian piano della sua mala sorte. E il contadino, di fuori, a confortarlo.

—Ora ajutami a uscirne,—disse alla fine Zi' Dima.

Ma quanto larga di pancia, tanto quella giara era stretta di collo. Gli parlava il cuore a quel contadino! Ma Zi' Dima, nella rabbia, non ci aveva fatto caso. Ora, prova e riprova, non trovava più modo a uscirne. E il contadino, invece di dargli ajuto, eccolo là, si torceva dalle risa. Imprigionato, imprigionato lì, nella giara da lui stesso sanata, e che ora—non c'era via di mezzo—per farlo uscire, doveva esser rotta daccapo e per sempre.

Alle risa, alle grida, sopravvenne don Lollò. Zi' Dima, dentro la giara, era come un gatto inferocito.

—Fatemi uscire!—urlava.—Corpo di Dio, voglio uscire! Subito! Datemi ajuto!

Don Lollò rimase dapprima come stordito. Non sapeva crederci.

—Ma come? Là dentro? S'è cucito là dentro?

S'accostò alla giara e gridò al vecchio:

—Ajuto? E che ajuto posso darvi? Vecchio stolido, ma come? non dovevate prender prima le misure? Su, provate, fuori un braccio, così! e la testa, su . . . no, piano! ma che! Come avete fatto? E la giara, adesso? Calma! Calma! Calma!—si mise a raccomandare tutt'intorno, come se la calma stessero per perderla gli altri e non lui.—Mi fuma la testa! Calma! Questo è caso nuovo . . . La mula!

Picchiò con le nocche delle dita su la giara. Sonava davvero come una campana.

—Bella! Rimessa a nuovo . . . Aspettate!—disse al prigioniero.—Va' a sellarmi la mula!—ordinò al contadino; e, grattandosi con le dita la fronte, seguitò a dire tra sé: «Ma vedete un po' che mi capita! Questa non è giara! quest'è ordigno del diavolo! Fermo! fermo lì!».

E accorse a regger la giara, in cui Zi' Dima, furibondo, si dibatteva come una bestia in trappola.

—Caso nuovo, caro mio, che deve risolvere l'avvocato! Io non mi fido. Vado e torno, abbiate pazienza! Nell'interesse vostro . . . Intanto, piano! calma! Io mi guardo i miei. E prima

the pincers he twisted the two ends. It took about an hour to pass them all through. He sweated rivers inside the jar. As he worked, he quietly lamented his evil fortune. And the farmhand, outside, kept consoling him.

"Now help me get out," Uncle Dima finally said.

But as wide as it was around the belly, that's how narrow that jar was at the neck. That farmhand had had a true premonition! Uncle Dima, in his rage, had paid no attention. Now, try and try again as he would, he found no way of getting back out. And the farmhand, instead of helping him—there he was, doubled up with laughter. Imprisoned, imprisoned there, in the jar he himself had repaired, and which now—there was no other way—to let him out, would have to be broken again and for good.

The laughter and shouting brought Don Lollò onto the scene. Uncle Dima, inside the jar, was like a maddened cat.

"Get me out!" he was howling. "For God's sake, I want to get out! Right away! Help me out!"

At first Don Lollò just stood there stunned. He couldn't believe it.

"But how? Inside? He riveted himself up inside?"

He went over to the jar and shouted to the old man:

"Help? And what help can I give you? Stupid old man, how could you? Shouldn't you have taken the measurements first? Come on, try, stick out an arm, like that! And your head, come on . . . no, easy does it! What? What have you done? And the jar, now? Keep calm! Keep calm! Keep calm!" he started to advise everyone around him, as if it were the others who were losing their composure and not he. "My head is on fire! Keep calm! This is a new case . . . The mule!"

He tapped on the jar with his knuckles. It really did ring like a bell.

"Beautiful! As good as new . . . Wait!" he said to the prisoner. "Go saddle my mule!" he ordered the farmhand; and, scratching his forehead with his fingers, he continued saying to himself: "But just look at what happens to me! This isn't a jar. It's a contrivance of the devil! Easy! Easy there!"

And he ran over to steady the jar, in which Uncle Dima was violently writhing like a trapped animal.

"A new case, my good man, which my lawyer needs to settle! I don't trust myself. I'll be back in a flash, be patient! It's in your own interests . . . Meanwhile, be still! Keep calm! I look after my

di tutto, per salvare il mio diritto, faccio il mio dovere. Ecco: vi pago il lavoro, vi pago la giornata. Tre lire. Vi bastano?

—Non voglio nulla!—gridò Zi' Dima.—Io voglio uscire!

—Uscirete. Ma io, intanto, vi pago. Qua, tre lire.

Le cavò dal taschino del panciotto e le buttò nella giara. Poi domandò, premuroso:

—Avete fatto colazione? Pane e companatico, subito! Non ne volete? Buttatelo ai cani! A me basta che ve l'abbia dato.

Ordinò che gli si desse; montò in sella, e via di trotto per la città. Chi lo vide, credette che andasse a chiudersi da sé al manicomio, tanto e in così strano modo gestiva, parlando fra sé.

Per fortuna, non gli toccò di fare anticamera nello studio dell'avvocato; ma gli toccò d'attendere un bel po' prima che questo finisse di ridere, quando gli ebbe esposto il caso. Delle risa si stizzì.

—Ma che c'è da ridere, scusi? A vossignoria non brucia! La giara è mia!

Ma quello seguitava a ridere e voleva che gli rinarrasse il caso, com'era stato, per farci su altre risate. Dentro, eh? S'era cucito dentro? E lui, don Lollò, che pretendeva? Te. . . tene. . . tenerlo là dentro . . . ah ah ah . . . tenerlo là dentro per non perderci la giara?

—Ce la devo perdere?—domandò lo Zirafa con le pugna serrate.—Il danno e lo scorno?

—Ma sapete come si chiama questo?—gli disse l'avvocato.—Si chiama sequestro di persona.

—Sequestro? E chi l'ha sequestrato?—esclamò lo Zirafa.—S'è sequestrato lui da sé! Che colpa ho io?

L'avvocato allora gli spiegò che erano due casi. Da un canto, lui, don Lollò, doveva subito liberare il prigioniero per non rispondere di sequestro di persona; dall'altro, il conciabrocche doveva rispondere del danno che veniva a cagionare con la sua imperizia o con la sua storditaggine.

—Ah!—rifiatò lo Zirafa.—Pagandomi la giara!

people. And before all else, in order to have a just claim, I do my duty. Here: I'm paying you for the job, I'm paying you for the day's work. Three *lire*. Is that enough?"

"I don't want a thing!" shouted Uncle Dima. "I want to get out!"

"You *will* get out. But in the meantime I'm paying you. Here, three *lire*."

He took them out of his vest pocket and threw them into the jar. Then he asked, solicitously:

"Have you had lunch? A lunch[4] over here, right away! You don't want any? Throw it to the dogs! It's enough for me that I gave it to you."

He ordered them to give the tinker lunch; he climbed into the saddle, and trotted off to town. Everyone who saw him thought he was going to commit himself to the insane asylum, from the extent and strangeness of his gesticulations, while talking to himself.

Luckily he didn't have to sit and wait at the lawyer's office; but he did have to wait a good while for the lawyer to stop laughing, once he had explained the case. He was annoyed at the laughter.

"But, tell me, what is there to laugh about? It doesn't affect *you!* The jar is mine!"

But the lawyer kept on laughing and wanted him to tell the whole story over again, just as it happened, so he could have another laugh. Inside, huh? He riveted himself up inside? And *he*, Don Lollò, what did he want to do? Kee. . . to kee. . . to keep him in there . . . ha, ha, ha . . . to keep him in there so as not to lose the jar?

"Do I have to lose it?" asked Zirafa with clenched fists. "The loss and the shame?"

"But do you know what this is called?" the lawyer said. "It's called 'illegal confinement.'"

"Confinement? And who confined him?" exclaimed Zirafa. "He confined himself! How am I to blame?"

The lawyer then explained to him that there were two cases. On the one hand, he, Don Lollò, was obliged to release the prisoner at once so as not to be liable to the charge of "illegal confinement"; on the other hand, the tinker was answerable for the damage he was causing through his lack of professionalism and his carelessness.

"Ah!" said Zirafa, with a sigh of relief. "By paying me for the jar!"

---

[4] Literally, "bread and accompaniments to bread."

—Piano!—osservò l'avvocato.—Non come se fosse nuova, badiamo!

—E perché?

—Ma perché era rotta!

—Nossignore!—negò quello.—Ora è sana. Meglio che sana, lo dice lui stesso! E se ora torno a romperla, non potrò più farla risanare. Giara perduta, signor avvocato!

Questi gli assicurò che se ne sarebbe tenuto conto, facendogliela pagare per quanto valeva nello stato in cui era adesso.

—Anzi,—gli consigliò,—fatela stimare avanti da lui stesso.

—Bacio le mani,—disse don Lollò, andando via di corsa.

Di ritorno, verso sera, trovò tutti i contadini in festa attorno alla giara abitata. Partecipava alla festa anche il cane di guardia. Zi' Dima s'era calmato, non solo, ma aveva preso gusto anche lui alla sua bizzarra avventura e rideva con la gajezza mala dei tristi.

Lo Zirafa scostò tutti e si sporse a guardare dentro la giara.

—Ah! Ci stai bene?

—Benone. Al fresco,—rispose quello.—Meglio che a casa mia.

—Piacere. Intanto ti avverto che questa giara mi costò quattr'onze, nuova. Quanto credi che possa costare adesso?

—Con me qua dentro?—domandò Zi' Dima.

I villani risero.

—Zitti!—gridò lo Zirafa.—Delle due l'una: o il tuo mastice serve, o non serve: se non serve, e tu sei un imbroglione; se serve, e la giara, così com'è, deve avere il suo prezzo. Che prezzo? Stimala tu.

Zi' Dima rimase un pezzo a riflettere, poi disse:

—Rispondo. Se lei me l'avesse fatta conciare col mastice solo, com'io volevo, io, prima di tutto, non mi troverei qua dentro, e la giara avrebbe su per giù lo stesso prezzo di prima. Così sconciata con questi puntacci, che ho dovuto darle per forza di qua dentro, che prezzo potrà avere? Un terzo di quanto valeva, sì o no.

"Not so fast!" the lawyer remarked. "It's not as if it were new, keep that in mind!"

"And why not?"

"Why, because it was broken!"

"No, sir!" Zirafa rebutted. "Now it's whole. Better than whole, he says so himself! And if I now break it again, I won't be able to have it mended again. It's a lost jar, counselor!"

The lawyer assured him that this would be taken into account, by demanding a payment equal to the jar's value in its present condition.

"In fact," he advised him, "have it appraised in advance by him himself."

"Many thanks, and goodbye,"[5] said Don Lollò, hurrying away.

Upon his return, toward evening, he found all the farmhands making merry around the inhabited jar. Even the watchdog was taking part in the fun. Not only had Uncle Dima calmed down; he, too, had begun to enjoy his unusual adventure and was laughing with the malicious gaiety that sad people have.

Zirafa made them all move away, and leaned over to look inside the jar.

"Ah! Are you comfortable?"

"Fine. In the cooler,"[6] he replied. "Better off than at home."

"Glad to hear it. Meanwhile I'll have you note that this jar cost me four *onze* new. How much do you think it would be worth now?"

"With me inside?" asked Uncle Dima.

The countryfolk laughed.

"Quiet!" shouted Zirafa. "It's one or the other: either your cement works or it doesn't work; if it doesn't work, you're a swindler; if it does work, the jar, just as it is, must have some value. What value? You judge."

Uncle Dima reflected for a while, then said:

"I'm answering. If you had allowed me to mend it with nothing but cement, the way I wanted, first of all I wouldn't be in here, and the jar would be worth just about the same as before. But sloppily mended with these ugly rivets that I was compelled to put in it from inside here, what value could it have? A third of its original value, more or less."

---

[5] *Bacio le mani* ("I kiss your hands"): a very formal salutation, frequently used in Sicily.

[6] A pun: literally, "in the cool" (that is, out of the heat of the sun); humorously, "in jail."

—Un terzo?—domandò lo Zirafa.—Un'onza e trentatré?

—Meno sì, più no.

—Ebbene,—disse don Lollò.—Passi la tua parola, e dammi diciassette lire.

—Cosa?—domandò Zi' Dima, come se non avesse intesso.

—Io rompo la giara per farti uscire,—rispose don Lollò,—e tu, dice l'avvocato, me la paghi per quanto vale: un'onza e trentatré.

—Io, pagare?—sghignò Zi' Dima.—Vossignoria scherza! Qua dentro ci faccio i vermi.

E, tratta di tasca con qualche stento la pipetta intartarita, l'accese e si mise a fumare, cacciando il fumo per il collo della giara.

Don Lollò ci restò brutto. Quest'altro caso, che Zi' Dima non volesse più uscir dalla giara, né lui né l'avvocato lo avevano previsto. E come si risolveva adesso? Fu lì lì per ordinar di nuovo:—La mula!—ma si trattenne a tempo, riflettendo ch'era già sera.

—Ah sì?—disse.—Ti vuoi domiciliare nella mia giara? Testimoni tutti voi qua! Non vuole uscire lui, per non pagarla; io son pronto a romperla! Intanto, poiché vuole star lì, domani io lo cito per alloggio abusivo, perché m'impedisce l'uso della giara!

Zi' Dima cacciò prima fuori un'altra boccata di fumo, poi rispose, placido:

—Nossignore. Non voglio impedirle niente, io. Che sto forse qua per piacere? Mi faccia uscire, ma pagare, niente! Neanche per ischerzo, vossignoria!

Don Lollò, in un impeto di rabbia, alzò un piede per avventare un calcio alla giara; ma s'arrestò; la afferrò invece con ambo le mani e la scrollò tutta, fremendo e gridando al vecchio:

—Pezzo da galera, chi l'ha fatto il male, io o tu? E devo pagarlo io? Muori di fame là dentro! Vedremo chi la vince!

E se n'andò, non pensando alle tre lire che gli aveva buttate la mattina dentro la giara. Con esse, per cominciare, Zi' Dima pensò di far festa quella sera insieme coi contadini che, avendo fatto tardi per quello strano accidente, rimanevano a passar la notte in campagna, all'aperto, su l'aja. Uno andò a far le spese a una taverna lì presso. A farlo apposta, c'era una luna che pareva fosse raggiornato.

"A third?" asked Zirafa. "One *onza*, thirty-three?"

"Maybe less, not more."

"All right," said Don Lollò. "Let your words be good, and give me seventeen *lire*."

"What?" asked Uncle Dima, as if he hadn't understood.

"I will break the jar to let you out," answered Don Lollò, "and you, as the lawyer says, pay me what it's worth: one *onza*, thirty-three."

"I should pay?" sneered Uncle Dima. "You're joking, sir. I'll rot in here."

And, with some difficulty pulling his little tartar-incrusted pipe out of his pocket, he lit and began smoking, driving the smoke out of the neck of the jar.

Don Lollò began to sulk. This additional possibility, that Uncle Dima would refuse to leave the jar, neither he nor the lawyer had foreseen. And how could things be settled now? He was just about to give the command "The mule!" again, but restrained himself in time, reflecting that it was already evening.

"Oh, is that so?" he said. "You want to take up residence in my jar? You're all witnesses here! He doesn't want to get out, to avoid paying for it; I'm ready to break it! Meanwhile, since he wants to stay there, tomorrow I'll present him with a summons for squatting on my property, because he's preventing me from using the jar!"

First Uncle Dima sent out another mouthful of smoke, then he replied, calmly:

"No, sir. I don't want to prevent you from doing anything. Am I here for my pleasure? Get me out, but I'm not paying a thing! Don't even say it as a joke, sir!"

Don Lollò, in a fit of rage, lifted one foot to give the jar a kick; but he stopped short; instead, he seized it with both hands and shook it vigorously, trembling and shouting to the old man:

"Scoundrel, who did the damage, you or me? And I'm supposed to pay for it? Die of hunger in there! We'll see who wins!"

And he went away, not thinking of the three *lire* he had thrown into the jar that morning. To begin with, it occurred to Uncle Dima to use that money to have a party that evening along with the farmhands, who, having stayed late because of that strange accident, were planning to spend the night in the countryside, outdoors, on the threshing floor. One of them went to make the purchases at a nearby tavern. As it turned out, the moon shone so brightly it seemed like daylight.

A una cert'ora don Lollò, andato a dormire, fu svegliato da un baccano d'inferno. S'affacciò a un balcone della cascina e vide su l'aja, sotto la luna, tanti diavoli: i contadini ubriachi che, presi per mano, danzavano attorno alla giara. Zi' Dima, là dentro, cantava a squarciagola.

Questa volta non si poté più reggere, don Lollò: si precipitò come un toro infuriato e, prima che quelli avessero tempo di pararlo, con uno spintone mandò a ruzzolar la giara giù per la costa. Rotolando, accompagnata dalle risa degli ubriachi, la giara andò a spaccarsi contro un olivo.

E la vinse Zi' Dima.

At a certain hour Don Lollò, who had gone to bed, was awakened by an infernal racket. Coming out onto a balcony of the farmhouse, he saw on the threshing floor, in the moonlight, a swarm of devils: the drunken farmhands who had linked hands and were dancing around the jar. Uncle Dima, inside, was singing at the top of his voice.

This time Don Lollò could no longer control himself: he dashed over like a maddened bull and, before they had time to ward him off, gave the jar a big push that sent it tumbling down the hillside. Rolling, to the accompaniment of the drunkards' laughter, the jar smashed up against an olive tree.

And Uncle Dima won.

NON È UNA COSA SERIA

Perazzetti? No. Quello poi era un genere particolare.

Le diceva serio serio, che non pareva nemmeno lui, guardandosi le unghie lunghissime, adunche, di cui aveva la cura più meticolosa.

È vero che poi, tutt'a un tratto, senz'alcuna ragione apparente . . . un'anatra, tal'e quale: scoppiava in certe risate, che parevano il verso di un'anatra; e ci guazzava dentro proprio come un'anatra.

Moltissimi trovavano appunto in queste risate la prova maggiore della pazzia di Perazzetti. Nel vederlo torcere con le lagrime agli occhi, gli amici gli domandavano:

—Ma perché?

E lui:

—Niente. Non ve lo posso dire.

A veder ridere uno così, senza che voglia dirne la ragione, si resta sconcertati, con un viso da scemi si resta e una certa irritazione in corpo, che nei così detti «urtati di nervi» può diventar facilmente stizza feroce e voglia di sgraffiare.

Non potendo sgraffiare, i così detti «urtati di nervi» (che sono poi tanti, oggidì) si scrollavano rabbiosamente e dicevano di Perazzetti:

—È un pazzo!

Se Perazzetti, invece, avesse detto loro la ragione di quel suo anatrare . . . Ma non la poteva dire, spesso, Perazzetti; veramente non la poteva dire.

Aveva una fantasia mobilissima e quanto mai capricciosa, la quale, alla vista della gente, s'imbizzarriva a destargli dentro, senza ch'egli lo volesse, le più stravaganti immagini, guizzi di comicissimi aspetti inesprimibili; a scoprirgli d'un subito certe riposte analogie, o a rappresentargli improvvisamente certi

IT'S NOT TO BE TAKEN SERIOUSLY

Perazzetti? No. He was certainly in a class of his own.

He would say things[1] with the utmost seriousness, so that you wouldn't even know it was him, while he looked at his extremely long, curved fingernails, of which he took the most meticulous care.

It's true that then, all of a sudden, for no apparent reason . . . exactly like a duck: he would burst out into certain fits of laughter that were like the quacking of a duck; and he would wallow around in that laughter just like a duck.

Many, many people found in that very laughter the best proof that Perazzetti was crazy. Seeing him writhe with tears in his eyes, his friends would ask him:

"But why?"

And he would reply:

"It's nothing. I can't tell you."

When people saw him laughing like that and refusing to say why, they got disconcerted, they stood there looking like fools and experienced a certain physical irritation, which in the case of the so-called "nervous types" còuld easily develop into a ferocious rage and an urge to scratch him.

Unable to scratch him, the so-called "nervous types" (and there are so many of them nowadays) would shake their heads furiously and say in reference to Perazzetti:

"He's a lunatic!"

If, instead, Perazzetti had told them the reason for that quacking of his . . . But frequently, Perazzetti couldn't tell them; he honestly couldn't tell them.

He had an extremely active and terrifically capricious imagination, which, when he saw other people, would fly out of control and, without his volition, would arouse in his mind the most outrageous images, flashes of inexpressibly hilarious visions; it would suddenly reveal to him certain hidden analogies, or unexpectedly indicate to

---

[1] The Italian text, highly idiomatic at this point, suggests (without stating outright) that Perazzetti is telling tall tales, or "whoppers."

contrasti così grotteschi e buffi, che la risata gli scattava irrefrenabile.

Come comunicare altrui il giuoco istantaneo di queste fuggevoli immagini impensate?

Sapeva bene Perazzetti, per propria esperienza, quanto in ogni uomo il fondo dell'essere sia diverso dalle fittizie interpretazioni di esso, che ciascuno se ne dà spontaneamente, o per inconscia finzione, per quel bisogno di crederci o d'esser creduti diversi da quel che siamo, o per imitazione degli altri, o per le necessità e le convenienze sociali.

Su questo fondo dell'essere egli aveva fatto studii particolari, e lo chiamava l'*antro della bestia*, della bestia originaria acquattata dentro a ognuno di noi, sotto tutti gli strati della coscienza, che gli sono man mano sovrapposti con gli anni. L'uomo, a toccarlo, a solleticarlo in questo o in quello strato, rispondeva con inchini, con sorrisi, porgeva la mano, diceva buon giorno e buona sera, dava magari in prestito cinque lire: ma guai ad andarlo a stuzzicare laggiù, nell'antro della bestia: scappava fuori il ladro, il farabutto, l'assassino. È vero che, dopo tanti secoli di civiltà, molti nel loro antro ospitavano ormai una bestia troppo mortificata: un porco che si diceva il rosario, una volpe che aveva perduta la coda.

In trattoria, per esempio, Perazzetti studiava le impazienze raffrenate degli avventori. Fuori, la creanza; dentro, l'asino che voleva subito la biada. E si divertiva un mondo a immaginare tutte le razze di bestie rintanate negli antri degli uomini di sua conoscenza: quello aveva certo dentro un formichiere e quello un porcospino e quell'altro un pollo d'India, e così via.

Spesso però le risate di Perazzetti avevano una ragione, dirò così, più costante; e questa davvero non era da spiattellare, là, a tutti; ma da confidare, se mai, in un orecchio pian piano a qualcuno. Confidata così, vi assicuro che promoveva inevitabilmente il più fragoroso scoppio di risa. La confidò una volta a un amico, presso al quale gli premeva di non passar per matto.

Io non posso dirvela forte; posso accennarvela appena; voi cercate d'intenderla a volo, giacché, detta forte, rischierebbe, tra l'altro, di parere una sconcezza, e non è.

Perazzetti non era un uomo volgare; anzi dichiarava d'avere

him certain contrasts that were so grotesque and comic that he would burst out laughing unrestrainedly.

How could he make other people share the instantaneous interplay of those fleeting, unpremeditated images?

Perazzetti knew clearly, from his own experience, how different the basic essence of every man is from the fictitious interpretations of that essence that each of us offers himself either spontaneously, or through unconscious self-deceit, out of that need to think ourselves or to be thought different from what we are, either because we imitate others or because of social necessities and conventions.

He had made a special study of that basic essence of being, and called it "the cave of the beast," of the primordial beast lurking inside each of us, beneath all the layers of our consciousness which have been gradually superimposed on it over the years. A man, when touched or tickled on this or that layer, would respond with bows, with smiles, would extend his hand, would say "good day" and "good evening," might even lend five *lire:* but woe to anyone who went and poked him down there, in the cave of the beast: out would come the thief, the impostor, the murderer. It's true that, after so many centuries of civilization, many people now sheltered in their cave an animal that was excessively subdued: a pig that said the rosary, a fox that had lost its tail.

In restaurants, for example, Perazzetti would study the customers' controlled impatience. On the outside, good manners; on the inside, the donkey who wanted his grain immediately. And he enjoyed himself no end imagining all the species of animals who had their lair in the caves belonging to the men he was acquainted with: this man surely had an anteater inside him, and that man a porcupine and that other man a turkey, and so on.

Often, however, Perazzetti's bursts of laughter had a reason that I might call more permanent; and, indeed, that reason couldn't be blurted out, just like that, to everybody; rather, it was to be confided, if at all, very quietly into someone's ear. When thus confided, I assure you that it inevitably provoked the noisiest outbreak of laughter. Once he confided it to a friend to whom he was eager to prove that he wasn't crazy.

I can't tell you the reason out loud; I can only give you some bare indication of it; try to comprehend it from my hint, because, if it were told out loud, among other things it might very well seem to be indecent, and it's not.

Perazzetti was not a vulgar man; on the contrary, he claimed to

una stima altissima dell'umanità, di tutto quanto essa, a dispetto della bestia originaria, ha saputo fare dai tempi dell'antica Grecia ai giorni nostri; ma Perazzetti non sapeva dimenticare che l'uomo, il quale è stato capace di crear tante bellezze, è pur costretto a obbedire ogni giorno a certe intime e brutte necessità naturali, che certamente non gli fanno onore.

Vedendo un pover'uomo, una povera donna in atto umile e dimesso, Perazzetti non ci pensava; ma quando vedeva certe donne che si davano arie di sentimento, certi uomini tronfii, gravidi di boria, era un disastro: subito, irresistibilmente, gli scattava dentro l'immagine di quelle intime e brutte necessità naturali, a cui anch'essi per forza dovevano ogni giorno ubbidire; li vedeva in quell'atto e scoppiava a ridere senza remissione.

Non c'era nobiltà d'uomo o bellezza di donna, che si potesse salvare da questo disastro nell'immaginazione di Perazzetti; anzi quanto più eterea e ideale gli si presentava una donna, quanto più composto a un'aria di maestà era un uomo, tanto più quella maledetta immagine si svegliava in lui all'improvviso.

Ora, con questo, immaginatevi Perazzetti innamorato.

E s'innamorava, il disgraziato, s'innamorava con una facilità straordinaria! Non pensava più a nulla, finiva d'esser lui, appena innamorato; diventava subito un altro, diventava quel Perazzetti che gli altri volevano, quale amava foggiarselo la donna nelle cui mani era caduto, non solo, ma quale amavano foggiarselo anche i futuri suoceri, i futuri cognati e perfino gli amici di casa della sposa.

Era stato fidanzato, a dir poco, una ventina di volte. E faceva schiattar dalle risa nel descrivere i tanti Perazzetti ch'egli era stato, uno più stupido e imbecille dell'altro: quello del pappagallo della suocera, quello de le stelle fisse della cognatina, quello dei fagiolini dell'amico non so chi.

Quando il calore della fiamma, che lo aveva messo per così dire in istato di fusione, cominciava ad attutirsi, ed egli a poco a poco cominciava a rapprendersi nella sua forma consueta e riacquistava coscienza di sé, provava dapprima stupore, sbigottimento nel contemplare la forma che gli avevano dato, la parte che gli avevano fatto rappresentare, lo stato d'imbecillità in cui lo avevano ridotto; poi, guardando la sposa, guardando la suocera, guardando il suocero, ricominciavano le terribili

have a very high esteem for humanity, for all that it has managed to accomplish from ancient Greek times to our own day, in spite of the primordial beast; but Perazzetti was unable to forget the fact that man, who has been capable of creating so many beautiful things, is still compelled daily to obey certain intimate and unseemly natural necessities, which surely do him no credit.

Seeing a poor man, a poor woman in a humble and modest attitude, Perazzetti didn't think about it; but when he saw certain women giving themselves sentimental airs, certain pompous men loaded with self-conceit, it was a disaster: immediately, irresistibly there leaped into his mind the image of those intimate and unseemly natural necessities, which even they definitely had to obey daily: he saw them in that posture and would burst out laughing mercilessly.

There was no masculine nobility or feminine beauty that could escape that disaster in Perazzetti's imagination; in fact, the more ethereal and idealized a woman's presence seemed to him, the more a man had put on an air of majesty, all the more did that accursed image awake within him unexpectedly.

Now, with this in mind, just imagine Perazzetti in love.

And fall in love he did, unlucky man, he fell in love with extraordinary ease! He no longer thought about anything, he was no longer himself, the moment he was in love; he immediately became another man, became that Perazzetti which others wished him to be, the sort of man that not only the woman into whose hands he had fallen wanted to mold him into, but also the sort of man that the future fathers-in-law, future brothers-in-law and even the friends of the bride's family wanted to mold him into.

He had been engaged at least twenty or so times. And he would make you split your sides laughing when he described all the different Perazzettis he had been, each one dumber and more idiotic than the last: the one with the mother-in-law's parrot, the one with the young sister-in-law's interest in the stars, the one with some friend or other's stringbeans.

Whenever the heat of passion, which had brought him into a state of fusion, so to speak, began to abate, and he gradually began to gell into his customary shape and recover self-consciousness, at first he felt amazement and alarm at observing the shape they had given him, the role they had made him play, the state of idiocy to which they had reduced him; then, as he looked at his fiancée, as he looked at the mother-in-law, as he looked at the father-in-law,

risate, e doveva scappare—non c'era via di mezzo—doveva scappare.

Ma il guaio era qua, che non volevano più lasciarlo scappare. Era un ottimo giovine, Perazzetti, agiato, simpaticissimo.

I drammi attraversati in quei suoi venti e più fidanzamenti, a raccoglierli in un libro, narrati da lui, formerebbero una delle più esilaranti letture dei giorni nostri. Ma quelle che per i lettori sarebbero risa, sono state purtroppo lagrime, lagrime vere per il povero Perazzetti, e rabbie e angosce e disperazione.

Ogni volta egli prometteva e giurava a se stesso di non ricascarci più; si proponeva di escogitare qualche rimedio eroico, che gl'impediva d'innamorarsi di nuovo. Ma che! Ci ricascava poco dopo, e sempre peggio di prima.

Un giorno finalmente scoppiò come una bomba la notizia, ch'egli aveva sposato. E aveva sposato nientemeno . . . Ma no, nessuno voleva crederci! Pazzie ne aveva fatte Perazzetti d'ogni genere; ma che potesse arrivare fino a tal punto, fino a legarsi per tutta la vita con una donna come quella . . .

Legarsi? Quando a uno dei tanti amici, andato a trovarlo in casa, gli scappò detto così, per miracolo Perazzetti non se lo mangiò.

—Legarsi? come legarsi? perché legarsi? Stupidi, scemi, imbecilli tutti quanti! Legarsi? Chi l'ha detto? Ti sembro legato? Vieni, entra qua . . . Questo è il mio solito letto, sì o no? Ti sembra un letto a due? Ehi, Cecchino! Cecchino!

Cecchino era il suo vecchio servo fidato.

—Di', Cecchino. Vengo ogni sera a dormire qua, solo?

—Sissignore, solo.

—Ogni sera?

—Ogni sera.

—Dove mangio?

—Di là.

—Con chi mangio?

—Solo.

—Mi fai tu da mangiare?

—Io, sissignore.

—E sono sempre lo stesso Celestino?

the terrible laughter would start all over again, and he had to flee—there was no other way—he had to flee.

But the trouble was that they were no longer willing to let him escape. He was an excellent young man, Perazzetti, well-to-do, extremely likable.

If the dramas enacted in those twenty or more engagements were assembled in a book as narrated by him, they would be among the most amusing reading materials of our generation. But what would be laughs for the reader were unfortunately tears, real tears for poor Perazzetti, fits of rage and of anguish, and despair.

Each time he promised and swore to himself that he wouldn't relapse; he resolved to think up some heroic cure that would prevent him from falling in love again. But no! He would relapse shortly afterward, and always worse than before.

Finally, one day the news that he had married burst like a bomb. And he had married none other than . . . But no, nobody wanted to believe it! Perazzetti had done all sorts of crazy things; but that he could go that far, to the point of tying himself for the rest of his life to a woman like that . . .

Tying himself? When one of his many friends, visiting him at home, came out with that expression, it was a wonder that Perazzetti didn't kill him.[2]

"Tie myself? What do you mean, tie myself? Why is it tying myself? You're all stupid, foolish idiots! Tie myself? Who said so? Do I look tied to you? Come with me, come in here . . . This is my regular bed, isn't it? Does it look like a double bed? Hey, Cecchino! Cecchino!"

Cecchino was his trusty old servant.

"Tell me, Cecchino. Do I come here every night to sleep, alone?"

"Yes, sir, alone."

"Every night?"

"Every night."

"Where do I eat?"

"In that room."

"With whom do I eat?"

"All alone."

"Do you prepare my food?"

"Yes, sir."

"And am I still the same Celestino?"

---

[2] Literally, "eat him up."

—Sempre lo stesso, sissignore.

Mandato via il servo, dopo questo interrogatorio, Perazzetti concluse, aprendo le braccia:

—Dunque . . .

—Dunque non è vero?—domandò quello.

—Ma sì, vero! verissimo! assoluto!—rispose Perazzetti.—L'ho sposata! L'ho sposata in chiesa e allo stato civile! Ma che per questo? Ti pare una cosa seria?

—No, anzi ridicolissima.

—E dunque!—tornò a concludere Perazzetti.—Escimi dai piedi! Avete finito di ridere alle mie spalle! Mi volevate morto, è vero? col cappio sempre alla gola? Basta, basta, cari miei! Ora mi son liberato per sempre! Ci voleva quest'ultima tempesta, da cui sono uscito vivo per miracolo . . .

L'ultima tempesta a cui alludeva Perazzetti era il fidanzamento con la figlia del capodivisione al Ministero delle finanze, Commendator Vico Lamanna; e aveva proprio ragione di dire Perazzetti che ne era uscito vivo per miracolo. Gli era toccato di battersi alla spada col fratello di lei, Lino Lamanna, bravo spadaccino; e poiché di Lino egli era amicissimo e sentiva di non aver nulla, proprio nulla contro di lui, s'era fatto infilzare generosamente come un pollo.

Pareva quella volta—e ci avrebbe messo chiunque la mano sul fuoco—che il matrimonio dovesse aver luogo. La signorina Ely Lamanna, educata all'inglese—come si poteva vedere anche dal nome—schietta, franca, solida, bene azzampata (leggi *scarpe all'americana*), era riuscita senza dubbio a salvarsi da quel solito disastro nell'immaginazione di Perazzetti. Qualche risata, sì, gli era scappata guardando il suocero commendatore, che anche con lui stava in aria e gli parlava alle volte con quella sua collosità pomatosa . . . Ma poi basta. Aveva confidato con garbo alla sposa il perché di quelle risate; ne aveva riso anche lei; e, superato quello scoglio, credeva anche lui, Perazzetti, che quella volta finalmente avrebbe raggiunto il tranquillo porto delle nozze (per modo di dire). La suocera era una buona vecchietta, modesta e taciturna, e Lino, il fra-

"Still the same, sir."

Sending away the servant, after that interrogation, Perazzetti concluded, opening his arms:

"And so . . . "

"So it's not true?" the other asked.

"Of course, it's true! True as can be! Absolutely true!" answered Perazzetti. "I married her! I married her in church and at the registry office! But what does that mean? You think it's something serious?"

"No, just the opposite, totally ridiculous."

"Well, there you have it!" Perazzetti concluded once more. "Get out of my way! You've all finished laughing behind my back! You pictured me dead, didn't you? With a noose always around my neck! Enough, enough, friends! Now I've freed myself for good! All it took was that last storm, from which I escaped alive by a miracle . . . "

The last storm to which Perazzetti alluded was his engagement to the daughter of the head of a division at the finance ministry, Commendatore[3] Vico Lamanna; and Perazzetti was perfectly right in saying that he had escaped it alive by a miracle. He had had to fight a sword duel with the woman's brother, Lino Lamanna, an excellent swordsman; and because he was a very good friend of Lino's and felt he had nothing, absolutely nothing against him, he had let himself be handsomely skewered like a chicken.

It seemed as if this time—and anyone would have called it a sure thing[4]—the wedding was definitely going to take place. Miss Elly Lamanna, brought up in English fashion—as could be seen even from her name—forthright, frank, solid, well-poised (read: American-style shoes), had doubtless succeeded in avoiding that usual disaster in Perazzetti's imagination. Yes, a bit of laughter had escaped him when looking at his father-in-law the Commendatore, who even with him remained on his high horse and would sometimes speak to him with that pomade-like stickiness of his . . . But enough of that. He had courteously confided to his fiancée the reason for those bursts of laughter; she had laughed over it herself; and when that reef had been passed, Perazzetti too believed that this time he would finally reach the safe harbor of matrimony (so to speak). The mother-in-law was a kind old lady, modest and taci-

---

[3] Member of an order of chivalry.

[4] Literally, "would have put his hand in the fire."

tello, pareva fatto apposta per medesimarsi in tutto e per tutto con lui.

Perazzetti e Lino Lamanna diventarono infatti fin dal primo giorno del fidanzamento due indivisibili. Più che con la sposa si può dire che Perazzetti stava col futuro cognato: escursioni, cacce, passeggiate a cavallo insieme, insieme sul Tevere alla società di canottaggio.

Tutto poteva immaginarsi, povero Perazzetti, tranne che questa volta il disastro dovesse venirgli da questa troppa intimità col futuro cognato, per un altro tiro dell'immaginazione sua morbosa e buffona.

A un certo punto, egli cominciò a scoprire nella fidanzata una rassomiglianza inquietante col fratello di lei.

Fu a Livorno, ai bagni, ov'era andato, naturalmente, coi Lamanna.

Perazzetti aveva veduto tante volte Lino in maglia in canotto; vide ora la sposa in costume da bagno. Notare che Lino aveva veramente un che di femineo, nelle anche.

Che impressione ebbe Perazzetti dalla scoperta di questa rassomiglianza? Cominciò a sudar freddo, cominciò a provare un ribrezzo invincibile al pensiero d'entrare in intimità conjugale con Ely Lamanna, che somigliava tanto al fratello. Gli si rappresentò subito come mostruosa, quasi contro natura, quella intimità, giacché vedeva il fratello nella fidanzata; e si torceva alla minima carezza ch'ella gli faceva, nel vedersi guardato con occhi ora incitanti e aizzosi, or che s'illanguidivano nella promessa d'una voluttà sospirata.

Poteva intanto gridarle Perazzetti:

—Oh Dio, per carità, smetti! finiamola! Io posso essere amicissimo di Lino, perché non debbo sposarlo; ma non posso più sposar te, perché mi parrebbe di sposare tuo fratello?

La tortura che soffrì questa volta Perazzetti fu di gran lunga superiore a tutte quelle che aveva sofferto per l'innanzi. Finì con quel colpo di spada, che per miracolo non lo mandò all'altro mondo.

E appena guarito della ferita, trovò il rimedio eroico che doveva precludergli per sempre la via del matrimonio.

—Ma come—voi dite—sposando?

Sicuro! Maddalena: quella del cane; sposando Maddalena, sicuro, quella povera scema che si vedeva ogni sera per via, parata con certi cappellacci carichi di verdura svolazzante, ti-

turn, and Lino, the brother, seemed perfectly suited to see eye to eye with him in every possible way.

Indeed, from the first day of the engagement, Perazzetti and Lino Lamanna became two inseparable companions. You might say that Perazzetti spent more time with his future brother-in-law than with his fiancée: outings, hunting trips, horseback rides together, together on the Tiber at the boating club.

He could imagine anything, poor Perazzetti, except that this time the disaster was to strike him because of his excessive closeness to his future brother-in-law, on account of another quirk of his morbid and ludicrous imagination.

At a certain point, he began to discover in his fiancée a disturbing resemblance to her brother.

It was at Livorno, at the seaside, where he had naturally gone with the Lamannas.

Perazzetti had seen Lino in a sporting jersey plenty of times when rowing; now he saw his fiancée in a bathing suit. It should be noted that Lino really did look ever so slightly feminine, in the hips.

What was the effect on Perazzetti when he discovered that resemblance? He broke out into a cold sweat, he began to feel an unconquerable repulsion at the thought of initiating marital intimacies with Elly Lamanna, who looked so much like her brother. He suddenly pictured those intimacies as something monstrous, almost unnatural, now that he saw the brother when looking at the fiancée; and he writhed at the slightest caress she gave him, seeing himself looked at by eyes now provocative and inciting, now languishing in the promise of a longed-for sensual pleasure.

But, meanwhile, could Perazzetti shout to her:

"Oh, for God's sake, quit it! Let's call it off! I can be very good friends with Lino, because I don't have to marry him; but I can no longer marry *you*, because it would be like marrying your brother."

The torture that Perazzetti suffered this time was far greater than all those he had suffered in the past. It ended up with that sword thrust, which by a miracle failed to send him to the next world.

And as soon as the wound had healed, he hit upon the heroic cure that was to bar the way to matrimony to him for good.

"But how," I hear you ask, "by getting married?"

Of course! Maddalena: the one with the dog; by marrying Maddalena, of course, that poor nitwit that you could see every night on the street, decked out in certain hideous hats loaded down with

rata da un barbone nero che non le lasciava mai il tempo di finir certe sue risatelle assassine alle guardie, ai giovanottini di primo pelo e ai soldati, per la fretta che aveva—maledetto cane—d'arrivare chi sa dove, chi sa a qual remoto angolo bujo . . .

In chiesa e allo stato civile la sposò; la tolse dalla strada; le assegnò due lire al giorno e la spedì lontano, in campagna.

Gli amici—come potete figurarvi—non gli dettero più pace per parecchio tempo. Ma Perazzetti era ritornato ormai tranquillo, a dirle serio serio, che non pareva nemmeno lui, guardandosi le unghie.

—Sì,—diceva.—L'ho sposata. Ma non è una cosa seria. Dormire, dormo solo, in casa mia; mangiare, mangio solo, in casa mia; non la vedo; non mi dà alcun fastidio . . . Voi dite per il nome? Sì: le ho dato il mio nome. Ma, signori miei, che cosa è un nome? Non è una cosa seria.

Cosa serie, a rigore, non ce n'erano per Perazzetti. Tutto sta nell'importanza che si dà alle cose. Una cosa ridicolissima, a darle importanza, può diventare seriissima, e viceversa, la cosa più seria, ridicolissima. C'è cosa più seria della morte? Eppure, per tanti che non le danno importanza . . .

Va bene; ma tra qualche giorno lo volevano vedere gli amici. Chi sa come se ne sarebbe pentito!

—Bella forza!—rispondeva Perazzetti.—Ma sicuro che me ne pentirò! Già già comincio a esserne pentito . . .

Gli amici, a questa uscita, levavano alte le grida:

—Ah! lo vedi?

—Ma imbecilli,—rimbeccava Perazzetti,—giusto quando me ne pentirò per davvero, risentirò il beneficio del mio rimedio, perché vorrà dire che mi sarò allora innamorato di nuovo, fino al punto di commettere la più grossa della bestialità: quella di prender moglie.

Coro:

—Ma se l'hai già presa!

Perazzetti:

—Quella? Eh via! Quella non è una cosa seria.

Conclusione:

Perazzetti aveva sposato per guardarsi dal pericolo di prender moglie.

fluttering greenery, pulled along by a black poodle that never gave her the time to finish those "killing" little laughs of hers, directed at policemen, young boys still wet behind the ears, and soldiers, because it was in such a hurry—damned dog—to get who knows where, to who knows what faraway dark corner . . .

He married her in church and at the registry office; he took her off the street; he gave her an allowance of two *lire* a day and shipped her off far away, into the country.

His friends—as you can imagine—gave him no peace for quite some time. But Perazzetti had now calmly returned to his habit of saying things with the utmost seriousness, so that you wouldn't even know it was him, while looking at his nails.

"Yes," he would say. "I married her. But it's nothing serious. As for sleeping, I sleep alone, at home; as for eating, I eat alone, at home; I don't see her; she doesn't bother me at all . . . You say, what about my name? Yes: I gave her my name. But, gentlemen, what's a name? It's not to be taken seriously."

Strictly speaking, nothing was serious to Perazzetti. Everything depends on the importance you attach to things. If you attach importance to the most ridiculous thing, it can become deadly serious, and vice versa, the most serious matter can become altogether ridiculous. Is there anything more serious than death? And yet, for those many people who attach no importance to it . . .

All right; but his friends wanted to see him a few days later. Who knows how he would regret it!

"No kidding!" Perazzetti would answer. "Of course I'll regret it! I'm already beginning to regret it . . . "

When he came out with that sally, his friends would begin to cry out:

"Ah! You see?"

"But, you fools," Perazzetti would retort, "at the exact moment I truly regret it, I'll reap the benefit of my cure, because that will mean I've fallen in love again, to the point of committing the most vulgar of bestial acts: that of taking a wife."

Chorus of voices:

"But you've already taken one!"

Perazzetti:

"That one? Go on, now! That one's not to be taken seriously."

Conclusion:

Perazzetti had gotten married to protect himself from the danger of taking a wife.

PENSACI, GIACOMINO!

Da tre giorni il professore Agostino Toti non ha in casa quella pace, quel riso, a cui crede ormai di aver diritto.

Ha circa settant'anni, sì, e dir che sia un bel vecchio, non si potrebbe neanche dire: piccoletto, con la testa grossa, calva, senza collo, il torso sproporzionato su due gambettine da uccello . . .

Il professor Toti lo sa bene, e non si lusinga affatto, perciò, che Maddalena, la bella mogliettina, che non ha ancora ventisei anni, lo possa amare per se stesso.

È vero che egli se l'è presa povera e l'ha inalzata: figliuola del bidello del liceo, è diventata moglie d'un professore ordinario di scienze naturali, tra pochi mesi con diritto al massimo della pensione; non solo, ma ricco anche da due anni per una fortuna insperata, per una vera manna dal cielo: un'eredità di quasi duecentomila lire, da parte d'un fratello spatriato da tanto tempo in Rumenia e morto scapolo colà.

Non per tutto questo però il professor Toti crede d'aver diritto alla pace e al riso. Egli è filosofo: sa che tutto questo non può bastare a una moglie giovine e bella.

Se l'eredità fosse venuta prima del matrimonio, egli magari avrebbe potuto pretendere da Maddalenina un po' di pazienza, che aspettasse cioè la morte di lui non lontana per rifarsi del sacrifizio d'aver sposato un vecchio. Ma son venute troppo tardi quelle duecentomila lire, due anni dopo il matrimonio, quando già . . . quando già il professor Toti filosoficamente aveva riconosciuto che non poteva bastare a compensare il sacrifizio della moglie la sola pensioncina ch'egli le avrebbe un giorno lasciata.

Avendo già concesso tutto prima, il professor Toti crede d'aver più che mai ragione di pretendere la pace e il riso ora, con l'aggiunta di quell'eredità vistosa. Tanto più, poi, in

THINK IT OVER, GIACOMINO!

For three days Professor[1] Agostino Toti hasn't had at home that peace, that laughter to which he thinks he is by now entitled.

Yes, he's about seventy, and you couldn't even say that he was a fine-looking old man: on the short side, with a big bald head, no neck, an outsize torso on two skinny legs like a bird's . . .

Professor Toti is well aware of this, and doesn't delude himself in the least, therefore, into thinking that Maddalena, his pretty little wife, who is not yet twenty-six, can love him for his own sake.

It's true that she was poor when he took her and that he improved her station in life: the daughter of a janitor in the high school, she became the wife of a permanent-staff teacher of natural sciences, with a claim to the maximum pension in a few months now; not only that, but also wealthy for the last two years thanks to an unexpected piece of good luck, truly like manna from heaven: an inheritance of nearly two hundred thousand *lire*, from a brother who had emigrated to Romania long ago and had died there a bachelor.

And yet, even with all that, Professor Toti wouldn't think he had a right to peace and laughter. He's a philosopher: he knows that all this wouldn't be enough for a young, pretty wife.

If his inheritance had arrived before the wedding, he might possibly have been able to ask Maddalena to have a little patience, that is, to wait for his death, not far off now, in order to be compensated for the sacrifice of having married an old man. But those two hundred thousand *lire* had come too late, two years after the wedding, when already . . . when Professor Toti had already philosophically realized that the small pension alone that he would leave her one day couldn't suffice to repay his wife for her sacrifice.

Having already made all those concessions, Professor Toti thinks he is more right than ever in claiming peace and laughter now, with the addition of that respectable inheritance. All the more so

---

[1] Toti is a *professore ordinario* in a *liceo*. A *liceo* corresponds more or less to an American high school, but even high-school teachers are addressed as "Professore" in Italy. At a university a *professore ordinario* would be a "full professor"; here it has been rendered as "permanent-staff teacher."

127

quanto che egli—uomo saggio veramente e dabbene—non si è contentato di beneficar la moglie, ma ha voluto anche beneficare . . . sì, lui, il suo buon Giacomino, già tra i più bravi alunni suoi al liceo, giovane timido, onesto, garbatissimo, bello come un cherubino.

Ma sì, ma sì—ha fatto tutto, ha pensato a tutto il vecchio professore Agostino Toti, filosoficamente. Giacomino Pugliese era sfaccendato, e l'ozio lo addolorava e lo avviliva; ebbene lui, il professor Toti, gli ha trovato posto nella Banca Agraria, dove ha investito le duecentomila lire dell'eredità.

C'è anche un bambino, ora, per casa, un angioletto di due anni e mezzo, a cui egli si è dedicato tutto, come uno schiavo innamorato. Ogni giorno, non gli par l'ora che finiscano le lezioni al liceo per correre a casa, a soddisfare tutti i capriccetti del suo piccolo tiranno. Veramente, dopo l'eredità, egli avrebbe potuto mettersi a riposo, rinunziando a quel massimo della pensione, per consacrare tutto il suo tempo al bambino. Ma no! Sarebbe stato un peccato! Dacché c'è, egli vuol portare fino all'ultimo quel suo giogo, che gli è stato sempre tanto gravoso! Se ha preso moglie proprio per questo, proprio perché recasse un beneficio a qualcuno ciò che per lui è stato un tormento tutta la vita!

Sposando con quest'unico intento di beneficare una povera giovane, egli ha amato quasi paternamente soltanto la moglie. E più che mai paternamente s'è messo ad amarla, da che è nato quel bambino, da cui quasi quasi amerebbe più d'esser chiamato nonno anziché papà. Questa bugia incosciente sui puri labbruzzi del bambino ignaro gli fa pena; gli pare che anche il suo amore per lui ne resti offeso. Ma come si fa? Bisogna pure che si prenda con un bacio quell'appellativo dalla boccuccia di Ninì, quel *papà* che fa ridere tutti i maligni, i quali non sanno capire le tenerezza sua per quell'innocente, la sua felicità per il bene che ha fatto e che seguita a fare a una donna, a un buon giovanotto, al piccino, e anche a sé—sicuro!—anche a sé—la felicità di vivere quegli ultimi anni in lieta e dolce compagnia, camminando per la fossa così, con un angioletto per mano.

because—being a truly wise and decent man—he wasn't satisfied with benefiting his wife, but also decided to benefit . . . yes, him, his good Giacomino, formerly one of his best students at the high school, a shy, honest, very courteous young man, handsome as a cherub.

Yes, yes—old Professor Agostino Toti has done everything, has thought of everything, philosophically. Giacomino Pugliese[2] had been unemployed, and his idleness was troubling him and depressing him; all right, he, Professor Toti, had found him a job in the Farmers' Bank, where he deposited the two hundred thousand *lire* he had inherited.

There's a child in the house, too, now, a little angel of two and a half, to whom he has become entirely devoted, like a loving slave. Every day he can't wait for the lessons at the high school to be over, so he can run home and humor his little tyrant's slightest whim. To tell the truth, after the inheritance he could have retired, giving up that maximum pension, so that he could spend all his time with the child. But no! It would have been a sin! Inasmuch as it exists, he wants to bear that yoke of his, which he has always found so burdensome, to the very end! After all, he took a wife for that very reason, just so someone could benefit from what had been a torment to him all his life!

Marrying with this single purpose, to benefit a poor young woman, he has loved his wife solely with a quasi-paternal affection. And he started loving her more paternally than ever from the time the child was born, the child by whom he would almost prefer to be called grandfather rather than daddy. This unwitting lie on the pure little lips of the ignorant child hurts him; he feels that even his love for him suffers from it. But what's to be done? He *must* receive with a kiss that name coming from Ninì's sweet little mouth, that "daddy" which gets a laugh from all the spiteful people who are unable to understand his loving feelings for that innocent creature, his happiness over the good that he has done and continues to do for a woman, a worthy young man, the little one, and himself as well—of course!—himself as well—the happiness of living these last years in cheerful, pleasant company, walking on the edge of the grave with a little angel holding his hand.

---

[2] In revisions of the story, called Giacomino Delisi. Perhaps the change was made to avoid confusion with Giacomo Pugliese, a thirteenth-century writer of the Sicilian School.

Ridano, ridano pure di lui tutti i maligni! Che gliene importa? Egli è felice.

Ma da tre giorni . . .

Che sarà accaduto? La moglie ha gli occhi gonfi e rossi di pianto; accusa un forte mal di capo; non vuole uscir di camera.

—Eh, gioventù! . . . gioventù! . . .—sospira il professor Toti, scrollando il capo con un risolino mesto e arguto negli occhi e sulle labbra.—Qualche nuvola . . . qualche temporaletto . . .

E con Ninì s'aggira per casa, afflitto, inquieto, anche un po' irritato, perché . . . via, proprio non si merita questo, lui, dalla moglie e da Giacomino. I giovani non contano i giorni: ne hanno tanti ancora innanzi a sé . . . Ma per un povero vecchio è grave perdita un giorno! E sono ormai tre, che la moglie lo lascia così per casa, come una mosca senza capo, e non lo delizia più con quelle ariette e canzoncine cantate con la vocetta limpida e fervida, e non gli prodiga più quelle cure, a cui egli è ormai avvezzo.

Anche Ninì è serio serio, come se capisca che la mamma non ha testa da badare a lui. Il professore se lo conduce da una stanza all'altra, e quasi non ha bisogno di chinarsi per dargli la mano, tant'è piccolino anche lui; lo porta innanzi al pianoforte, tocca qua e là qualche tasto, sbuffa, sbadiglia, poi siede, fa galoppare un po' Ninì su le ginocchia, poi torna ad alzarsi: si sente tra le spine. Cinque o sei volte ha tentato di forzar la mogliettina a parlare.

—Male, eh? ti senti proprio male?

Maddalenina seguita a non volergli dir nulla: piange; lo prega di accostar gli scuri del balcone e di portarsi Ninì di là: vuole star sola e al bujo.

—Il capo, eh?

Poverina, le fa tanto male il capo . . . Eh, la lite dev'essere stata grossa davvero!

Il professor Toti si reca in cucina e cerca d'abbordar la servetta, per avere qualche notizia da lei; ma fa larghi giri, perché sa che la servetta gli è nemica; sparla di lui, fuori, come tutti gli altri, e lo mette in berlina. Non riesce a saper nulla neanche dalla servetta.

E allora il professor Toti prende una risoluzione eroica: reca Ninì dalla mamma e la prega che glielo vesta per benino.

Let them laugh, let all the spiteful people laugh at him! What does that matter to him? He is happy.

But for three days . . .

What can have happened? His wife's eyes are swollen and red from crying; she says she has a bad headache; she doesn't want to leave her room.

"Ah, youth! . . . youth! . . . " Professor Toti sighs, shaking his head with a sad, sly smile in his eyes and on his lips. "Some cloud . . . some little thunderstorm . . . "

And with Ninì he wanders around the house, troubled, nervous, also a little irritated, because . . . no, he really doesn't deserve such treatment from his wife and from Giacomino. Young people don't count the days: they have so many still ahead of them . . . But for a poor old man the loss of a day is serious! And it's been three now that his wife has been leaving him alone in the house this way, like a fly without a head, and no longer treating him to those little airs and songs sung in her clear, impassioned little voice, and no longer lavishing those cares on him to which he is now accustomed.

Ninì, too, is as serious as can be, as if he understands that his Mommy's mind is too occupied to pay attention to him. The Professor takes him along from one room to the other, and has practically no need to stoop down to give him his hand, he's so small himself; he leads him in front of the piano, presses down a few keys here and there, snorts, yawns, then sits down, gives Ninì a ride on his knees for a while, then stands up again: he's on pins and needles. Five or six times he has tried to force his little wife to speak.

"Bad, eh? You're really feeling bad?"

Little Maddalena persists in not wanting to tell him anything; she weeps; she asks him to close the balcony shutters and take Ninì to another room: she wants to be alone in the dark.

"Your head, eh?"

Poor thing, her head aches so . . . Ah, the quarrel must have been really a major one!

Professor Toti moves on to the kitchen and tries to start a conversation with the young maid, to get some information out of her; but he beats around the bush, because he knows that the maid is hostile to him; she speaks ill of him, outside the house, like all the rest, and criticizes him. He fails to learn anything, even from the maid.

And then Professor Toti makes a heroic resolution: he takes Ninì to his mother and asks her to dress him up nicely.

—Perché?—domanda ella.

—Lo porto a spassino,—risponde lui.—Oggi è festa . . .
Qua s'annoja, povero bimbo!

La mamma non vorrebbe. Sa che la trista gente ride vedendo il vecchio professore col piccino per mano; sa che qualche malvagio insolente è arrivato finanche a dirgli:—Ma
quanto gli somiglia, professore, il suo figliuolo!

Il professor Toti però insiste.

—No, a spassino, a spassino . . .

E si reca col bimbo in casa di Giacomino Pugliese.

Questi abita insieme con una sorella nubile, che gli ha fatto
da madre. Ignorando la ragione del beneficio recato al fratello, la signorina Agata era prima molto grata al professor
Toti; ora invece—religiosissima com'ella è—lo tiene in conto
d'un diavolo, né più né meno, perché ha indotto il suo Giacomino in peccato mortale.

Il professor Toti deve aspettare un bel po', col piccino dietro
la porta, dopo aver sonato. La signorina Agata è venuta a
guardar dalla spia ed è scappata. Senza dubbio, è andata ad
avvertire il fratello della visita, e ora tornerà a dire che Giacomino non è in casa.

Eccola. Vestita di nero, cerea, stecchita, arcigna, appena
aperta la porta, investe, tutta vibrante il professore.

—Ma come . . . scusi . . . viene a cercarlo pure in casa
adesso? . . . E che vedo! anche col bambino? ha portato anche
il bambino?

Il professor Toti non s'aspetta una simile accoglienza; resta
intronato; guarda la signorina Agata, guarda il piccino, sor-
ride, balbetta:

—Per . . . perché? . . . che è? . . . non posso . . . non . . . non
posso venire a . . .

—Non c'è!—s'affretta a riprendere quella, asciutta e
dura.—Giacomino non c'è.

—Va bene,—dice, chinando il capo, il professor Toti.—Ma
lei, signorina . . . mi scusi . . . lei mi tratta in un modo che . . .
non so! Io non credo d'aver fatto né a suo fratello, né a lei . . .

—Ecco, professore,—lo interrompe, un po' rabbonita, la
signorina Agata.—Noi, creda pure, le siamo . . . le siamo gra-
tissimi, ma anche lei dovrebbe comprendere . . .

Il professor Toti socchiude gli occhi, torna a sorridere, alza

"Why?" she asks.

"I'm taking him for a little walk," he replies. "Today is a holiday . . . He's bored here, poor kid!"

His mother is unwilling. She knows that evil-minded people laugh when they see the old Professor walking hand in hand with the little one; she knows that one insolent scoundrel went so far as to say to him: "My, how your son resembles you, Professor!"

But Professor Toti insists.

"No, for a walk, for a walk . . . "

And with the child he goes to Giacomino Pugliese's house.

Giacomino lives together with a sister of marriageable age who has been a mother to him. Unaware of the reason for the kindnesses showered on her brother, Miss Agata was at first very grateful to Professor Toti; now, instead—being extremely religious—she puts him on a par with the devil, neither more nor less, because he has led her Giacomino into mortal sin.

Professor Toti has to wait in front of the door with the little one for quite some time after ringing the bell. Miss Agata came to look through the peephole and fled. No doubt she went to inform her brother of the visit, and now she'll come back and say that Giacomino isn't home.

Here she is. Dressed in black, with a waxen complexion, thin as a stick, sullen, as soon as the door is open she attacks the Professor, all aquiver.

"How's this? . . . Excuse me . . . Now you're coming to see him in his own house, too? . . . And what's this I see? With the child, too? You brought the child, too?"

Professor Toti wasn't expecting this kind of reception; he's dumbfounded; he looks at Miss Agata, looks at the little one, smiles, stammers:

"Wh. . . why? . . . What's wrong? . . . Can't I . . . can't . . . can't I come to . . . "

"He's not in!" she hurriedly resumes, in her arid, harsh manner. "Giacomino's not in."

"All right," says Professor Toti, bowing his head. "But you, Miss . . . forgive me . . . you treat me in a fashion that . . . I don't know! I don't think I've dealt with either your brother or you . . . "

"Now, Professor," Miss Agata interrupts him, somewhat appeased. "Believe me, we're . . . we're extremely grateful to you, but even *you* ought to understand . . . "

Professor Toti half-closes his eyes, smiles again, raises one hand

una mano e poi si tocca parecchie volte con la punta delle dita il petto, per significarle che, quanto a comprendere, lasci fare a lui.

—Sono vecchio, signorina,—dice,—e comprendo . . . tante cose comprendo io! e guardi, prima di tutte, questa: che certe furie bisogna lasciarle svaporare, e quando nascono malintesi, la miglior cosa è chiarire . . . chiarire, signorina, chiarire francamente, senza sotterfugi, senza riscaldarsi . . . Non le pare?

—Certo, sì . . .—riconosce, almeno così in astratto, la signorina Agata.

—E dunque,—riprende il professor Toti,—mi lasci entrare e mi chiami Giacomino.

—Ma se non c'è!

—Vede? No. Non mi deve dire che non c'è. Giacomino è in casa, e lei me lo deve chiamare. Chiariremo tutto con calma . . . glielo dica: con calma! Io son vecchio e comprendo tutto, perché sono stato anche giovane, signorina. Con calma, glielo dica. Mi lasci entrare.

Introdotto nel modesto salotto, il professor Toti siede con Ninì tra le gambe, rassegnato ad aspettare anche qua un bel pezzo, che la sorella persuada Giacomino.

—No, qua, Ninì . . . buono!—dice di tratto in tratto al bimbo, che vorrebbe andare a una mensoletta, dove luccicano certi gingilli di porcellana; e intanto si scapa a pensare che diamine può essere accaduto di così grave in casa sua, senza ch'egli se ne sia accorto per nulla. Maddalenina è così buona! Che male può ella aver fatto, da provocare un così aspro e forte risentimento, qua, anche ne la sorella di Giacomino?

Il professor Toti, che ha creduto finora a una bizza passeggera, comincia a impensierirsi e a costernarsi sul serio.

Oh, ecco Giacomino finalmente! Dio, che viso alterato! che aria rabbuffata! E come? Ah, questo no! Scansa freddamente il bambino che gli è corso incontro gridando con le manine tese:

—*Giamì! Giamì!*

—Giacomino!—esclama, ferito, con severità il professor Toti.

—Che ha da dirmi, professore?—s'affretta a domandargli quello, schivando di guardarlo negli occhi.—Io sto male . . . Ero a letto . . . Non sono in grado di parlare e neanche di sostener la vista d'alcuno . . .

and then touches his chest several times with his fingertips to indicate that, when it comes to understanding, he's the one for the job.

"I'm old, Miss," he says, "and I do understand . . . I understand so many things! And look, first and foremost, I understand this: that it's necessary to let certain angers evaporate and, when misunderstandings arise, the best thing is to clarify matters . . . to clarify them, Miss, clarify them frankly, without subterfuges, without getting heated up . . . Don't you agree?"

"Of course I do . . . ," Miss Agata acknowledges, at least in the abstract.

"And so," resumes Professor Toti, "let me in and call Giacomino for me."

"But I tell you he's not in!"

"You see? No. You mustn't tell me he's not in. Giacomino is at home, and you must call him for me. We'll clarify everything calmly . . . tell him that: calmly! I'm old and I understand everything, because I was also young once, Miss. Calmly, tell him that. Let me in."

Ushered into the humble parlor, Professor Toti sits down with Ninì between his knees, resigned to waiting a long time here, too, while Giacomino's sister is persuading him to come.

"No, here, Ninì . . . that's a good boy!" he says from time to time to the child, who would like to go over to a shelf on which some porcelain knickknacks are sparkling; and meanwhile he racks his brains wondering what the devil could have happened in his house that was so serious, without his having noticed it at all. Little Maddalena is so good-natured! What wrong could she have committed to cause such a fierce and strong resentment, here, even in Giacomino's sister?

Professor Toti, who up to now has thought it was a passing spat, is starting to get worried and seriously alarmed.

Ah, here is Giacomino finally! God, what an angry face! What a ruffled manner! What's this? Oh, no, not that! He coldly shuns the child, who has run to meet him with his little hands outstretched, crying:

"'Giamì! Giamì!'"

"Giacomino!" Professor Toti, who is hurt, exclaims with severity.

"What do you have to say to me, Professor?" Giacomino quickly asks him, avoiding looking him in the eye. "I'm unwell . . . I was in bed . . . I'm in no shape to talk or even bear the sight of anybody . . . "

—Ma il bambino?!

—Ecco,—dice Giacomino; e si china a baciare Ninì.

—Ti senti male?—riprende il professor Toti, un po' rac-
consolato da quel bacio.—Lo supponevo. E son venuto per
questo. Il capo, eh? Siedi, siedi . . . Discorriamo. Qua, Ninì . . .
Senti che *Giamì* ha la bua? Sì, caro, la bua . . . qua, povero
Giamì . . . Sta' bonino; ora andiamo via. Volevo doman-
darti—soggiunge, rivolgendosi a Giacomino,—se il direttore
della Banca Agraria ti ha detto qualche cosa.

—No, perché?—fa Giacomino, turbandosi ancor più.

—Perché ieri gli ho parlato—risponde con un risolino mi-
sterioso il professor Toti.—Il tuo stipendio non è molto
grasso, figliuol mio. E sai che una mia parolina . . .

Giacomino Pugliese si torce su la sedia, stringe le pugna
fino ad affondarsi le unghie nel palmo delle mani.

—Professore, io la ringrazio,—dice,—ma mi faccia il favore, la carità di non incomodarsi più per me, ecco!

—Ah sì?—risponde il professor Toti con quel risolino ancora su la bocca.—Bravo! Non abbiamo più bisogno di nessuno, eh? Ma se io volessi farlo per mio piacere? Caro mio,
ma se non debbo più curarmi di te, di chi vuoi che mi curi
io? Sono vecchio, Giacomino! E ai vecchi—badiamo, che non
siano egoisti!—ai vecchi piace di vedere i giovani, come te
meritevoli, farsi avanti nella vita per loro mezzo; e godono
della loro allegria, delle loro speranze, del posto ch'essi
prendono man mano nella società. Io poi per te . . . via, tu lo
sai . . . ti considero come un figliuolo . . . Che cos'è? Piangi?

Giacomino ha nascosto infatti il volto tra le mani e sussulta
come per un impeto di pianto che vorrebbe frenare.

Ninì lo guarda sbigottito, poi, rivolgendosi al professore,
dice:

—*Giamì, bua* . . .

Il professore si alza e fa per posare una mano su la spalla
di Giacomino; ma questi balza in piedi, quasi ne provi ribrezzo,
mostra il viso scontraffatto come per una fiera risoluzione improvvisa, e gli grida esasperatamente:

—Non mi s'accosti! Professore, se ne vada, la scongiuro, se
ne vada! Lei mi sta facendo soffrire una pena d'inferno! Io

"But the child?!"

"There," Giacomino says; and he stoops down to kiss Ninì.

"You're not well?" Professor Toti resumes, somewhat comforted by that kiss. "I thought as much. And that's why I came. Your head, eh? Sit down, sit down . . . Let's have a talk. Here, Ninì . . . You hear? 'Giamì' is 'sick.'[3] Yes, dear, 'sick' . . . here, poor 'Giamì' . . . Be good; we're leaving right away. I meant to ask you," he adds, addressing Giacomino, "whether the director of the Farmers' Bank told you anything."

"No, why?" says Giacomino, becoming even more perturbed.

"Because I spoke to him yesterday," says Professor Toti with a mysterious little smile. "Your salary isn't all that big, son. And you know that a word from me . . . "

Giacomino Pugliese writhes on his chair and clenches his fists till he sinks his nails into the palms of his hands.

"Professor, I thank you," he says, "but do me the favor, the very great favor, of no longer troubling yourself over me, won't you?"

"Oh, really?" answers Professor Toti with that little smile still on his lips. "Good man! We no longer need anybody, eh? But what if I wanted to do it for my own pleasure? My good man, if I'm not to take care of you any more, whom do you want me to take of? I'm old, Giacomino! And old people—assuming they're not selfish!—old people like to see deserving youngsters like you get ahead in life with their help; and they get enjoyment out of the youngsters' happiness, their hopes, the position they gradually assume in society. Now, with regard to you, I . . . come now, you know it . . . I look on you as a son . . . What's wrong? You're crying?"

Indeed, Giacomino has hidden his face in his hands and is shaken as if by an attack of weeping that he'd like to hold back.

Ninì looks at him in dismay, then, addressing the Professor, says: "'Giamì,' sick . . . "

The Professor gets up and starts to put a hand on Giacomino's shoulder; but the young man leaps to his feet as if repelled at the thought, shows his face, which is distorted as if by a sudden fierce resolution, and shouts at him in exasperation:

"Don't come near me! Professor, go away, I beg of you, go away! You're making me suffer the torments of hell! I don't deserve this

---

[3] *"Bua,"* somewhat like English "boo-boo," is baby talk for an injury or other discomfort.

non merito codesto suo affetto e non lo voglio, non lo voglio . . . Per carità, se ne vada, si porti via il bambino e si scordi
che io esisto!

Il professor Toti resta sbalordito; domanda:

—Ma perché?

—Glielo dico subito!—risponde Giacomino.—Io sono fidanzato, professore! Ha capito? Sono fidanzato!

Il professor Toti vacilla, come per una mazzata sul capo;
alza le mani; balbetta:

—Tu? fi. . . fidanzato?

—Sissignore,—dice Giacomino.—E dunque, basta . . .
basta per sempre! Capirà che non posso più . . . vederla qui . . .

—Mi cacci via?—domanda, quasi senza voce, il professor
Toti.

—No!—s'affretta a rispondergli Giacomino, dolente.—Ma
è bene che lei . . . che lei se ne vada, professore . . .

Andarsene? Il professore casca a sedere su una seggiola. Le
gambe gli si sono come stroncate sotto. Si prende la testa tra
le mani e geme:

—Oh Dio! Ah che rovina! Dunque per questo? Oh povero
me! Oh povero me! Ma quando? come? senza dirne nulla?
con chi ti sei fidanzato?

—Qua, professore . . . da un pezzo . . .—dice Giacomino.—Con una povera orfana, come me . . . amica di mia
sorella . . .

Il professor Toti lo guarda, inebetito, con gli occhi spenti,
la bocca aperta, e non trova la voce per parlare.

—E . . . e . . . e si lascia tutto . . . così . . . e . . . e non si pensa
più a . . . a nulla . . . non si . . . non si tien più conto di nulla . . .

Giacomino si sente rinfacciare con queste parole l'ingrati-
tudine, e si ribella, fosco:

—Ma scusi! che mi voleva schiavo, lei?

—Io, schiavo?—prorompe, ora, con uno schianto nella
voce, il professor Toti.—Io? E lo puoi dire? Io che ti ho fatto
padrone della mia casa? Ah, questa, questa sì che è vera ingra-
titudine! E che forse t'ho beneficato per me? che ne ho avuto
io, se non il dileggio di tutti gli sciocchi che non sanno capire
il sentimento mio? Dunque non lo capisci, non lo hai capito
neanche tu, il sentimento di questo povero vecchio, che sta
per andarsene e che era tranquillo e contento di lasciar tutto
a posto, una famigliuola bene avviata, in buone condizioni . . .
felice? Io ho settant'anni; io domani me ne vado, Giacomino!
Che ti sei levato di cervello, figliuolo mio! Io vi lascio tutto,

affection of yours and I don't want it, I don't want it . . . For heaven's sake, go away, take away the child and forget that I exist!"

Professor Toti stands there amazed; he asks:

"But why?"

"I'll tell you right away!" Giacomino answers. "I'm engaged, Professor! Understand? I'm engaged!"

Professor Toti staggers, as if hit on the head with a club; he raises his hands; stammers:

"You? En. . . engaged?"

"Yes, sir," says Giacomino. "And so, enough . . . enough for always! You'll understand that I can no longer . . . see you here . . . "

"You're throwing me out?" Professor Toti asks, almost tonelessly.

"No!" Giacomino hurriedly replies, in his sorrow. "But it would be good for you . . . for you to go away, Professor . . . "

Go away? The professor plumps down on a chair. His legs seem to have been knocked out from under him. He takes his head in his hands and moans:

"Oh, God! Ah, what a catastrophe! And so this was the reason? What shall I do? What shall I do? But when? How? Without saying a thing? To whom are you engaged?"

"Here, Professor . . . for some time," says Giacomino. "To a poor orphan like myself . . . a friend of my sister's . . . "

Professor Toti looks at him numbly, with his eyes dulled, his mouth open, and can't summon up his voice to go on speaking.

"And . . . and . . . and everything is abandoned . . . like this . . . and . . . and no more thought is given to . . . to anything . . . no more . . . no more account is taken of anything . . . "

Giacomino feels that he is being reproached with ingratitude, and he protests, gloomily:

"Just a moment! You wanted me to be a slave?"

"I . . . a slave?" Professor Toti now bursts out, with a crack in his voice. "I? And you can say that? I, who made you master in my own house? Ah, this, yes, this is true ingratitude! And was it perhaps for my sake that I benefited you? What did I get out of it, except the mockery of all the fools who can't understand my feelings? And so you don't understand them, not even you have understood them, the feelings of this poor old man who is about to depart from the scene and who was calmly contented to leave everything arranged, a little family that was doing well, in comfortable circumstances . . . happy? I'm seventy years old; tomorrow I'll be gone, Giacomino! You've lost your mind, son! I'm leaving you two every-

qua . . . Che vai cercando? Non so ancora, non voglio saper
chi sia la tua fidanzata; sarà magari un'onesta giovine, perché
tu sei buono . . . ; ma pensa che . . . pensa che . . . non è possibile che tu abbia trovato di meglio, Giacomino, sotto tutti i riguardi . . . Non ti dico soltanto per l'agiatezza assicurata . . .
Ma tu hai già la tua famigliuola, in cui non ci sono che io solo
di più, ancora per poco . . . io che non conto per nulla . . . Che
fastidio vi do io? Io sono come il padre . . . Io posso anche, se
volete . . . per la vostra pace . . . Ma dimmi com'è stato? che
è accaduto? come ti s'è voltata la testa, così tutt'a un tratto?
Dimmelo! dimmelo . . .

E il professor Toti s'accosta a Giacomino e vuol prendergli
un braccio e scuoterglielo; ma quegli si restringe tutto in sé,
quasi rabbrividendo, e si schermisce.

—Professore!—grida.—Ma come non capisce, come non
s'accorge che tutta codesta sua bontà . . .

—Ebbene?

—Mi lasci stare! non mi faccia dire! Come non capisce
che certe cose si possono far solo di nascosto, e non son più
possibili alla luce, con lei che sa, con tutta la gente che
ride?

—Ah, per la gente?—esclama il professore.—E tu . . .

—Mi lasci stare!—ripete Giacomino, al colmo dell'orgasmo,
scotendo in aria le braccia.—Guardi! Ci sono tant'altri giovani
che han bisogno d'ajuto, professore!

Il Toti si sente ferire fin nell'anima da queste parole, che
sono un'offesa atroce e ingiusta per sua moglie; impallidisce,
allividisce, e tutto tremante dice:

—Maddalenina è giovine, ma è onesta, perdio! e tu lo sai!
Maddalenina ne può morire . . . perché è qui, è qui, il suo
male, nel cuore . . . dove credi che sia? È qui, è qui, ingrato!
Ah, la insulti, per giunta? E non ti vergogni? e non ne senti
rimorso di fronte a me? Puoi dirmi questo in faccia? tu? Credi
che ella possa passare, così, da uno all'altro, come niente?
madre di questo piccino? Ma che dici? Come puoi parlar
così?

Giacomino lo guarda strasecolato, allibito.

—Io?—dice.—Ma lei piuttosto, professore, scusi, lei, lei,

thing, here . . . What are you still looking for? I don't know yet, I don't want to know, who your fiancée is; I'm sure she's a respectable young woman, because *you* are so fine . . . ; but just think that . . . just think that . . . it isn't possible for you to have found anything better, Giacomino, from any point of view . . . I don't mean merely because of the guaranteed financial comfort . . . But you already have your own little family, of which I'm the only super-fluous member, and that not for long . . . and I don't count at all . . . What bother do I give you two? I'm like your father . . . If you like, I can even . . . for your peace of mind . . . But tell me how it came about. What happened? How did your head turn so suddenly? Tell me! Tell me . . . "

And Professor Toti goes over to Giacomino and wants to take him by the arm and shake it; but Giacomino tenses up, as if shuddering, and wards him off.

"Professor!" he shouts. "How is it that you don't understand, that you don't realize that all this kindness of yours . . . "

"Well?"

"Let me be! Don't make me say it! How is it you don't understand that certain things can be done only clandestinely, and are no longer possible in the full light of the day, with you knowing about them, with all the people laughing over them?"

"Oh, it's on account of the people?" exclaims the Professor. "And you . . . "

"Let me be!" Giacomino repeats, at the peak of his excitement, waving his arms in the air. "Look! There are so many other young men in need of assistance, Professor!"

Toti feels hurt to the bottom of his heart by these words, which are a horrible, unjust insult to his wife; he turns pale, he becomes livid, and, trembling all over, he says:

"Little Maddalena is young, but she's respectable, damn it! And you know it! Maddalena may die of this . . . because her pain is here, here, in the heart . . . Where do you think it is? It's here, it's here, you ingrate! Ah, now you're insulting her, on top of everything else? And you're not ashamed? And you don't feel any remorse on my account? You have the nerve to say that to my face? You? You think she can change hands like that, from one man to another, and think nothing of it? The mother of this little one? But what are you saying? How can you talk that way?"

Giacomino looks at him, shocked and astounded.

"I?" he says. "But, Professor, forgive me, it's actually *you*,

come può parlare così? Ma dice sul serio? che sono io? sono il marito di sua moglie? e lei che è? mio suocero? Ma scusi!

Il professor Toti si stringe ambo le mani su la bocca, strizza gli occhi, squassa il capo e rompe in un pianto disperato. Ninì anche lui, allora, si mette a piangere. Il professore lo sente, corre a lui, lo abbraccia.

—Ah, povero Ninì mio . . . ah che sciagura, Ninì mio, che rovina! E che sarà della tua mamma ora? e che sarà di te, Ninì mio, con una mammina come la tua, inesperta, senza guida . . . Ah, che baratro!

Solleva il capo, e, guardando tra le lagrime Giacomino:

—Piango,—dice,—perché mio è il rimorso; io t'ho protetto, io t'ho accolto in casa, io le ho parlato sempre tanto bene di te, io . . . io le ho tolto ogni scrupolo d'amarti . . . e ora che ella ti amava sicura . . . madre di questo piccino . . . tu . . .

S'interrompe e, fiero, risoluto, convulso:

—Bada, Giacomino!—dice.—Io son capace di presentarmi con questo piccino per mano in casa della tua fidanzata!

Giacomino, che suda freddo, pur su la brace ardente, nel sentirlo parlare e piangere così, a questa minaccia giunge le mani, gli si fa innanzi e scongiura:

—Professore, professore, ma lei vuol dunque proprio coprirsi di ridicolo?

—Di ridicolo?—grida il professore.—E che vuoi che me n'importi, quando vedo la rovina d'una povera donna, la rovina tua, la rovina d'una creature innocente? Vieni, vieni, andiamo, su via, Ninì, andiamo!

Giacomino gli si para davanti:

—Professore, lei non lo farà!

—Io lo farò!—gli grida con viso fermo il professor Toti.—E per impedirti il matrimonio son anche capace di farti cacciare dalla Banca! Ti do tre giorni di tempo.

E, voltandosi su la soglia, col piccino per mano:

—Pensaci, Giacomino! Pensaci!

you—how can *you* talk like that? Are you serious? What am I? Am I the husband of your wife? And what are you? My father-in-law? Come, now!"

Professor Toti clasps both hands to his mouth, presses his eyes shut, shakes his head and breaks out into despairing tears. Then Ninì, too, starts to cry. The Professor hears him, runs to him, embraces him.

"Ah, my poor Ninì . . . oh, what a disaster, my Ninì, what a catastrophe! And what will become of your Mommy now? And what will become of you, my Ninì, with a little mother like yours, inexperienced, with no one to guide her . . . ? Oh, what hell!"

He lifts his head, and, looking at Giacomino through his tears:

"I'm crying," he says, "because the remorse is mine. I protected you, I took you into my home, I always spoke so well of you to her, I . . . I removed all the scruples she had about loving you . . . and now that she was safely in love with you . . . the mother of this little one . . . you . . . "

He breaks off and, sternly, resolutely, nervously:

"Watch out, Giacomino!" he says. "I'm capable of showing up at your fiancée's house hand in hand with this little one!"

Giacomino, in a cold sweat even though on hot coals from hearing him speak and cry like that, at that threat puts his hands together, moves in front of him and beseeches him:

"Professor, Professor, do you really want to cover yourself with ridicule?"

"With ridicule?" shouts the Professor. "And what difference do you want that to make to me, when I see the destruction of a poor woman, your destruction, the destruction of an innocent baby? Come, come, we're going, come now, Ninì, we're going!"

Giacomino comes up to him.

"Professor, you won't do that!"

"I *will* do it!" Professor Toti shouts to him with a resolute expression. "And to prevent that marriage of yours, I'm even capable of having you thrown out of the bank! I give you three days' time."

And, turning around on the threshold, holding the little one by the hand:

"Think it over, Giacomino! Think it over!"

LA TRAGEDIA D'UN PERSONAGGIO

Persisto nella mia vecchia abitudine di fare udienza ogni domenica mattina ai personaggi delle mie future novelle.

Tre ore, dalle sette alle dieci.

M'accade quasi sempre di trovarmi in cattiva compagnia.

Non so perché, di solito accorre a queste mie udienze la gente più scontenta del mondo, o afflitta da strani mali, o ingarbugliata in speciosissimi casi, con la quale è veramente una pena trattare.

Io ascolto tutti con sopportazione infinita; prendo nota de' nomi e delle condizioni di ciascuno; tengo conto dei loro sentimenti e delle loro aspirazioni; li interrogo con buona grazia e mi sforzo quanto più posso di contentarli, cioè di volerli in me, nell'opera mia, cosi come essi in sè e per sè si vogliono.

Ma bisogna anche aggiungere ch'io poi non sono, per mia indole e per mia disgrazia, di facile contentatura. Pazienza, buona grazia, sì; ma esser gabbato non mi piace. E voglio penetrare in fondo, con lunga e sottile indagine.

Ora avviene che a certe mie domande quelli s'impuntino, aombrino, recalcitrino furiosamente, perché sembra loro ch'io provi gusto a scomporli dalla serietà con cui mi si presentano.

Che c'entra questo?

Con pazienza, con buona grazia m'ingegno di far vedere e toccar con mano che c'entra benissimo, perché si fa presto a volersi in un modo o in un altro; tutto sta poi se possiamo essere quali ci vogliamo. Ove quel potere manchi, per forza questa volontà deve apparir ridicola e vana.

Non se ne vogliono persuadere.

E allora io, che in fondo sono di buon cuore, li compatisco. Ma è mai possibile il compatimento di certe sventure, se non a patto che se ne rida?

Orbene, i personaggi delle mie novelle vanno sbandendo per il mondo che io sono uno scrittore crudelissimo e spietato.

A CHARACTER'S TRAGEDY

I persist in my old habit of giving audience every Sunday morning to the characters of my future short stories.

Three hours, from seven to ten.

I almost always find myself in bad company.

I don't know why, but usually those who attend my audiences are the most discontented people in the world, either suffering from strange maladies, or entangled in the most singular situations, people with whom it's really a torment to deal.

I listen to them all with infinite forbearing; I take down each one's name and circumstances; I take into account their feelings and aspirations; I question them courteously and make the greatest possible effort to satisfy them; that is, to accept them in my own mind and in my writings just as they see themselves in their own mind as individuals.

But I must also add that, by my nature and to my misfortune, I myself am not easily pleased. Patience, courtesy—yes, I have those; but I don't like being hoodwinked. And it's my custom to get to the bottom of each matter, making a long, detailed investigation.

Now, it's often the case that at certain questions I pose they jib, they take umbrage, they resist furiously, because they think that I'm getting enjoyment out of demolishing the serious front with which they come to me.

"What does that have to do with anything?"

Using my patience and my courtesy, I do my best to make them see and perceive that my question was perfectly à propos, because it's easy for anyone to *wish* to be one kind of person or another; the real question is whether we *can* be the way we want to be. When the power to do so is lacking, the wish must necessarily appear ridiculous and vain.

They can't be convinced of this.

And then, being basically good-hearted, I'm sorry for them. But is it ever possible to feel sorry for certain misfortunes unless you can laugh at them at the same time?

Well, the characters of my stories go around spreading the word everywhere that I am an extremely cruel and merciless writer. It

Ci vorrebbe un critico di buona volontà che facesse vedere quanto compatimento sia sotto a quel riso.

Ma dove sono oggi i critici di buona volontà?

È bene avvertire che alcuni personaggi, in queste udienze, balzano innanzi agli altri e s'impongono con tanta prepotenza, ch'io mi vedo costretto qualche volta a lasciarli entrar prima e lì per lì nella vita.

Parecchi di questa lor furia poi si pentono amaramente e si raccomandano a me per avere accomodato chi un difetto e chi un altro. Ma io grido loro che scontino ora il loro peccato originale e aspettino ch'io non abbia più tanta folla attorno e abbia tempo e modo di ritornare a loro.

Tra quelli che rimangono indietro, in attesa, sopraffatti, chi sospira, chi s'oscura, chi si stanca e se ne va a picchiare alla porta di qualche altro scrittore. Mi è avvenuto non di rado di ritrovar ne le novelle di parecchi miei colleghi certi personaggi che prima s'erano presentati a me; come pure m'è avvenuto di ravvisarvene certi altri, i quali, non contenti del modo com'io li avevo trattati, han voluto provare di fare altrove una miglior figura.

Non me ne lagno, perché solitamente di nuovi me ne vengono incontro due o tre per settimana, che si aggiungono al non esiguo numero degli aspettanti. E spesso la ressa è tanta, ch'io debbo dar retta a più d'uno contemporaneamente. Se non che, a un certo punto, lo spirito, così diviso e frastornato, si ricusa a quel doppio o triplo allevamento e grida esasperato che, o uno alla volta, piano piano, riposatamente, o via a monte tutt'e tre!

Ricordo sempre con quanta remissione aspettò il suo turno un povero vecchietto arrivatomi da lontano, un certo maestro Icilio Saporini, spatriato in America nel 1849, alla caduta della Repubblica romana, per aver musicato un inno patriottico, e ritornato in Italia dopo quarantacinque anni, quasi ottantenne, per morirvi! Cerimonioso, col suo vocino di zanzara, lasciava passar tutti innanzi a sé. E finalmente, un giorno ch'ero ancor convalescente d'una lunga malattia, me lo vidi entrare in camera, umile umile, con un timido sorrisetto su le labbra:

—Se posso . . . Se non le dispiace . . .

Oh sì, caro vecchietto! Aveva scelto il momento più opportuno. E lo feci morire subito subito in una novelletta intitolata *Musica vecchia*.

*

would take a critic possessed of good will to make people see how much sympathy underlies that laughter.

But where are the critics possessed of good will nowadays?

It should be noted that some characters at these audiences leap ahead of the others and make their presence felt with such self-importance that I sometimes find myself compelled to let them enter life out of turn, right on the spot.

A number of them later bitterly regret this furore of theirs and implore me to patch up whatever defect each one has. But I yell at them, saying that now they must atone for their original sin and wait until there is no longer such a big crowd around me and I have the time and the means to get back to them.

Among those who remain behind waiting, feeling overwhelmed, some sigh, some grow sullen, some get tired and go off to knock at some other writer's door. Not seldom I have happened to find in the stories of several colleagues of mine certain characters that had called on me first; just as I have also happened to recognize certain others, who, dissatisfied with the way I had treated them, decided to try and cut a better figure elsewhere.

I don't complain of this, because usually two or three come to see me every week, joining the far from tiny number of those waiting. And often there is such a mob that I have to give my attention to more than one at the same time. Unless, at some point, my mind becomes so distracted and bewildered that it rejects that double or triple nurturing and shouts in its exasperation: "Either one at a time, quietly and calmly, or all three of you can get lost!"

I always remember how meekly one poor old man awaited his turn, after coming a long way to see me: a certain composer named Icilio Saporini, who had emigrated to America in 1849 after the fall of the Roman Republic because he had set a patriotic hymn to music, and had come back to Italy to die forty-five years later, aged almost eighty. Ceremonious, with a tiny voice like a mosquito's, he would let everyone else get ahead of him. And finally, one day when I was still recovering from a long illness, I saw him come into my room, humble as can be, with a timid little smile on his lips:

"If I may . . . If it isn't any trouble . . . "

Of course, dear old man! He had chosen the most opportune moment. And I had him die just as fast as possible in a little story titled "Old Music."[1]

*

---

[1] "Musica vecchia," first published in 1910.

Quest'ultima domenica sono entrato nello scrittojo, per l'udienza, un po' più tardi del solito.

Un lungo romanzo inviatomi in dono, e che aspettava da più d'un mese d'esser letto, mi tenne sveglio fino alle tre del mattino per le tante considerazioni che mi suggerì un personaggio di esso, l'unico vivo tra molte ombre vane.

Rappresentava un pover'uomo, un certo dottor Fileno, che credeva d'aver trovato il più efficace rimedio a ogni sorta di mali, una ricetta infallibile per consolar se stesso e tutti gli uomini d'ogni publica o privata calamità.

Veramente, più che rimedio o ricetta, era un metodo, questo del dottor Fileno, che consisteva nel leggere da mane a sera libri di storia e nel veder nella storia anche il presente, cioè come già lontanissimo nel tempo. E con questo metodo egli era guarito di tutti i mali, si era liberato d'ogni pena e d'ogni fastidio, e aveva trovato—senza bisogno di morire—la pace: una pace austera e serena, soffusa di quella certa mestizia senza rimpianto che serberebbero ancora i cimiteri su la faccia della terra, anche quando tutti gli uomini vi fossero morti.

Non si sognava neppure il dottor Fileno di trarre dal passato ammaestramenti per il presente, perché sapeva che sarebbe stato tempo perduto e da sciocchi. La storia è composizione ideale d'elementi raccolti secondo la natura, le antipatie, le simpatie, le aspirazioni, le opinioni degli storici. Come dunque applicare questa composizione ideale alla realtà viva, effettiva, in cui gli elementi sono ancora scomposti e sparpagliati? Nè si sognava parimenti di trarre dal presente norme o previsioni per l'avvenire. Il dottor Fileno anzi faceva proprio il contrario. Si poneva idealmente nell'avvenire per guardare il presente e lo vedeva come passato.

Gli era morta, per esempio, da pochi giorni una figliuola. Un amico era andato a trovarlo per condolersi con lui della sciagura. Ebbene, lo aveva trovato già così consolato, come se quella figliuola gli fosse morta da cent'anni.

La sua sciagura, ancor calda calda, egli la aveva senz'altro allontanata nel tempo, respinta e composta nel passato.

Ma bisognava vedere da quale altezza e con quanta dignità ne parlava!

In somma, di quel suo metodo il dottor Fileno s'era fatto

This past Sunday I went into my study, for the audience, a little later than usual.

A long novel that had been sent to me as a gift and had been waiting over a month for me to read it kept me up till three in the morning because of the many reflections aroused in me by one of its characters, the only living one among a crowd of empty shadows.

His role was that of an unfortunate man, a certain Dr. Fileno, who thought he had found the most effective cure for every kind of ailment, an infallible prescription for consoling himself and all men for every public or private calamity.

To tell the truth, rather than a cure or a prescription, this discovery of Dr. Fileno's was a method, which consisted of reading history books from morning till night and of looking on the present as history, too—that is, as something already very remote in time. And with this method he had been cured of all his ills, he had freed himself from every sorrow and every annoyance, and had found peace without the necessity of dying: an austere, serene peace, permeated with that certain sadness without regret which the cemeteries on the earth's surface would still retain even after all the people on earth had died out.

Dr. Fileno hadn't even the slightest thought of deriving lessons from the past for the present, because he knew it would be a waste of time and a game for fools. History is an idealized amalgam of elements gathered together in accordance with the nature, likes, dislikes, aspirations and opinions of historians. How, then, can this idealized amalgam be applied to living, effective reality, in which the elements are still separate and scattered? Nor, similarly, did he have any thought of deriving from the present any norms or predictions for the future. In fact, Dr. Fileno did just the opposite. In his mind he placed himself in the future in order to look back at the present, which he viewed as the past.

For example, a few days earlier a daughter of his had died. A friend had come to see him to condole with him over his misfortune. Well, he had found him as consoled already as if that daughter had died a hundred years before.

He had just taken that misfortune of his, while it was still recent and painful, and had distanced it in time, had relegated it to, and filed it away in, the past.

But you had to see from what a height and with how much dignity he spoke about it!

In short, Dr. Fileno had made a sort of telescope for himself out

come un cannocchiale. Lo apriva, ma non si metteva già a guardare verso l'avvenire, dove sapeva che non avrebbe veduto nulla; persuadeva l'anima sua a esser contenta di porsi a mirare dalla lente più grande, volta all'avvenire, attraverso la piccola, appuntata al presente. E la sua anima così guardava col cannocchiale rivoltato, e il presente subito le s'impiccioliva, lontano lontano.

Il dottor Fileno attendeva da varii anni a comporre un libro, che avrebbe fatto epoca certamente. Il libro aveva appunto per titolo *La filosofia del lontano.*

Durante la lettura del romanzo m'era apparso manifesto che l'autore, tutto inteso ad annodare artificiosamente una delle trame più solite, non aveva saputo assumere intera coscienza di questo personaggio, il quale, contenendo in sé esso solo il germe d'una vera e propria creazione, era riuscito a un certo punto a prender la mano all'autore e a stagliarsi per un lungo tratto con possente e straordinario rilievo su i comunissimi casi narrati e rappresentati; poi, all'improvviso, sformato, s'era lasciato piegare e adattare alle esigenze d'una falsa e sciocca soluzione.

Ero rimasto a lungo, nel silenzio della notte, con l'imagine di questo personaggio innanzi agli occhi, a fantasticare. Perdio, c'era tanta materia in esso, da trarne fuori un capolavoro! Se l'autore non lo avesse così indegnamente trascurato e misconosciuto, se avesse fatto di lui il centro della narrazione, anche tutti quegli elementi artificiosi di cui s'era valso, si sarebbero trasformati, sarebbero diventati subito vivi. E una gran pena e un gran dispetto s'erano impadroniti di me per quella vita miseramente mancata.

Entrando tardi nello scrittojo, lo trovai più del solito ingombro. Ma non ingombro soltanto. Vi era uno scompiglio, una mischia. Quel dottor Fileno s'era cacciato in mezzo ai miei personaggi aspettanti, i quali, adirati e indispettiti, gli erano saltati addosso e cercavano di cacciarlo via, di strapparlo indietro.

—Ohé! – gridai.—Signori miei, che modo è questo? Dottor Fileno, io ho già sprecato con lei troppo tempo, scusi! Lei non m'appartiene. Mi lasci attendere in pace adesso ai miei personaggi, e se ne vada. Capirà che questi han ragione di considerarlo qui e di trattarlo come un intruso e come un disturbatore. Se ne vada!

Una così intensa e disperata angoscia si dipinse nel volto

of that method of his. He would open it, but now not with the intention of looking toward the future, where he knew he would see nothing. He convinced his mind that it should be contented to look through the larger lens, which was pointed at the future, toward the smaller one, which was pointed at the present. And so his mind looked through the "wrong" end of the telescope, and immediately the present became small and very distant.

Dr. Fileno had been looking forward for several years to writing a book that would certainly create a stir. And, in fact, the title of the book was *The Philosophy of Distance.*

While reading the novel it had seemed evident to me that the author, exclusively concerned with artificially weaving one of the most well-worn plots, had been unable to become fully aware of this character, who, containing within himself alone the germ of a true and real creation, had succeeded to some extent in taking over from the author and, for a large part of the book, in standing out in powerful and extraordinary relief against the extremely humdrum events being narrated and performed; then, suddenly denatured, he had allowed himself to be molded and adapted to the exigencies of a false and foolish conclusion.

I had remained for some time, in the silence of the night, with the image of this character before my eyes, giving my imagination free rein. Damn it all, there was enough material in him to produce a masterpiece! If the author hadn't neglected and disregarded him so undeservingly, if he had made him the center of the narrative, all those artificial elements he had had recourse to would also have been transformed, would suddenly have taken on life. And a great sorrow and a great vexation had seized upon me for the sake of that miserably failed life.

Coming into my study late, I found it more crowded than usual. It was disorganized, a muddle. That Dr. Fileno had thrust himself into the midst of my waiting characters, who, angry and irritated, had jumped on him and were trying to drive him away, to pull him back.

"Hey!" I yelled. "Ladies and gentlemen, is this any way to behave? Dr. Fileno, I've already wasted too much time on you, you know! You don't belong to me. Let me now listen to my characters in peace and quiet, and go away. You surely understand that they are right in looking on you and treating you as an intruder and disturber of the peace. Go away!"

Such an intense, despairing anguish was portrayed in Dr. Fileno's

del dottor Fileno, che subito tutti quegli altri, i miei personaggi che ancora stavano a trattenerlo, impallidirono mortificati e si ritrassero.

—Non mi scacci, per carità, non mi scacci! Mi accordi cinque soli minuti d'udienza, e si lasci persuadere, per carità!

Perplesso e pur compreso di pietà, io gli domandai:

—Ma persuadere di che? Sono persuaso appieno ch'ella, caro dottore, meritava di capitare in migliori mani. Che vuole ch'io le faccia? Mi son doluto già abbastanza della sua sorte; ora me ne condolgo con lei personalmente, e basta.

—E basta? Ah, no, perdio!—scattò il dottor Fileno con un fremito d'indignazione per tutta la persona.—Lei dice così perché non son cosa sua! La sua noncuranza, il suo disprezzo mi sarebbero, creda, assai men crudeli, che codesta passiva commiserazione, indegna d'un artista, mi scusi! Nessuno può sapere meglio di lei, che noi siamo esseri vivi, più vivi di quelli che respirano e vestono panni; forse meno reali, ma più veri! Si nasce alla vita in tanti modi, caro signore; e lei sa bene che la natura si serve dello strumento della fantasia umana per proseguire la sua opera di creazione. E chi nasce mercè quest'attività creatrice, che ha sede nello spirito dell'uomo, è ordinato da natura a una vita superiore a quella di chi nasce dal grembo mortale d'una donna. Chi nasce personaggio, chi ha la ventura di nascere personaggio vivo, può infischiarsi anche della morte. Non muore più! Morrà l'uomo, lo scrittore, che è stato lo strumento naturale della creazione; la creatura non muore più! E per vivere eterna, non ha mica bisogno di straordinarie doti o d'opere prodigiose. Mi dica lei chi era Sancho Panza! Mi dica lei chi era don Abbondio! E vivono eterni perché—vivi germi—ebbero la ventura di trovare una matrice feconda, una fantasia che li seppe allevare e nutrire.

—Ma sì, caro dottore: tutto questo sta bene,—io gli dissi.—Son pienamente d'accordo. Ma, scusi, non vedo ancora che cosa ella voglia da me.

—No? Proprio no?—fece il dottor Fileno.—Ho forse sbagliato strada? Son caduto per caso nel mondo della Luna? Che razza di scrittore è lei? Ma dunque sul serio lei non comprende

face that suddenly all those others, those characters of mine who were still in the act of restraining him, turned pale with mortification and drew back.

"Don't throw me out, for heaven's sake don't throw me out! Grant me just five minutes' audience, and let me persuade you, I beg of you!"

Perplexed and yet filled with pity, I asked him:

"But persuade me about what? I am fully persuaded that you, dear Doctor, deserved to fall into better hands. What do you want me to do for you? I have already lamented your fate sufficiently; now I condole with you personally, and that's the end of it."

"The end of it? No, by God!" exclaimed Dr. Fileno with a shudder of indignation all over his body. "You say that because I'm not one of yours! Believe me, if you showed nonchalance or contempt, it would be much less cruel than this passive pity, unworthy of an artist, if you allow me to say so! No one is in a better position than you to know that we are living beings, more alive than those who breathe and wear clothes; perhaps less real, but truer! There are so many ways of coming to life, sir; and you know very well that nature makes use of the human imagination as a tool for pursuing its work of creation. And anyone who is born thanks to this creative activity which has its seat in the human spirit is ordained by nature for a life that is higher than the life of those born from the mortal womb of a woman. Whoever is born as a character, whoever has the good fortune to be born as a living character, can even thumb his nose at death. He will no longer die! The man will die, the writer who was the natural instrument of his creation; but the creature will no longer die! And in order to live eternally, he hasn't the slightest need of extraordinary gifts or prodigious feats. Tell me, who was Sancho Panza? Tell me, who was Don Abbondio?[2] And yet they live eternally because—as living germs—they had the good fortune to find a fertile womb, an imagination that was able to raise and nourish them.

"Yes, yes, dear Doctor: all that is quite so," I said. "I agree entirely. But, forgive me, I don't yet see what you want of *me*."

"No? You really don't?" said Dr. Fileno. "Have I perhaps come to the wrong place? Have I by chance landed on the world of the Moon? What kind of writer are you? So you seriously don't under-

---

[2] A character in *I promessi sposi* (The Betrothed), the great early nineteenth-century novel by Alessandro Manzoni.

l'orrore della tragedia mia? Avere il privilegio inestimabile di
nascere personaggio, oggi come oggi, oggi che la vita materiale
è così irta di vili difficoltà che ostacolano, deformano, ammi-
seriscono ogni esistenza; avere il privilegio di nascere personaggio vivo, ordinato dunque, anche nella mia piccolezza,
all'immortalità, e sissignore, cadere in quelle mani, esser
condannato a perire iniquamente, a soffocare in quel mondo
d'artificio dove non posso trar respiro né dare un passo, perché è tutto finto, falso, combinato, posticcio! Parole e carta!
Carta e parole! Un uomo, se si trova avviluppato in condizioni
di vita a cui non possa o non sappia adattarsi, può scappare,
fuggire: ma un povero personaggio, no: è lì fissato, inchiodato
a un martirio senza fine! Aria! aria! vita! Ma guardi ... *Fileno* ... mi ha messo nome *Fileno* ... Le pare sul serio che io
mi possa chiamar Fileno? Imbecille, imbecille! Neppure il
nome ha saputo darmi! Io, Fileno! E poi, già, io, io, l'autore
della *Filosofia del lontano*, proprio io dovevo andare a finire in
quel modo indegno per sciogliere tutto quello stupido garbu-
glio di casi là! Dovevo sposarla io, è vero? quell'oca di Graziella,
invece del notajo Negroni! Ma mi faccia il piacere! Questi
sono delitti, caro signore, delitti che si dovrebbero scontare a
lagrime di sangue! Ora invece che avverrà? Niente. Silenzio.
O forse qualche stroncatura in due o tre giornaletti ... Forse
qualche critico esclamerà: «Quel povero Fileno, peccato!
Quello sì era un buon personaggio!». E tutto finirà così. Condannato a morte, io, l'autore della *Filosofia del lontano*, che
quell'imbecille non ha trovato modo neanche di farmi
stampare a mie spese! Eh già, se no, sfido! come avrei potuto
sposare più quell'oca di Graziella? Ah, non mi faccia pensare!
Su, su, all'opera, all'opera, caro signore! Mi riscatti lei, subito
subito! mi faccia viver lei che ha compreso bene tutta la vita
che è in me!

A questa proposta avventata furiosamente come conclusione del lunghissimo sfogo, io restai un pezzo balordo, a mirare in faccia il dottor Fileno.

—Si fa scrupolo?—mi domandò, scombujandosi.

—Si fa scrupolo? Ma è perfettamente legittimo, sa! È suo
diritto sacrosanto riprendermi e darmi la vita che quell'imbecille non ha saputo darmi! È suo e mio diritto, capisce?

—Sarà suo diritto, caro dottore,—io gli risposi,—e sarà

stand the horror of my tragedy? To have the inestimable privilege of being born as a character, now of all times, when material life is so beset with tawdry difficulties which create obstacles for, denature and impoverish every existence; to have the privilege of being born as a living character, and therefore, petty as I may be, ordained for immortality and—just think of it!—to fall into those hands, to be condemned to perish unjustly, to suffocate in that artificial world in which I can't draw a free breath or take one step, because it's all made up, fake, contrived, a sham! Words and paper! Paper and words! If a man finds himself entangled in circumstances of living to which he is physically or mentally unable to adapt, he can escape, run away; but a poor character can't: he's stuck there, nailed to an endless martyrdom! Air! Air! Life! Just look . . . 'Fileno' . . . He gave me the name 'Fileno' . . . Do you seriously think that I can be called Fileno? The imbecile, the imbecile! He couldn't even give me a proper name! I, Fileno! And then, I, I, the author of *The Philosophy of Distance*, I of all people had to end up in that wretched way in order to unravel that whole stupid tangle of incidents! Did *I* really have to marry her, that ninny Graziella, instead of the notary Negroni? Don't give me that! These are crimes, my good man, crimes that should be atoned for with tears of blood! Now, what will happen instead? Nothing. Silence. Or perhaps some bad reviews in two or three minor newspapers. Maybe some critic will exclaim: "That poor Fileno, what a shame! *He* really was a good character." And that will be the end of the whole thing. Condemned to death—I, the author of *The Philosophy of Distance*, which that imbecile didn't even see his way to have me publish at my own expense! Otherwise, tell me, how could I have married that ninny Graziella after that? Oh, don't even let me think about it! Come, come, get to work, get to work, my dear sir! Redeem me, at once, at once! You, who have clearly understood all the life there is in me, let me live!"

On hearing this proposal, furiously flung out as the conclusion to this very lengthy outburst, I was stunned for a while and just stared at Dr. Fileno's face.

"Do you have qualms about it?" he asked, growing disturbed. "Do you have any qualms? It's perfectly legitimate, you know! It's your sacrosanct right to take me over and give me the life that that imbecile was unable to give me! It's your right and mine, understand?"

"It may be your right, dear Doctor," I replied, "and it may even

anche legittimo, come lei crede; ma queste cose, sa? io non le faccio. È inutile che insista. Non le faccio. Provi a rivolgersi altrove.

—E a chi vuole che mi rivolga, se lei . . .

—Ma io non so! Provi. Forse non stenterà molto a trovarne qualcuno perfettamente convinto della legittimità di quel diritto. Se non che, mi ascolti un po', caro dottor Fileno. È lei, sì o no, veramente l'autore della *Filosofia del lontano?*

—E come no?—disse il dottor Fileno tirandosi un passo indietro e ponendosi ambo le mani sul petto.—Oserebbe metterlo in dubbio? Capisco, capisco! È sempre per colpa di quel mio assassino! Ha dato appena appena, in succinto, di passata, un'idea delle mie teorie, non supponendo neppur lontanamente tutto il partito che c'era da cavare da quella mia scoperta del cannocchiale rivoltato!

Parai le mani per arrestarlo, sorridendo e dicendo:

—Va bene . . . va bene . . . ma, e lei, scusi?

—Io? Come, io?

—Si lamenta del suo autore; ma ha saputo lei, caro dottore, trar partito veramente della sua teoria? Ecco, volevo dirle proprio questo. Mi lasci dire. Se Ella crede sul serio, come me, alla virtù della sua filosofia, perché non la applica un po' al suo caso? Ella va cercando, oggi, tra noi, uno scrittore che la consacri all'immortalità. Ma ci guardi tutti, a uno a uno, ponendo me, s'intende, in coda a tutti. E insieme con noi sottoponga al suo famoso cannocchiale rivoltato i fatti più notevoli, le questioni più ardenti e le più mirabili opere dei giorni nostri. Caro il mio dottore, ho gran paura ch'Ella non vedrà più niente né nessuno. E dunque, via, si consoli, o piuttosto, si rassegni, e mi lasci attendere ai miei poveri personaggi, i quali, saranno cattivi, saranno scontrosi, ma non hanno almeno la sua stravagante ambizione.

be legitimate, as you believe; but I just don't do things like that. There's no use your insisting. I don't do that. Try applying to somebody else."

"And to whom would you have me apply, if you . . . "

"I don't know! Try. Maybe you won't have much trouble finding someone who is perfectly convinced of the legitimacy of that right. Or else there's this: listen a moment, dear Dr. Fileno. Yes or no, are you really the author of *The Philosophy of Distance?*"

"Of course!" said Dr. Fileno, taking a step backward and placing both hands on his chest. "Do you dare doubt it? I understand, I understand! As usual, it's the fault of that man who murdered me! He just barely, in summary, in passing, gave an idea of my theories, not even remotely imagining all the benefit that could be derived from that discovery of mine of looking through the wrong end of the telescope!"

I put out my hands to stop him, smiling and saying:

"All right . . . all right . . . but, tell me, what about *you?*"

"I? Where do *I* come in?"

"You're complaining about your author; but, my dear Doctor, were *you* really able to derive benefit from your theory? There, that's exactly what I wanted to say to you. Let me speak. If you seriously believe, as I do, in the efficacy of your philosophy, why don't you apply a little of it to your own case? Here you are, seeking out from among us a writer who will make you immortal. But look at us all, one by one, putting me at the very end of the line, naturally. And, along with us, look through your celebrated wrong-end-of-the-telescope at the most notable events, the most burning questions and the most admirable accomplishments of our day. My dear Doctor, I'm very much afraid that you will no longer see anything or anybody. And so, come now, cheer up or, rather, resign yourself, and let me listen to my own poor characters, who may be a bad lot and may be peevish, but at least don't have your wild ambition."

LA RALLEGRATA

Appena il capostalla se n'andò, bestemmiando più del solito, Fofo si volse a Nero, suo compagno di mangiatoja, nuovo arrivato, e sospirò:

«Ho capito! Gualdrappe, fiocchi e pennacchi. Cominci bene, caro mio! Oggi è di prima classe.»

Nero voltò la testa dall'altra parte. Non sbruffò, perchè era un cavallo bene educato. Ma non voleva dar confidenza a quel Fofo.

Veniva da una scuderia principesca, lui, dove uno si poteva specchiare nei muri: greppie di faggio a ogni posta, campanelle d'ottone, battifianchi imbottiti di cuojo e colonnini col pomo lucente.

Mah!

Il giovane principe, tutto dedito a quelle carrozze strepitose, che fanno—pazienza, puzzo—ma anche fumo di dietro e scappano sole, non contento che già tre volte gli avessero fatto correre il rischio di rompersi il collo, subito appena colpita di paralisi la vecchia principessa (che di quelle diavole là, oh benedetta!, non aveva voluto mai sapere), s'era affrettato a disfarsi, tanto di lui, quanto di Corbino, gli ultimi rimasti nella scuderia, per il placido landò della madre.

Povero Corbino, chi sa dov'era andato a finire, dopo tant'anni d'onorato servizio!

Il buon Giuseppe, il vecchio cocchiere, aveva loro promesso che, andando a baciar la mano con gli altri vecchi servi fidati alla principessa, relegata ormai per sempre in una poltrona, avrebbe interceduto per essi.

Ma che! Dal modo con cui il buon vecchio, ritornato poco dopo, li aveva accarezzati al collo e sui fianchi, subito l'uno e l'altro avevano capito che ogni speranza era perduta e la loro sorte decisa. Sarebbero stati venduti.

E difatti . . .

Nero non comprendeva ancora, dove fosse capitato. Male, proprio male, no. Certo, non era la scuderia della principessa. Ma una buona scuderia era anche questa. Più di venti cavalli,

A PRANCING HORSE

The moment the head groom left, cursing more than usual, Fofo turned toward Blackie, his newly arrived mangermate, and sighed:

"I get it! Saddlecloths, tassels and plumes. You're off to a good start, fellow! It's a first-class one today."

Blackie turned his head in the other direction. He didn't snort, because he was a well-brought-up horse. But he didn't want to confide in that Fofo.

He came from a princely stable, he did, where it was possible to see your reflection on the walls: beechwood cribs for every stall, brass rings, partition bars padded with leather and posts with shiny rounded tops.

Oh, well!

The young Prince, entirely devoted to those noisy carriages which create not only (bear with me!) a stink but also a trail of smoke at the rear, and which dash off on their own power, wasn't satisfied with having already three times run the risk of breaking his neck: just as soon as the old Princess (who, bless her, had never wanted to have anything to do with those devils) had been stricken with paralysis, he had lost no time in getting rid of him (Blackie) as well as Raven Black, the last two horses left in the stable, for his mother's tranquil landau.

Poor Raven Black, who knows where he had ended up, after so many years of honorable service!

Kind Giuseppe, the old coachman, had promised them that he would go and, together with the other old, trusted servants, kiss the hand of the Princess, who was now confined to an armchair for good, and would intercede for them.

But no! From the way in which the kind old man, who had returned quickly, had patted their necks and flanks, immediately both of them had understood that all hope was lost and their fate decided. They would be sold.

And indeed . . .

Blackie still failed to comprehend where he had gotten to. It wasn't bad, not really bad. Of course, it wasn't the Princess' stable. But this was a good stable, too. More than twenty horses, all black

tutti mori e tutti anzianotti, ma di bella presenza, dignitosi e pieni di gravità. Oh, per gravità, forse ne avevano anche troppa!

Che anch'essi comprendessero bene l'ufficio a cui erano addetti, Nero dubitava. Gli pareva che tutti quanti, anzi, stessero di continuo a pensarci, senza tuttavia venirne a capo. Quel dondolio lento di code prolisse, quel raspare di zoccoli, di tratto in tratto, certo erano di cavalli cogitabondi.

Solo quel Fofo era sicuro, sicurissimo d'aver capito bene ogni cosa.

Bestia volgare e presuntuosa!

Brocco di reggimento, scartato dopo tre anni di servizio, perché—a suo dire—un tanghero di cavalleggere abruzzese lo aveva sgroppato, non faceva che parlare e parlare e parlare.

Nero, col cuore ancor pieno di rimpianto per il suo vecchio amico Corbino, non poteva soffrirlo. Più di tutto lo urtava quel tratto confidenziale, e poi la continua maldicenza su i compagni di stalla.

Dio, che lingua!

Di venti, non se ne salvava uno! Questo era così, quello cosà . . .

«La coda . . . guardami là, per piacere, se quella è una coda! se quello è un modo di muovere la coda! Che brio, eh?

«Cavallo da medico, te lo dico io.

«E là, là, guardami là quel bel truttrù calabrese, come crolla con grazia le orecchie di porco . . . E che bel ciuffo! e che bella barbozza! Brioso anche lui, non ti pare?

«Ogni tanto si sogna di non esser castrone, e vuol fare all'amore con quella cavalla là, tre poste a destra, la vedi? con la testa di vecchia, bassa davanti e la pancia fin'a terra.

«Ma quella è una cavalla? Quella è una vacca, te lo dico io. E se sapessi come la va con passo di scuola! Pare che si scotti gli zoccoli, toccando la terra! . . . Eppure, certe saponate, amico mio! Già, perché è di bocca fresca . . . Deve ancor pareggiare i cantoni, figurati!»

Invano Nero dimostrava in tutti i modi a quel Fofo di non

and on the old side, but with a good presence, dignified and full of gravity. Oh, as for gravity, they may even have had too much!

Blackie doubted whether even they understood properly the work to which they were assigned. On the contrary, it seemed to him that they were all constantly thinking about it, but without coming to any conclusion. That slow swaying of flowing tails, that scraping of hooves, from time to time, were unerring indicators of horses in deep reflection.

Only that Fofo was sure, perfectly sure, that he had fully understood everything.

Vulgar and presumptuous animal!

An old army horse, rejected after three years of service, because—to hear him tell it—some light-cavalry bumpkin from the Abruzzi had broken his wind, he did nothing but talk and talk and talk.

Blackie, with his heart still full of regret for his old friend Raven Black, couldn't stand Fofo. What jarred him most of all was that familiar behavior of his, and then his constant criticism of their stablemates.

God, what a tongue!

Not one of the twenty escaped! This one was like this, that one was like that . . .

"That tail . . . just look over there, if you please, and tell me whether that's a tail! If that's any way to move one's tail! Some energy, huh?

"That's a doctor's horse, I'm telling you.

"And over there, there, look at that fine Calabrian nag, how gracefully he wiggles his pig's ears . . . And what a fine forelock! And what a fine chin groove! He's another live wire, don't you think?

"Every once in a while he dreams he's not a gelding, and he wants to make love to that mare over there, three stalls to the right, see her?—with a face that looks so old, low in the forequarters, with her belly scraping the ground.

"But would you even call that a mare? That's a cow, let me tell you. And if you knew how she moves, as if in riding school! She looks as if her hooves were scalded whenever she touched the ground! . . . And yet, does she get foamed up! Sure, because she has a tender mouth. She has yet to grow her incisors to an even height, imagine that!"

It did Blackie no good to show that Fofo in every possible way

dargli ascolto. Fofo imperversava sempre più.

Per fargli dispetto.

«Sai dove siamo noi? Siamo in un ufficio di spedizione. Ce n'è di tante specie. Questo è detto delle pompe funebri.

«Pompa funebre sai che vuol dire? Vuol dire tirare un carro nero di forma curiosa, alto, con quattro colonnini che reggono il cielo, tutto adorno di balze e paramenti e dorature: insomma, un bel carrozzone di lusso; ma roba sprecata, non credere, tutta roba sprecata, perché dentro vedrai che non ci sale mai nessuno.

«Solo il cocchiere, serio serio, in serpe.

«E si va piano, sempre di passo. Ah, non c'è pericolo che tu sudi e ti strofinino al ritorno, né che il cocchiere ti dia mai una frustata o ti solleciti in qualche altro modo!

«Piano—piano—piano.

«Dove devi arrivare, arrivi sempre a tempo.

«E quel carro lì—io l'ho capito bene—dev'essere per gli uomini oggetto d'una particolare venerazione.

«Nessuno, come t'ho detto, ardisce di montarci sopra; e tutti, appena lo vedono fermo innanzi a una casa, s'arrestano a mirarlo con certi visi lunghi spauriti; e tanti gli vengono attorno anche coi ceri accesi; e poi, appena cominciamo a muoverci, tutti dietro, zitti zitti, lo accompagnano.

«Spesso, anche, davanti a noi, c'è la banda, una banda, caro mio, che ti suona una certa musica, da far cascare a terra le budella.

«Tu, ascolta bene, tu hai il vizio di sbruffare e di muover troppo la testa. Ebbene, codesti vizii te li devi levare. Se sbruffi per nulla, figuriamoci che sarà quando ascolterai quella musica!

«Il nostro è un servizio piano, non si nega; ma vuole compostezza e solennità. Niente sbruffi, niente beccheggio. È già troppo, che ti concedano di dondolar la coda, appena appena.

«Perché il carro che noi tiriamo, torno a dirtelo, è molto rispettato. Vedrai che tutti, come ci vedono passare, si levano il cappello.

«Sai come ho capito, che si debba trattare di spedizione? L'ho capito da questo.

«Circa due anni fa, me ne stavo fermo, con uno de' nostri

that he was paying him no mind. Fofo would just rage on all the
more.

To spite him.

"You know where we are? We're in a shipping agency. There
are all kinds. This one is called the funeral type.

"You know what funeral means? It means pulling a black wagon
with a peculiar shape—high, with four posts that support the can-
opy—and decorated all over with flounces and curtains and gild-
ing: in short, a big, beautiful, luxury carriage; but it's all a waste,
I assure you, all a waste, because you'll see that no one ever gets
into it.

"There's only the coachman, looking as serious as he can, on his
box.

"And they move slowly, always at a walking pace. Oh, there's no
danger of your working up a sweat and getting a rubdown when
you come back, or that the coachman will ever give you a lash or
hurry you up in any other way!

"Slow—slow—slow.

"You always get where you need to get to in plenty of time.

"And that wagon—I understand it clearly—must be something
held in special veneration by man.

"As I mentioned, no one dares to get inside; and, as soon as it's
seen standing in front of a house, everybody stops and stares at it
with long, frightened faces; many people even gather around it
with lighted tapers; and then, as soon as we start to move, all of
them accompany it from behind, in total silence.

"Often there's a band in front of us, too, a band, my friend,
playing a kind of music that makes your guts drop out.

"Listen, you've got the bad habit of snorting and moving your
head too much. Well, you've got to get rid of habits like that. If
you snort for no reason, just imagine what will happen when you
hear that music!

"Our work is easy, there's no denying; but it takes orderliness
and solemnity. No snorting, no pitching. It's already too much when
they allow you to shake your tail, just barely.

"Because the wagon that we're pulling, I'm telling you again, is
highly respected. You'll find out that, on seeing us pass by, everybody lifts his hat.

"Do you know how I understood that it must be connected with
shipping? I understood it from this.

"About two years ago, I was standing still, with one of our cano-

carri a padiglione, innanzi alla gran cancellata dell'edificio, che è la nostra meta costante.

«La vedrai, questa gran cancellata! Ci sono dietro tanti alberi neri, a punta, che se ne vanno lunghi e dritti, in due file interminabili, lasciando di qua e di là certi bei prati verdi, con tanta buon'erba grassa, da mangiare; ma roba sprecata anche quella: guai se, passando, ci allunghi le labbra!

«Basta. Me ne stavo lì fermo, allorché mi si accostò un povero mio antico compagno di servizio al reggimento, ridotto assai male: a tirare, figurati, un traino ferrato, di quei lunghi, bassi e senza molle.

«Dice:

« – Mi vedi? Ah Fofo, non ne posso proprio più!

«—Che servizio?—gli domando io.

«E lui:

«—Trasporto casse, tutto il giorno, da un ufficio di spedizione alla dogana.

«—Casse?—dico io.—Che casse?

«—Pesanti!—fa lui.—Ah, pesanti! Casse piene di roba da spedire . . .

«Fu per me una rivelazione.

«Perché devi sapere, che una certa cassa lunga lunga, la trasportiamo anche noi. La introducono pian piano (tutto, sempre, pian piano) entro il nostro carro, dalla parte di dietro; e mentre si fa quest'operazione, la gente attorno si scopre il capo e sta a mirar sbigottita. Chi sa perché! Ma certo, se traffichiamo di casse anche noi, deve trattarsi di spedizione, non ti pare?

«Che diavolo contiene quella cassa? Pesa oh, non credere! Fortuna, che ne trasportiamo sempre una alla volta . . .

«Roba da spedire, certo. Ma che roba, se—appena la vedono—tutti quelli che passano fanno tanti atti di rispetto, e la spedizione avviene con tanta pompa e tanto accompagnamento?

«A un certo punto, di solito (non sempre), ci fermiamo davanti a un fabbricato maestoso, che forse è l'ufficio di dogana per le spedizioni nostre. Dal portone si fanno avanti certi uomini parati con una sottana nera e la camicia di fuori (che saranno, suppongo, i doganieri); la cassa è tratta dal carro; tutti di nuovo si scoprono il capo; e quelli segnano sulla cassa il lasciapassare.

«Dove vada tutta questa roba preziosa, che noi spe-

pied wagons, in front of the big railing of the building that is our normal destination.

"You'll see that big railing! Behind it there are many dark, pointed trees that extend in two long, straight, endless lines, leaving some beautiful green lawns here and there with plenty of good, rich grass to eat; but that's all wasted, too: woe to you if you put out your lips toward it as you pass by.

"Enough of that. I was standing still there when a poor old comrade of mine from my days of army service came up beside me; he had really come down in the world: imagine, he was pulling an iron-fitted truck, one of those long, low, springless ones.

"He said:

"'Do you see me? Oh, Fofo, I'm really worn out!'

"'What line of work?' I asked him."

"And he:

"'Transporting boxes, all day long, from a shipping agency to the customs office.'

"'Boxes?' I said. 'What boxes?'

"'Heavy ones!' he said. 'Really heavy! Boxes full of goods to be shipped . . . '

"That was a relevation to me.

"Because you ought to know that we, too, transport a kind of very long box. They place it very slowly (everything always goes very slowly) into our wagon, from the back; and while that procedure is going on, the people all around take off their hats and just stare in an awed way. Who knows why? But surely, if we, too, deal in boxes, it must be connected with shipping, don't you think so?

"What the devil does that box contain? It's heavy, just you believe me! Lucky that we always transport one at a time . . .

"Merchandise to be shipped, certainly. But what kind of merchandise, if—as soon as it comes into view—every passerby gives so many indications of respect, and the shipping is done with so much pomp and ceremony?

"At a given moment, usually (not always), we stop in front of a majestic building that may be the customs office for our shipments. From the doorway there step forward certain men decked out in a black underskirt, with their shirt worn outside (I suppose they're the customs officers); the box is taken out of the wagon; everybody takes his hat off again; and those men mark the box with an official permit.

"Where all those precious goods that we ship go to—that, you

diamo—questo, vedi—non sono riuscito ancora a capirlo. Ma ho un certo dubbio, che non lo capiscano bene neanche gli uomini, e mi consolo.

«Veramente, la magnificenza delle casse e la solennità della pompa potrebbero far supporre, che qualche cosa gli uomini debbano sapere su queste loro spedizioni. Ma li vedo troppo incerti e sbigottiti. E dalla lunga abitudine, che ormai ho con essi, ho ricavato questa esperienza: che tante cose fanno gli uomini, caro mio, senza punto sapere perché le facciano!»

Come Fofo, quella mattina, alle bestemmie del capostalla s'era figurato: gualdrappe, fiocchi e pennacchi. Tir'a quattro. Era proprio di prima classe.

«Hai visto?»

Nero si trovò attaccato con Fofo al timone. E Fofo, naturalmente, seguitò a seccarlo con le sue eterne spiegazioni.

Ma era seccato anche lui, quella mattina, della soperchieria del capostalla, che nei tiri a quattro lo attaccava sempre al timone e mai alla bilancia.

«Che cane! Perché, tu intendi bene, questi due, qua davanti a noi, sono per comparsa. Che tirano? Non tirano un corno! Tiriamo noi. Si va tanto piano! Ora si fanno una bella passeggiatina per sgranchirsi le gambe, parati di gala ... E guarda un po' che razza di bestie mi tocca di vedermi preferire! Le riconosci?»

Eran quei due mori, che Fofo aveva qualificati cavallo da medico e truttrù calabrese.

«Codesto calabresaccio ... Ce l'hai davanti tu, per fortuna! Sentirai, caro; t'accorgerai che di porco non ha soltanto le orecchie, e ringrazierai il capostalla, che lo protegge e gli dà doppia profenda ... Ci vuol fortuna a questo mondo, non sbruffare. Cominci fin d'adesso? Quieto con la testa! Ih, se fai così, oggi, caro mio, a furia di strappate di briglia, tu farai sangue dalla bocca, te lo dico io. Ci sono i discorsi, oggi. Vedrai che allegria! Un discorso, due discorsi, tre discorsi ... M'è

see, I haven't yet managed to understand. But I have some suspicion that not even the humans understand it perfectly, and I console myself.

"To tell the truth, the magnificence of the boxes and the solemnity of the proceedings could lead you to believe that the humans must know *something* about these shipments of theirs. But they look too uncertain and awed to me. And from the long acquaintance I now have with them, I have derived this much experience: humans do many, many things, my friend, without knowing at all why they do them!"

As Fofo had deduced that morning from the head groom's curses: saddlecloths, tassels and plumes. Four horses to draw the carriage. It was really a first-class job.

"Did you see?"

Blackie found himself harnessed between the shafts with Fofo. And Fofo, naturally, continued to bore him with his eternal explanations.

But he, too, was bothered that morning by the imposition put on him by the head groom, who, when there were four horses, always harnessed him between the shafts and never to the splinter bar for extra horses.[1]

"What a dog! Because, you realize, these two here in front of us are just for show. What do they pull? They don't pull a damn thing! We're the ones who pull. And we go so slowly! Now they're taking a nice little walk to stretch their legs, all decked out in gala . . . And just look at what sort of animals I'm forced to see get the preference over myself! Recognize them?"

They were the two black horses that Fofo had dubbed "doctor's horse" and "Calabrian nag."

"That damned Calabrian . . . You have him in front of *you*, lucky you! You'll smell him, my friend; you'll become aware that his ears aren't the only piglike thing about him, and you'll thank the head groom, who protects him and gives him double rations of fodder . . . It takes luck in this world—don't snort. Are you starting already? Keep your head still! Whew, if you act like that today, my friend, you'll get so many tugs on the reins that you'll have a bloody mouth, I'm telling you. There will be speeches today. You'll see how jolly it is! One speech, two speeches, three speeches . . . I've

---

[1] Using different terms, Fofo and Blackie are "wheelers" and the other two horses are "leaders."

capitato il caso d'una prima classe anche con cinque discorsi!
Roba da impazzire . . . Tre ore di fermo, con tutte queste ga-
lanterie addosso, che ti levano il respiro: le gambe impastojate,
la coda imprigionata, le orecchie tra due fori . . . Allegro, con
le mosche che ti mangiano sotto la coda! Che sono i discorsi?
Mah! Ci capisco poco, dico la verità . . . Queste di prima classe,
debbono essere spedizioni molto complicate. E forse, con quei
discorsi, fanno la spiega. Una non basta, e ne fanno due;
non bastano due, e ne fanno tre. Arrivano a farne fino a
cinque, come t'ho detto: mi ci son trovato io, che mi veniva
di sparar calci, caro mio, a dritta e a manca, e poi di mettermi
a rotolar per terra come un matto . . . Forse oggi sarà
lo stesso. Gran gala! Hai visto il cocchiere, com'è parato
anche lui? E ci sono anche i famigli, i torcieri . . . Di', tu sei
sitoso?»

«Non capisco . . .»

«Via, pigli ombra facilmente? Perché vedrai che, tra poco,
i ceri accesi te li metteranno proprio sotto il naso . . . Piano,
uh . . . piano! che ti piglia? Vedi? Una prima strappata . . .
T'ha fatto male? Eh, ne avrai molte tu oggi, te lo dico io . . .
Ma che fai? sei matto? Non allungare il collo così! (Bravo,
cocco, nuoti? giochi alla morra?). Sta' fermo . . . Ah sì? Pigliati
queste . . . Ohé, dico, bada, fai strappar la bocca a me! Ma
questo è matto! Dio, Dio, quest'è matto davvero! Ansa, rigna,
annitrisce, fa ciambella, che cos'è? Guarda che rallegrata! È
matto! è matto! fa la rallegrata, tirando un carro di prima
classe!»

Nero pareva veramente impazzito: ansava, nitriva, scal-
pitava, fremeva tutto. In fretta, in furia, giù dal carro
dovettero precipitarsi i famigli a trattenerlo davanti al
portone del palazzo, ove dovevano arrestarsi, tra una gran
calca di signori incamatiti, in abito lungo e cappello a
cilindro.

—Che avviene?—si gridava da ogni parte.—Uh, guarda,
s'impenna un cavallo del carro mortuario!

even come across a first-class funeral with five speeches! Enough to make you crazy . . . Three hours of standing still, with all these decorations on you that don't allow you to breathe: your legs cramped, your tail imprisoned, your ears between two holes . . . Jolly, with the flies biting you under your tail! What are the speeches? Who knows? I really don't understand, to tell the truth . . . These first-class shipments must be very complicated ones. And maybe, in those speeches, they're giving the instructions. One isn't enough, and they make two; two aren't enough, and they make three. They sometimes make as many as five, as I said: there I was, my friend, with an urge to kick out right and left, and then start rolling on the ground like a madcap . . . Maybe it will be the same today. Full gala! Did you see the coachmen, how he's tricked out, too? And there are also the ushers, the taper-bearers . . . Tell me, are you skittish?"

"I don't understand . . . "

"You know: do you shy easily? Because, you'll see, in a little while they'll put the lighted tapers right under your nose . . . Easy, there . . . easy! What's got into you? You see? The first tug on the reins . . . Did it hurt you? Well, you'll get a lot of them today, let me tell you . . . But what are you doing? Are you crazy? Don't stretch out your neck like that! (Nice baby, are you swimming?[2] Are you playing a kicking game?)[3] "Stay still . . . Oh, really? Take that tug, and that! Hey! Watch out, now you're making them tug at my mouth, too! Say, this one is crazy! My God, my God, this one is really crazy! He's panting, he's neighing, he's whinnying, he's turning in a circle; what's going on? Look at him prancing! He's crazy, he's crazy! Going into a prance while he's pulling a first-class wagon!"

Blackie did indeed seem to have lost his mind; he was panting, neighing, pawing the ground and trembling all over. The lackeys had to leap down from the carriage in hot haste to hold him still in front of the doorway of the manor house where they were to stop, amid a large throng of stiff gentlemen in frockcoats and top hats.

"What's going on?" was the cry everywhere. "Oh, look, a horse of the funeral carriage is rearing up!"

---

[2] The original text has *ruoti*, but this was surely a typographical error; later versions have *nuoti*.

[3] Literally, "playing *morra*" (the game of how-many-fingers-am-I-holding-up?).

E tutta la gente, in gran confusione, si fece intorno al carro, curiosa, costernata, meravigliata, scandalizzata. I famigli non riuscivano ancora a tener fermo Nero. Il cocchiere s'era levato in piedi e tirava furiosamente le briglie. Invano. Nero seguitava a zampare, nitrire, friggeva, con la testa volta verso il portone del palazzo.

Si quietò, solo quando sopravvenne da quel portone un vecchio servitore in livrea, il quale, scostati i famigli, lo prese per la briglia, e subito, riconosciutolo, si diede a esclamare con le lagrime agli occhi:

—Ma è Nero! è Nero! Ah, povero Nero . . . Ma sicuro, che fa così . . . Il cavallo della signora! il cavallo della povera principessa! Ha riconosciuto il palazzo . . . sente l'odore della sua scuderia . . . Povero Nero, povero Nero . . . buono, buono . . . sì, vedi? sono io, il tuo vecchio Giuseppe . . . Sta' buono, sì . . . Povero Nero, tocca a te di portartela, vedi? la tua padrona . . . Tocca a te, poverino, che ti ricordi ancora . . . Sarà contenta lei d'essere trasportata da te per l'ultima volta . . .

Si voltò poi al cocchiere, che, imbestialito per la cattiva figura che la Casa di pompe funebri faceva davanti a tutti quei signori, seguitava a tirar furiosamente le briglie, minacciando frustate, e gli gridò:

—Basta! Smettila! Lo reggo qua io . . . È manso come una pecora . . . Mettiti a sedere. Lo guiderò io per tutto il tragitto . . . Andremo insieme, eh Nero? a lasciar la nostra buona signora . . . Pian piano, al solito, eh? E tu starai buono, per non farle male, povero vecchio Nero, che ti ricordi ancora . . . L'hanno già chiusa nella cassa; ora la portano giù . . .

Fofo, che dall'altra parte del timone se ne stava a sentire, a questo punto domandò, stupito:

«Dentro la cassa, la tua padrona?»

Nero gli sparò un calcio di traverso.

Ma Fofo era troppo assorto nella nuova rivelazione, per aversene a male.

«Ah, dunque, noi . . .» seguitò a dir tra sè, «ah, dunque, noi . . . guarda, guarda . . . lo volevo dire io . . . Questo vecchio piange; tant'altri ho visto piangere, altre volte . . . e tanti visi sbigottiti . . . e quella musica languida . . . Capisco tutto, adesso, capisco tutto . . . Per questo il nostro servizio è così piano! Solo quando gli uomini piangono, possiamo stare allegri e andar riposati nojaltri . . .»

E gli venne la tentazione di fare una rallegrata anche lui.

And all the people, in great confusion, surrounded the carriage, curious, dismayed, surprised, shocked. The ushers had not yet managed to hold Blackie still. The coachman had risen to his feet and was pulling the reins furiously. In vain. Blackie kept on lashing out with his hooves and neighing; he was foaming, with his head turned toward the doorway of the house.

He only calmed down when there came out of that door and arrived on the scene an old servant in livery, who, shoving aside the ushers, took him by the bridle and immediately, on recognizing him, started to exclaim with tears in his eyes:

"Why, it's Blackie! It's Blackie! Oh, poor Blackie . . . Why, of course he acts this way . . . The mistress' horse! The late Princess' horse! He recognized the house . . . he smells the odor of his own stable . . . Poor Blackie, poor Blackie . . . behave, behave . . . yes, you see? It's me, your old Giuseppe . . . Behave, yes . . . Poor Blackie, it's up to you to carry her—see?—your mistress . . . It's up to you, poor thing, you who still remember . . . She'll be pleased to be conveyed by you for the last time . . . "

Then he turned to the coachman, who, infuriated by the bad showing that the funeral establishment was making in front of all those gentlemen, was continuing to tug violently on the reins and threatening to whip the horse, and shouted at him:

"Enough! Stop! I've got him under control here . . . He's gentle as a lamb . . . Sit back down. I'll guide him the whole way . . . We'll go together—right, Blackie?—to leave our kind mistress . . . Slowly and quietly, as usual, right? And you'll behave, so you don't hurt her, poor old Blackie, you who still remember . . . They've already enclosed her in the box; now they're carrying her down . . . "

At this moment Fofo, who was listening to all this from the other side of the shafts, asked in amazement:

"It's your mistress inside the box?"

Blackie gave him a sidelong kick.

But Fofo was too absorbed by this new revelation to be offended.

"Ah, so we . . . ," he kept on saying to himself, "ah, so we . . . what about that! . . . it's what *I* meant to say . . . This old man is crying; I've seen so many others crying, other times . . . and so many awed faces . . . and that depressing music . . . Now I understand it all, I understand it all . . . *That's* why our work is so easy! It's only when humans cry that *we* can be cheerful and relaxed . . . "

And he too felt the temptation to prance.

LA SIGNORA FROLA E IL SIGNOR PONZA, SUO GENERO

Ma insomma, ve lo figurate? c'è da ammattire sul serio tutti quanti a non poter sapere chi tra i due sia il pazzo, se questa signora Frola o questo signor Ponza, suo genero. Cose che capitano soltanto a Valdana, città disgraziata, calamita di tutti i forestieri eccentrici!

Pazza lei o pazzo lui; non c'è via di mezzo: uno dei due dev'esser pazzo per forza. Perché si tratta niente meno che di questo... Ma no, è meglio esporre prima con ordine.

Sono, vi giuro, seriamente costernato dell'angoscia in cui vivono da tre mesi gli abitanti di Valdana, e poco m'importa della signora Frola e del signor Ponza, suo genero. Perché, se è vero che una grave sciagura è loro toccata, non è men vero che uno dei due, almeno, ha avuto la fortuna d'impazzirne e l'altro l'ha ajutato, seguita ad ajutarlo, così che non si riesce, ripeto, a sapere quale dei due veramente sia pazzo; e certo una consolazione meglio di questa non se la potevano dare. Ma dico di tenere così, sotto quest'incubo, un'intera cittadinanza, vi par poco? togliendole ogni sostegno al giudizio, per modo che non possa più distinguere tra fantasma e realtà. Un'angoscia, un perpetuo sgomento. Ciascuno si vede davanti ogni giorno, quei due; li guarda in faccia; sa che uno dei due è pazzo; li studia, li squadra, li spia e, niente! non poter scoprire quale dei due; dove sia il fantasma, dove la realtà. Naturalmente, nasce in ciascuno il sospetto pernicioso che tanto vale allora la realtà quanto il fantasma, e che ogni realtà può benissimo essere un fantasma e viceversa. Vi par poco? Nei panni del signor prefetto, io darei senz'altro, per la salute

MRS. FROLA AND MR. PONZA,
HER SON-IN-LAW

But after all, can you imagine? Everybody may really go mad because they can't decide which of the two is the crazy one, that Mrs. Frola or that Mr. Ponza, her son-in-law. Things like this only happen in Valdana, an unlucky town that attracts every kind of eccentric outsider!

She is crazy or *he* is crazy; there's no middle ground: one of the two *must* be crazy. Because what's involved is nothing less than this . . . No, it's better to start off explaining things in their proper order.

I assure you, I'm seriously alarmed by the anxiety in which the inhabitants of Valdana have been living for three months, and I'm not much concerned for Mrs. Frola and Mr. Ponza, her son-in-law. Because, even if it's true that a grave misfortune has befallen them, it's no less true that one of them, at least, has had the good luck to be driven crazy by it and the other one has aided and is continuing to aid the victim, in such a way that, I repeat, no one can manage to know for sure which of the two is really crazy; and, certainly, they couldn't have comforted each other in a better way than that. But I ask you, do you think it's nothing to keep the entire citizenry under such a nightmarish burden, knocking out all the props of their reasoning capacity so that they can no longer distinguish between illusion and reality? It's anguish, perpetual dismay. Everyone sees those two daily, looks at their faces, knows that one of the two is crazy, studies them, scrutinizes them, spies on them and—no use! Impossible to discover which of the two it is; where illusion lies, where reality lies. Naturally, there arises in each mind the pernicious suspicion that, in that case, reality counts for no more than illusion does, and that every reality may very well be an illusion, and vice versa. You think it's nothing? If I were in the governor's[1] shoes, for the mental well-being of the inhabitants of Valdana I

---

[1] *Prefetto*, chief officer of a *provincia* (Italy is divided into "provinces" administratively).

dell'anima degli abitanti di Valdana, lo sfratto alla signora Frola e al signor Ponza, suo genero.

Ma procediamo con ordine.

Questo signor Ponza arrivò a Valdana, or sono tre mesi, segretario di prefettura. Prese alloggio nel casone nuovo all'uscita del paese, quello che chiamano «il Favo». Lì. All'ultimo piano, un quartierino. Tre finestre che danno su la campagna, alte, tristi (ché la facciata di là, all'aria di tramontana, su tutti quegli orti pallidi, chi sa perché, benché nuova, s'è tanto intristita) e tre finestre interne, di qua, sul cortile, ove gira la ringhiera del ballatojo diviso da tramezzi a grate. Pendono da quella ringhiera, lassù lassù, tanti panierini pronti a esser calati col cordino, a un bisogno.

Nello stesso tempo, però, con maraviglia di tutti, il signor Ponza fissò nel centro della città, e propriamente in Via dei Santi n. 15, un altro quartierino mobigliato di tre camere e cucina. Disse che doveva servire per la suocera, signora Frola. E difatti questa arrivò cinque o sei giorni dopo; e il signor Ponza si recò ad accoglierla, lui solo, alla stazione e la condusse e la lasciò lì, sola.

Ora, via, si capisce che una figliuola, maritandosi, lasci la casa della madre per andare a convivere col marito, anche in un'altra città; ma che questa madre poi, non reggendo a star lontana dalla figliuola, lasci il suo paese, la sua casa, e la segua, e che nella città dove tanto la figliuola quanto lei sono forestiere vada ad abitare in una casa a parte, questo non si capisce più facilmente; o si deve ammettere tra suocera e genero una così forte incompatibilità da rendere proprio impossibile la convivenza, anche in queste condizioni.

Naturalmente a Valdana dapprima si pensò così. E certo chi scapitò per questo nell'opinione di tutti fu il signor Ponza. Della signora Frola, se qualcuno ammise che forse doveva averci anche lei un po' di colpa, o per scarso compatimento o per qualche caparbietà o intolleranza, tutti considerarono l'amore materno che la traeva appresso alla figliuola, pur condannata a non poterle vivere accanto.

Gran parte ebbe in questa considerazione per la signora Frola e nel concetto che subito del signor Ponza s'impresse

wouldn't hesitate to give Mrs. Frola and Mr. Ponza, her son-in-law, their walking papers.

But let's proceed in an orderly fashion.

This Mr. Ponza arrived in Valdana three months ago as a secretary in the governor's office. He took lodgings in the new apartment house at the edge of town, the one called "the Honeycomb." There. On the top floor, a tiny flat. Three windows looking out at the countryside, high, sad windows (because the housefront on that side, exposed to the north wind, facing all those pallid market gardens, although it's new, has become so deteriorated, who knows why?), and three inner windows, on this side, facing the courtyard, which is encircled by the railing of the top gallery, divided into sections by grated partitions. Hanging from that railing, all the way up, are a large number of little baskets ready to be lowered on ropes as needed.

At the same time, however, to everyone's amazement, Mr. Ponza rented another small furnished flat, three rooms and kitchen, in the center of town, Number 15 Via dei Santi, to be exact. He said it was to be used by his mother-in-law, Mrs. Frola. And she did indeed arrive five or six days later; and Mr. Ponza, all alone, went to meet her at the station, took her to the apartment and left her there by herself.

Now, please! You can understand it if a daughter, on getting married, leaves her mother's house to go and live with her husband, even in another town; but when that mother, not bearing to remain far from her daughter, leaves her hometown, her own house, and follows her, and when, in the town where both she and her daughter are strangers, she goes to live in a separate house, *that* is no longer so easily understood; or else one must assume such a strong incompatibility between mother-in-law and son-in-law that their all living together is impossible, even under these circumstances.

Naturally, that's what people in Valdana thought at first. And certainly the one who came off the worst in everyone's opinion because of this was Mr. Ponza. When it came to Mrs. Frola, if someone granted that she might perhaps be partly to blame in this, either through a lack of indulgence or through some obstinacy or intolerance, everybody was favorably impressed by the maternal love that drew her close to her daughter, even though condemned not to be able to live by her side.

A great part was played in this favoring of Mrs. Frola and in the image of Mr. Ponza that was immediately stamped on everyone's

nell'animo di tutti, che fosse cioè duro, anzi crudele, anche l'aspetto dei due, bisogna dirlo. Tozzo, senza collo, nero come un africano, con folti capelli ispidi su la fronte bassa, dense e aspre sopracciglia giunte, grossi mustacchi lucidi da questurino, e negli occhi cupi, fissi, quasi senza bianco, un'intensità violenta, esasperata, a stento contenuta, non si sa se di doglia tetra o di dispetto della vista altrui, il signor Ponza non è fatto certamente per conciliarsi la simpatia o la confidenza. Vecchina gracile, pallida, è invece la signora Frola, dai lineamenti fini, nobilissimi, e un'aria malinconica, ma d'una malinconia senza peso, vaga e gentile, che non esclude l'affabilità con tutti.

Ora di questa affabilità, naturalissima in lei, la signora Frola ha dato subito prova in città, e subito per essa nell'animo di tutti è cresciuta l'avversione per il signor Ponza; giacché chiaramente è apparsa a ognuno l'indole di lei, non solo mite, remissiva, tollerante, ma anche piena d'indulgente compatimento per il male che il genero le fa; e anche perché s'è venuto a sapere che non basta al signor Ponza relegare in una casa a parte quella povera madre, ma spinge la crudeltà fino a vietarle anche la vista della figliuola.

Se non che, non crudeltà, non crudeltà, protesta subito nelle sue visite alle signore di Valdana la signora Frola, ponendo le manine avanti, veramente afflitta che si possa pensar questo di suo genero. E s'affretta a decantarne tutte le virtù, a dirne tutto il bene possibile e immaginabile: quale amore, quante cure, quali attenzioni egli abbia per la figliuola, non solo, ma anche per lei, sì, sì, anche per lei; premuroso, disinteressato . . . Ah, non crudele, no, per carità! C'è solo questo: che vuole tutta, tutta per sé la mogliettina, il signor Ponza, fino al punto che anche l'amore, che questa deve avere (e l'ammette, come no?) per la sua mamma, vuole che le arrivi non direttamente, ma attraverso lui, per mezzo di lui, ecco. Sì, può parere crudeltà, questa, ma non è; è un'altra cosa, un'altra cosa ch'ella, la signora Frola, intende benissimo e si strugge di non sapere esprimere. Natura, ecco . . . ma no, forse una specie di malattia . . . come dire? Dio mio, basta guardarlo negli occhi. Fanno in prima una brutta impressione, forse, quegli occhi; ma dicono tutto a chi, come lei, sappia leggere in essi: la pienezza chiusa, dicono, di tutto un mondo d'amore in lui, nel quale la moglie deve vivere senza mai uscirne minimamente,

mind—namely, that he was a hard, no! a cruel man—by their physical appearance as well, it must be said. Thickset, neckless, dark as an African, with thick, coarse hair hanging over his low forehead, dense, bristly eyebrows that meet over his nose, a big shiny mustache like a policeman's, and in his eyes—melancholy, staring, almost without any white—a violent, exasperated, barely restrained intensity—whether from sad pain or from irritation at other people's glances, it was hard to say—Mr. Ponza is certainly one whose looks don't make him readily liked or trusted. On the other hand, Mrs. Frola is a frail, pale little old lady, with elegant, very noble features and an air of melancholy, but a weightless, vague and sweet melancholy that doesn't keep her from being affable to everyone.

Now, as soon as she came to town, Mrs. Frola exhibited this affability, so natural in her, and, because of that, the aversion for Mr. Ponza immediately increased in everybody's mind; because everyone clearly perceived her character—as not only gentle, humble, tolerant, but also full of indulgent understanding for the wrong that her son-in-law is doing her; and also because it came to be known that Mr. Ponza is not satisfied to relegate that poor mother to a separate house, but also pushes his cruelty to the point of forbidding her to see her daughter.

Except that, on her visits to the ladies of Valdana, Mrs. Frola immediately protests: "Not cruelty, not cruelty," thrusting out her little hands, sincerely distressed that people can think such a thing about her son-in-law. And she hurriedly praises all his virtues, saying all the good about him that's possible and imaginable: how much love, how much care, how many attentions he lavishes not only on her daughter but also on her, yes, yes, also on her; solicitous, selfless . . . Oh, not cruel, no, for heaven's sake! There's only this: that Mr. Ponza wants to have his wife entirely to himself, to such an extent that he wants even the love she must have for her mother (and he admits it, of course) to reach her not directly but through him, as intermediary, that's it! Yes, this may look like cruelty, but it's not; it's something else, something that she, Mrs. Frola, understands perfectly and is anguished at being unable to express. His nature, that's what . . . but no, perhaps a kind of illness . . . how to put it? My goodness, you just have to look at his eyes. At first those eyes may make a bad impression; but they say it all to anyone who can read them as she can: they speak of the sealed-up fullness of a whole world of love within him, in which his wife must live without ever leaving it for a moment, and into which no one else, not even

e nel quale nessun altro, neppure la madre, deve entrare. Gelosia? Sì, forse; ma a voler definire volgarmente questa totalità esclusiva d'amore. Egoismo? Ma un egoismo che si dà tutto, come un mondo, alla propria donna! Egoismo, in fondo, sarebbe forse quello di lei a voler forzare questo mondo chiuso d'amore, a volervisi introdurre per forza, quand'ella sa che la figliuola è felice, così adorata ... Questo a una madre può bastare! Del resto, non è mica vero ch'ella non la veda, la sua figliuola. Due o tre volte al giorno la vede: entra nel cortile della casa; suona il campanello e subito la sua figliuola s'affaccia di lassù.

—Come stai, Tildina?

—Benissimo, mamma. Tu?

—Come Dio vuole, figliuola mia. Giù, giù il panierino!

E nel panierino, sempre due parole di lettera, con le notizie della giornata. Ecco, le basta questo. Dura ormai da quattr'anni questa vita, e ci s'è già abituata la signora Frola. Rassegnata, sì. E quasi non ne soffre più.

Com'è facile intendere, questa rassegnazione della signora Frola, quest'abitudine ch'ella dice d'aver fatto al suo martirio, ridondano a carico del signor Ponza, suo genero, tanto più, quanto più ella col suo lungo discorso si affanna a scusarlo.

Con vera indignazione perciò, e anche dirò con paura, le signore di Valdana che hanno ricevuto la prima visita della signora Frola, accolgono il giorno dopo l'annunzio di un'altra visita inattesa, del signor Ponza, che le prega di concedergli due soli minuti d'udienza, per una «doverosa dichiarazione», se non reca loro incomodo.

Affocato in volto, quasi congestionato, con gli occhi più duri e più tetri che mai, un fazzoletto in mano che stride per la sua bianchezza, insieme coi polsini e il colletto della camicia, sul nero della carnagione, del pelame e del vestito, il signor Ponza, asciugandosi di continuo il sudore che gli sgocciola dalla fronte bassa e dalle gote raschiose e violacee, non già per il caldo, ma per la violenza evidentissima dello sforzo che fa su se stesso e per cui anche le grosse mani dalle unghie lunghe gli tremano; in questo e in quel salotto, davanti a quelle signore che lo mirano quasi atterrite, domanda prima se la signora Frola, sua suocera, è stata a visita da loro il giorno avanti; poi, con pena, con sforzo, con agitazione di punto in punto crescenti, se ella ha parlato loro della figliuola e se ha

her mother, must enter. Jealousy? Yes, perhaps; but only if you want to give a cheap name to this exclusive totality of love. Selfishness? If so, it's a selfishness that makes him give all of himself, like a world, to his own lady! When you get to the bottom of it, you might call it selfishness in *her* that she desires to break open this closed world of love, to make her way into it by force, when she knows that her daughter is happy and so adored . . . That should be enough for a mother! Besides, it's not at all true that she doesn't see her daughter. She sees her two or three times a day: she goes into the courtyard of the building; she rings the bell and immediately her daughter comes to the window up there.

"How are you, Tildina?"

"Fine, Mother. And you?"

"As God wishes, daughter. Send down the basket!"

And in the basket there's always a short note with the events of the day. There! that's enough for her. This life has been going on for four years now, and Mrs. Frola has already gotten used to it. Yes, she's resigned to it. And she practically no longer suffers from it.

As you can easily understand, this resigned attitude of Mrs. Frola's, her saying that she has gotten used to her torment, redounds all the more to the discredit of Mr. Ponza, her son-in-law, the more that she strains herself to excuse him in that long speech of hers.

Therefore it is with real indignation and, I may add, even with fear, that the ladies of Valdana to whom Mrs. Frola paid her first visit receive the notice on the following day of another unexpected visit, from Mr. Ponza, who begs them to grant him just two minutes of audience, for a "dutiful declaration," if it's not inconvenient.

Red in the face, almost as if he were having a stroke, with his eyes harder and sadder than ever, in his hand a handkerchief whose whiteness, like that of his cuffs and shirt collar, clashes with the darkness of his skin, body hair and suit, Mr. Ponza, continually wiping away the perspiration dripping from his low forehead and stubbly, purplish cheeks—not from the heat, but from the very evident violence of the control he is exerting over himself, which also causes a trembling in his large hands with their long nails—in this parlor and in that, in front of those ladies staring at him as if in fright, first asks whether Mrs. Frola, his mother-in-law, came to visit them the day before; then, with his sorrow, effort and agitation constantly increasing, asks whether she spoke to them about her

detto ch'egli le vieta assolutamente di vederla e di salire in casa sua.

Le signore, nel vederlo così agitato, com'è facile immaginare, s'affrettano a rispondergli che la signora Frola, sì, è vero, ha detto loro di quella proibizione di veder la figlia, ma anche tutto il bene possibile e immaginabile di lui, fino a scusarlo, non solo, ma anche a non dargli nessun'ombra di colpa per quella proibizione stessa.

Se non che, invece di quietarsi, a questa risposta delle signore, il signor Ponza si agita di più; gli occhi gli diventano più duri, più fissi, più tetri; le grosse gocciole di sudore più spesse; e alla fine, facendo uno sforzo ancor più violento su se stesso, viene alla sua «dichiarazione doverosa».

La quale è questa, semplicemente: che la signora Frola, poveretta, non pare, ma è pazza.

Pazza da quattro anni, sì. E la sua pazzia consiste appunto nel credere che egli non voglia farle vedere la figliuola. Quale figliuola? È morta, è morta da quattro anni la figliuola; e la signora Frola, appunto per il dolore di questa morte, è impazzita; per fortuna, impazzita, sì, giacché la pazzia è stata per lei lo scampo del suo disperato dolore. Naturalmente non poteva scamparne, se non così, cioè credendo che non sia vero che la sua figliuola è morta e che sia lui, invece, suo genero, che non vuole più fargliela vedere.

Per puro dovere di carità verso un'infelice, egli, il signor Ponza, seconda da quattro anni, a costo di molti e gravi sacrifici, questa pietosa follia: tiene, con dispendio superiore alle sue forze, due case: una per sé, una per lei; e obbliga la sua seconda moglie, che per fortuna caritatevolmente si presta volentieri, a secondare anche lei questa follia. Ma carità, dovere, ecco, fino a un certo punto: anche per la sua qualità di pubblico funzionario, il signor Ponza non può permettere che si creda di lui, in città, questa cosa crudele e inverosimile: ch'egli cioè, per gelosia o per altro, vieti a una povera madre di vedere la propria figliuola.

Dichiarato questo, il signor Ponza s'inchina innanzi allo sbalordimento delle signore, e va via. Ma questo sbalordimento delle signore non ha neppure il tempo di scemare un po', che rieccoti la signora Frola con la sua aria dolce di vaga malinconia a domandare scusa se, per causa sua, le buone signore si sono prese qualche spavento per la visita del signor Ponza, suo genero.

E la signora Frola, con la maggior semplicità e naturalezza

daughter and told them that he absolutely forbids her to see her and go up to his apartment.

The ladies, seeing him so upset, as you may easily imagine, quickly reply that it's true, yes, Mrs. Frola did tell them about being forbidden to see her daughter, but also said all the good about him that's possible and imaginable, to the extent of not only excusing him, but also not giving him a shred of blame for that very prohibition.

Except that, instead of calming down at this reply from the ladies, Mr. Ponza gets even more upset; his eyes become harder, more staring, sadder; the big drops of sweat fall more heavily; and finally, making an even more violent effort at self-control, he comes to his "dutiful declaration."

Which is simply this: that Mrs. Frola, poor woman, doesn't look it, but she's crazy.

Yes, she's been crazy for four years. And her madness takes this very form: her belief that he refuses to allow her to see her daughter. What daughter? She's dead, her daughter died four years ago; and it was precisely from her grief at that death that Mrs. Frola went mad; yes, and it's a good thing she went mad, because for her, madness was the release from her desperate sorrow. Naturally she could only escape it in this manner; namely, by believing that it wasn't true her daughter had died, and that instead it's he, her son-in-law, who won't let her see her any more.

Purely out of a duty of charity toward an unhappy creature, he, Mr. Ponza, has for four years, at the cost of many serious sacrifices, been humoring that pathetic delusion: at an expense beyond his means, he maintains two households, one for him and one for her; and he makes his second wife, who by good luck is charitably willing to go along, humor that delusion, too. But charity, duty—look, they can go only so far: in his capacity as a civil servant as well, Mr. Ponza can't permit the people in town to think such a cruel and improbable thing about him; namely, that out of jealousy or any other reason, he forbids a poor mother to see her own daughter.

After this declaration, Mr. Ponza makes a bow to those bewildered ladies, and leaves. But this bewilderment of the ladies doesn't even have the time to diminish a little, when there appears Mrs. Frola again with her gentle air of vague melancholy, asking forgiveness if, on her account, the kind ladies were somewhat frightened by the visit of Mr. Ponza, her son-in-law.

And Mrs. Frola, with the greatest simplicity and naturalness in

del mondo, dichiara a sua volta, ma in gran confidenza, per carità! poiché il signor Ponza è un pubblico funzionario, e appunto per questo ella la prima volta s'è astenuta dal dirlo, ma sì, perché questo potrebbe seriamente pregiudicarlo nella carriera; il signor Ponza, poveretto—ottimo, ottimo, inappuntabile segretario alla prefettura, compito, preciso in tutti i suoi atti, in tutti i suoi pensieri, pieno di tante buone qualità—il signor Ponza, poveretto, su quest'unico punto non . . . non ragiona più; ecco; il pazzo è lui, poveretto; e la sua pazzia consiste appunto in questo: nel credere che sua moglie sia morta da quattro anni e nell'andar dicendo che la pazza è lei, la signora Frola che crede ancora viva la figliuola. No, non lo fa per coonestare in certo qual modo innanzi agli altri quella sua gelosia quasi maniaca e quella crudele proibizione a lei di veder la figliuola, no; crede, crede sul serio il poveretto che sua moglie sia morta e che questa che ha con sé sia una seconda moglie. Caso pietosissimo! Perché veramente col suo troppo amore quest'uomo rischiò in prima di distruggere, d'uccidere la giovane moglietta delicatina, tanto che si dovette sottrargliela di nascosto e chiuderla a insaputa di lui in una casa di salute. Ebbene, il pover'uomo, a cui già per quella frenesia d'amore s'era anche gravemente alterato il cervello, ne impazzì; credette che la moglie fosse morta davvero: e questa idea gli si fissò talmente nel cervello, che non ci fu più verso di levargliela, neppure quando, ritornata dopo circa un anno florida come prima, la moglietta gli fu ripresentata. La credette un'altra; tanto che si dovette con l'ajuto di tutti, parenti e amici, simulare un secondo matrimonio, che gli ha ridato pienamente l'equilibrio delle facoltà mentali.

Ora la signora Frola crede d'aver qualche ragione di sospettare che da un pezzo suo genero sia del tutto rientrato in sé e ch'egli finga, finga soltanto di credere che sua moglie sia una seconda moglie, per tenersela così tutta per sé, senza contatto con nessuno, perché forse tuttavia di tanto in tanto gli balena la paura che di nuovo gli possa esser sottratta nascostamente.

Ma sì. Come spiegare, se no, tutte le cure, le premure che ha per lei, sua suocera, se veramente egli crede che è una seconda moglie quella che ha con sé? Non dovrebbe sentir l'obbligo di tanti riguardi per una che, di fatto, non sarebbe più sua suocera, è vero? Questo, si badi, la signora Frola lo

the world, declares in her turn, but in strict confidence, for heaven's sake! because Mr. Ponza is a civil servant and for that very reason she refrained from saying this the first time, yes, because this could seriously damage his career; Mr. Ponza, poor man—an excellent, excellent irreproachable secretary at the governor's office, perfect, precise in all his actions, in all his thoughts, full of so many good qualities—Mr. Ponza, poor man, in this matter alone is no longer . . . no longer in his right mind; there you have it; the crazy one is he, poor man; and his madness takes this very form: his belief that his wife died four years ago and his going around saying that the crazy one is she, Mrs. Frola, who believes her daughter is still alive. No, he isn't doing this in order somehow to justify to others that almost maniacal jealousy of his and that cruelty of forbidding her to see her daughter; no, the poor man believes, seriously believes that his wife is dead and the one he has with him is a second wife. A most pitiful case! Because, to tell the truth, with his excessive love this man at first ran the risk of destroying, of killing his young, fragile little wife, so much so that it was necessary to get her out of his hands secretly and put her into a nursing home without his knowledge. Well, the poor man, whose mind had already been seriously weakened by this frenzied love, went mad from this; he thought his wife had really died: and this idea became so fixed in his mind that there was no longer any way to remove it, not even when his wife, back home after about a year, and as healthy as before, was brought before him. He thought she was a different woman; so that, with the aid of everybody, relatives and friends, it was necessary to simulate a second wedding, which fully restored the balance of his mental faculties.

Now, Mrs. Frola believes she has some right to suspect that for some time her son-in-law has been completely himself again and that he is pretending, only pretending to believe that his wife is a second wife, in order to keep her entirely to himself, without contact with anyone, because perhaps from time to time he nevertheless is smitten with the fear that she may be secretly taken away from him again.

Yes! Otherwise, how could you explain all the care, all the solicitude, he has for her, his mother-in-law, if he really believes that the woman he has with him is a second wife? He ought not to feel the obligation of so much consideration for a woman who in fact would no longer be his mother-in-law, right? Note that Mrs. Frola

dice, non per dimostrare ancor meglio che il pazzo è lui; ma per provare anche a se stessa che il suo sospetto è fondato.

—E intanto,—conclude con un sospiro che su le labbra le s'atteggia in un dolce mestissimo sorriso,—intanto la povera figliuola mia deve fingere di non esser lei, ma un'altra; e anch'io sono obbligata a fingermi pazza credendo che la mia figliuola sia ancora viva. Mi costa poco, grazie a Dio, perché è là, la mia figliuola, sana e piena di vita; la vedo, le parlo; ma sono condannata a non poter convivere con lei, e anche a vederla e a parlarle da lontano, perché egli possa credere, o fingere di credere che la mia figliuola, Dio liberi, è morta e che questa che ha con sé è una seconda moglie. Ma torno a dire, che importa se a questo patto siamo riusciti a ridar la pace a tutti e due? So che la mia figliuola è adorata, contenta; la vedo; le parlo; e mi rassegno per amore di lei e di lui a vivere così e a passare anche per pazza, signora mia, pazienza . . .

Dico, non vi sembra che a Valdana ci sia proprio da restare a bocca aperta, a guardarci tutti negli occhi, come insensati? A chi credere dei due? Chi è il pazzo? Dov'è la realtà? dove il fantasma?

Lo potrebbe dire la moglie del signor Ponza. Ma non c'è da fidarsi se, davanti a lui, costei dice d'esser seconda moglie; come non c'è da fidarsi se, davanti alla signora Frola, conferma d'esserne la figliuola. Si dovrebbe prenderla a parte e farle dire a quattr'occhi la verità. Non è possibile. Il signor Ponza—sia o no lui il pazzo—è realmente gelossissimo e non lascia veder la moglie a nessuno. La tiene lassù, come in prigione, sotto chiave; e questo fatto è senza dubbio in favore della signora Frola; ma il signor Ponza dice che è costretto a far così, e che sua moglie stessa anzi glielo impone, per paura che la signora Frola non le entri in casa all'improvviso. Può essere una scusa. Sta anche di fatto che il signor Ponza non tiene neanche una serva in casa. Dice che lo fa per risparmio, obbligato com'è a pagar l'affitto di due case; e si sobbarca intanto a farsi da sé la spesa giornaliera; e la moglie, che a suo dire non è la figlia della signora Frola, si sobbarca anche lei per pietà di questa, cioè d'una povera vecchia che fu suocera di suo marito, a badare a tutte le faccende di casa, anche alle più umili, privandosi dell'ajuto d'una serva. Sembra a tutti un po'

says this, not to give an even better proof that *he* is the crazy one; but to prove even to herself that her suspicion is well founded.

"And meanwhile," she concludes with a sigh that on her lips assumes the form of a sweet, very sad smile, "meanwhile my poor daughter has to pretend she's not herself but someone else; and I am also obliged to pretend I'm crazy to believe my daughter is still alive. It doesn't cost me much, thank God, because my daughter is there, well and full of life; I see her, I speak to her; but I'm condemned not to be able to live with her, and also to see her and speak to her only from a distance, so that he can keep on believing, or pretending to believe, that my daughter, God forbid, is dead and the woman he has with him is a second wife. But I say once more, what's the difference if, on these terms, we have succeeded in restoring peace of mind to both of them? I know that my daughter is adored, contented; I see her; I speak to her; and I resign myself, out of love for her and for him; to live this way and even to be considered a madwoman, madam—patience! . . . "

I ask you, don't you think that things are at such a pass in Valdana that we all go around with open mouths, looking each other in the eye, like lunatics? Who of the two is to be believed? Who is the crazy one? Where is the reality, where the illusion?

Mr. Ponza's wife would be able to tell us. But there's no trusting her when, in his presence, she says she is the second wife; just as there's no trusting her when, in Mrs. Frola's presence, she confirms the statement that she's her daughter. It would be necessary to take her aside and make her tell the truth privately. But that's impossible. Mr. Ponza—whether or not he's the crazy one—is really very jealous and doesn't let anybody see his wife. He keeps her up there, as if in prison, under lock and key; and without a doubt this fact is in Mrs. Frola's favor; but Mr. Ponza says he is compelled to do this, in fact that his wife herself makes him do it, for fear that Mrs. Frola will unexpectedly come into the house. That may be an excuse. But it's also a fact that Mr. Ponza doesn't even have one maid in the house. He says he does it to save money, obliged as he is to pay rent on two apartments; and in the meantime he himself assumes the burden of doing the daily marketing; and his wife, who according to her own statements is not Mrs. Frola's daughter, out of pity for her—that is, for a poor old woman who was formerly her husband's mother-in-law—also takes it upon herself to attend to all the household chores, even the most humble, doing without the aid of a servant. It seems a bit much to everybody. But it's also

troppo. Ma è anche vero che questo stato di cose, se non con la pietà, può spiegarsi con la gelosia di lui.

Intanto, il signor Prefetto di Valdana s'è contentato della dichiarazione del signor Ponza. Ma certo l'aspetto e in gran parte la condotta di costui non depongono in suo favore, almeno per le signore di Valdana più propense tutte quante a prestar fede alla signora Frola. Questa, difatti, viene premurosa a mostrar loro le letterine affettuose che le cala giù col panierino la figliuola, e anche tant'altri privati documenti, a cui però il signor Ponza toglie ogni credito, dicendo che le sono stati rilasciati per confortare il pietoso inganno.

Certo è questo, a ogni modo: che dimostrano tutt'e due, l'uno per l'altra, un meraviglioso spirito di sacrifizio, commoventissimo; e che ciascuno ha per la presunta pazzia dell'altro la considerazione più squisitamente pietosa. Ragionano tutt'e due a meraviglia; tanto che a Valdana non sarebbe mai venuto in mente a nessuno di dire che l'uno dei due era pazzo, se non l'avessero detto loro: il signor Ponza della signora Frola, e la signora Frola del signor Ponza.

La signora Frola va spesso a trovare il genero alla Prefettura per aver da lui qualche consiglio, o lo aspetta all'uscita per farsi accompagnare in qualche compera: e spessissimo, dal canto suo, nelle ore libere e ogni sera il signor Ponza va a trovare la signora Frola nel quartierino mobigliato; e ogni qual volta per caso l'uno s'imbatte nell'altra per via, subito con la massima cordialità si mettono insieme; egli le dà la destra e, se stanca, le porge il braccio, e vanno così, insieme, tra il dispetto aggrondato e lo stupore e la costernazione della gente che li studia, li squadra, li spia e, niente!, non riesce ancora in nessun modo a comprendere quale sia il pazzo dei due, dove sia il fantasma, dove la realtà.

true that if this state of affairs can't be explained by pity, it can be explained by his jealousy.

Meanwhile, the governor of Valdana has been satisfied with Mr. Ponza's declaration. But surely the latter's appearance and in large part his conduct do not speak in his favor, at least for the ladies of Valdana, who are all more inclined to give credence to Mrs. Frola. Indeed, that lady comes solicitously to show them the loving notes that her daughter sends down to her in the little basket, as well as many other private documents, the credibility of which, however, is totally denied by Mr. Ponza, who says that they were delivered to her to bolster the pious deception.

One thing is certain anyway: that both of them manifest a marvelous, deeply moving spirit of sacrifice for each other; and that each of them has the most exquisitely compassionate consideration for the presumed madness of the other. Both of them state their case with wonderful rationality; so that it would never have occurred to anyone in Valdana to say that either of them was crazy, if they hadn't said it themselves: Mr. Ponza about Mrs. Frola, and Mrs. Frola about Mr. Ponza.

Mrs. Frola often goes to see her son-in-law at the governor's office to get some advice from him, or waits for him when he comes out so he can accompany her to do some shopping; and very often, for his part, in his free time and every evening Mr. Ponza goes to visit Mrs. Frola in her little furnished flat; and every time they accidentally run into each other in the street they immediately continue on together with the greatest cordiality; he lets her walk on the right and, if she's tired, he offers his arm, and so they go off together, amid the sullen anger, amazement and dismay of the people who study them, scrutinize them, spy on them, but—no use!—cannot yet in any way manage to understand which of the two is the crazy one, where the illusion is, where the reality.

A CATALOG OF SELECTED
DOVER BOOKS
IN ALL FIELDS OF INTEREST

A CATALOG OF SELECTED DOVER
BOOKS IN ALL FIELDS OF INTEREST

CONCERNING THE SPIRITUAL IN ART, Wassily Kandinsky. Pioneering work by father of abstract art. Thoughts on color theory, nature of art. Analysis of earlier masters. 12 illustrations. 80pp. of text. 5⅜ × 8½. 23411-8 Pa. $3.95

ANIMALS: 1,419 Copyright-Free Illustrations of Mammals, Birds, Fish, Insects, etc., Jim Harter (ed.). Clear wood engravings present, in extremely lifelike poses, over 1,000 species of animals. One of the most extensive pictorial sourcebooks of its kind. Captions. Index. 284pp. 9 × 12. 23766-4 Pa. $11.95

CELTIC ART: The Methods of Construction, George Bain. Simple geometric techniques for making Celtic interlacements, spirals, Kells-type initials, animals, humans, etc. Over 500 illustrations. 160pp. 9 × 12. (USO) 22923-8 Pa. $9.95

AN ATLAS OF ANATOMY FOR ARTISTS, Fritz Schider. Most thorough reference work on art anatomy in the world. Hundreds of illustrations, including selections from works by Vesalius, Leonardo, Goya, Ingres, Michelangelo, others. 593 illustrations. 192pp. 7⅛ × 10¼. 20241-0 Pa. $8.95

CELTIC HAND STROKE-BY-STROKE (Irish Half-Uncial from "The Book of Kells"): An Arthur Baker Calligraphy Manual, Arthur Baker. Complete guide to creating each letter of the alphabet in distinctive Celtic manner. Covers hand position, strokes, pens, inks, paper, more. Illustrated. 48pp. 8¼ × 11.
24336-2 Pa. $3.95

EASY ORIGAMI, John Montroll. Charming collection of 32 projects (hat, cup, pelican, piano, swan, many more) specially designed for the novice origami hobbyist. Clearly illustrated easy-to-follow instructions insure that even beginning papercrafters will achieve successful results. 48pp. 8¼ × 11. 27298-2 Pa. $2.95

THE COMPLETE BOOK OF BIRDHOUSE CONSTRUCTION FOR WOOD-WORKERS, Scott D. Campbell. Detailed instructions, illustrations, tables. Also data on bird habitat and instinct patterns. Bibliography. 3 tables. 63 illustrations in 15 figures. 48pp. 5¼ × 8½. 24407-5 Pa. $1.95

BLOOMINGDALE'S ILLUSTRATED 1886 CATALOG: Fashions, Dry Goods and Housewares, Bloomingdale Brothers. Famed merchants' extremely rare catalog depicting about 1,700 products: clothing, housewares, firearms, dry goods, jewelry, more. Invaluable for dating, identifying vintage items. Also, copyright-free graphics for artists, designers. Co-published with Henry Ford Museum & Greenfield Village. 160pp. 8¼ × 11. 25780-0 Pa. $9.95

HISTORIC COSTUME IN PICTURES, Braun & Schneider. Over 1,450 costumed figures in clearly detailed engravings—from dawn of civilization to end of 19th century. Captions. Many folk costumes. 256pp. 8⅜ × 11¾. 23150-X Pa. $11.95

STICKLEY CRAFTSMAN FURNITURE CATALOGS, Gustav Stickley and L. & J. G. Stickley. Beautiful, functional furniture in two authentic catalogs from 1910. 594 illustrations, including 277 photos, show settles, rockers, armchairs, reclining chairs, bookcases, desks, tables. 183pp. 6½ × 9¼. 23838-5 Pa. $8.95

AMERICAN LOCOMOTIVES IN HISTORIC PHOTOGRAPHS: 1858 to 1949, Ron Ziel (ed.). A rare collection of 126 meticulously detailed official photographs, called "builder portraits," of American locomotives that majestically chronicle the rise of steam locomotive power in America. Introduction. Detailed captions. xi + 129pp. 9 × 12. 27393-8 Pa. $12.95

AMERICA'S LIGHTHOUSES: An Illustrated History, Francis Ross Holland, Jr. Delightfully written, profusely illustrated fact-filled survey of over 200 American lighthouses since 1716. History, anecdotes, technological advances, more. 240pp. 8 × 10¾. 25576-X Pa. $11.95

TOWARDS A NEW ARCHITECTURE, Le Corbusier. Pioneering manifesto by founder of "International School." Technical and aesthetic theories, views of industry, economics, relation of form to function, "mass-production split" and much more. Profusely illustrated. 320pp. 6⅛ × 9¼. (USO) 25023-7 Pa. $8.95

HOW THE OTHER HALF LIVES, Jacob Riis. Famous journalistic record, exposing poverty and degradation of New York slums around 1900, by major social reformer. 100 striking and influential photographs. 233pp. 10 × 7⅞. 22012-5 Pa $10.95

FRUIT KEY AND TWIG KEY TO TREES AND SHRUBS, William M. Harlow. One of the handiest and most widely used identification aids. Fruit key covers 120 deciduous and evergreen species; twig key 160 deciduous species. Easily used. Over 300 photographs. 126pp. 5⅜ × 8½. 20511-8 Pa. $3.95

COMMON BIRD SONGS, Dr. Donald J. Borror. Songs of 60 most common U.S. birds: robins, sparrows, cardinals, bluejays, finches, more—arranged in order of increasing complexity. Up to 9 variations of songs of each species. Cassette and manual 99911-4 $8.95

ORCHIDS AS HOUSE PLANTS, Rebecca Tyson Northen. Grow cattleyas and many other kinds of orchids—in a window, in a case, or under artificial light. 63 illustrations. 148pp. 5⅜ × 8½. 23261-1 Pa. $3.95

MONSTER MAZES, Dave Phillips. Masterful mazes at four levels of difficulty. Avoid deadly perils and evil creatures to find magical treasures. Solutions for all 32 exciting illustrated puzzles. 48pp. 8¼ × 11. 26005-4 Pa. $2.95

MOZART'S DON GIOVANNI (DOVER OPERA LIBRETTO SERIES), Wolfgang Amadeus Mozart. Introduced and translated by Ellen H. Bleiler. Standard Italian libretto, with complete English translation. Convenient and thoroughly portable—an ideal companion for reading along with a recording or the performance itself. Introduction. List of characters. Plot summary. 121pp. 5¼ × 8½. 24944-1 Pa. $2.95

TECHNICAL MANUAL AND DICTIONARY OF CLASSICAL BALLET, Gail Grant. Defines, explains, comments on steps, movements, poses and concepts. 15-page pictorial section. Basic book for student, viewer. 127pp. 5⅜ × 8½. 21843-0 Pa. $3.95

BRASS INSTRUMENTS: Their History and Development, Anthony Baines. Authoritative, updated survey of the evolution of trumpets, trombones, bugles, cornets, French horns, tubas and other brass wind instruments. Over 140 illustrations and 48 music examples. Corrected and updated by author. New preface. Bibliography. 320pp. 5⅜ × 8½. 27574-4 Pa. $9.95

HOLLYWOOD GLAMOR PORTRAITS, John Kobal (ed.). 145 photos from 1926–49. Harlow, Gable, Bogart, Bacall; 94 stars in all. Full background on photographers, technical aspects. 160pp. 8⅜ × 11¼. 23352-9 Pa. $11.95

MAX AND MORITZ, Wilhelm Busch. Great humor classic in both German and English. Also 10 other works: "Cat and Mouse," "Plisch and Plumm," etc. 216pp. 5⅜ × 8½. 20181-3 Pa. $5.95

THE RAVEN AND OTHER FAVORITE POEMS, Edgar Allan Poe. Over 40 of the author's most memorable poems: "The Bells," "Ulalume," "Israfel," "To Helen," "The Conqueror Worm," "Eldorado," "Annabel Lee," many more. Alphabetic lists of titles and first lines. 64pp. 5^{3}⁄16 × 8¼. 26685-0 Pa. $1.00

SEVEN SCIENCE FICTION NOVELS, H. G. Wells. The standard collection of the great novels. Complete, unabridged. First Men in the Moon, Island of Dr. Moreau, War of the Worlds, Food of the Gods, Invisible Man, Time Machine, In the Days of the Comet. Total of 1,015pp. 5⅜ × 8½. (USO) 20264-X Clothbd. $29.95

AMULETS AND SUPERSTITIONS, E. A. Wallis Budge. Comprehensive discourse on origin, powers of amulets in many ancient cultures: Arab, Persian, Babylonian, Assyrian, Egyptian, Gnostic, Hebrew, Phoenician, Syriac, etc. Covers cross, swastika, crucifix, seals, rings, stones, etc. 584pp. 5⅜ × 8½. 23573-4 Pa. $12.95

RUSSIAN STORIES/PYCCKNE PACCKA3bl: A Dual-Language Book, edited by Gleb Struve. Twelve tales by such masters as Chekhov, Tolstoy, Dostoevsky, Pushkin, others. Excellent word-for-word English translations on facing pages, plus teaching and study aids, Russian/English vocabulary, biographical/critical introductions, more. 416pp. 5⅜ × 8½. 26244-8 Pa. $8.95

PHILADELPHIA THEN AND NOW: 60 Sites Photographed in the Past and Present, Kenneth Finkel and Susan Oyama. Rare photographs of City Hall, Logan Square, Independence Hall, Betsy Ross House, other landmarks juxtaposed with contemporary views. Captures changing face of historic city. Introduction. Captions. 128pp. 8¼ × 11. 25790-8 Pa. $9.95

AIA ARCHITECTURAL GUIDE TO NASSAU AND SUFFOLK COUNTIES, LONG ISLAND, The American Institute of Architects, Long Island Chapter, and the Society for the Preservation of Long Island Antiquities. Comprehensive, well-researched and generously illustrated volume brings to life over three centuries of Long Island's great architectural heritage. More than 240 photographs with authoritative, extensively detailed captions. 176pp. 8¼ × 11. 26946-9 Pa. $14.95

NORTH AMERICAN INDIAN LIFE: Customs and Traditions of 23 Tribes, Elsie Clews Parsons (ed.). 27 fictionalized essays by noted anthropologists examine religion, customs, government, additional facets of life among the Winnebago, Crow, Zuni, Eskimo, other tribes. 480pp. 6⅛ × 9¼. 27377-6 Pa. $10.95

FRANK LLOYD WRIGHT'S HOLLYHOCK HOUSE, Donald Hoffmann. Lavishly illustrated, carefully documented study of one of Wright's most controversial residential designs. Over 120 photographs, floor plans, elevations, etc. Detailed perceptive text by noted Wright scholar. Index. 128pp. 9¼ × 10¾.
27133-1 Pa. $11.95

THE MALE AND FEMALE FIGURE IN MOTION: 60 Classic Photographic Sequences, Eadweard Muybridge. 60 true-action photographs of men and women walking, running, climbing, bending, turning, etc., reproduced from rare 19th-century masterpiece. vi + 121pp. 9 × 12.
24745-7 Pa. $10.95

1001 QUESTIONS ANSWERED ABOUT THE SEASHORE, N. J. Berrill and Jacquelyn Berrill. Queries answered about dolphins, sea snails, sponges, starfish, fishes, shore birds, many others. Covers appearance, breeding, growth, feeding, much more. 305pp. 5¼ × 8¼.
23366-9 Pa. $7.95

GUIDE TO OWL WATCHING IN NORTH AMERICA, Donald S. Heintzelman. Superb guide offers complete data and descriptions of 19 species: barn owl, screech owl, snowy owl, many more. Expert coverage of owl-watching equipment, conservation, migrations and invasions, etc. Guide to observing sites. 84 illustrations. xiii + 193pp. 5⅜ × 8½.
27344-X Pa. $7.95

MEDICINAL AND OTHER USES OF NORTH AMERICAN PLANTS: A Historical Survey with Special Reference to the Eastern Indian Tribes, Charlotte Erichsen-Brown. Chronological historical citations document 500 years of usage of plants, trees, shrubs native to eastern Canada, northeastern U.S. Also complete identifying information. 343 illustrations. 544pp. 6½ × 9¼.
25951-X Pa. $12.95

STORYBOOK MAZES, Dave Phillips. 23 stories and mazes on two-page spreads: Wizard of Oz, Treasure Island, Robin Hood, etc. Solutions. 64pp. 8¼ × 11.
23628-5 Pa. $2.95

NEGRO FOLK MUSIC, U.S.A., Harold Courlander. Noted folklorist's scholarly yet readable analysis of rich and varied musical tradition. Includes authentic versions of over 40 folk songs. Valuable bibliography and discography. xi + 324pp. 5⅜ × 8½.
27350-4 Pa. $7.95

MOVIE-STAR PORTRAITS OF THE FORTIES, John Kobal (ed.). 163 glamor, studio photos of 106 stars of the 1940s: Rita Hayworth, Ava Gardner, Marlon Brando, Clark Gable, many more. 176pp. 8⅜ × 11¼.
23546-7 Pa. $10.95

BENCHLEY LOST AND FOUND, Robert Benchley. Finest humor from early 30s, about pet peeves, child psychologists, post office and others. Mostly unavailable elsewhere. 73 illustrations by Peter Arno and others. 183pp. 5⅜ × 8½.
22410-4 Pa. $5.95

YEKL and THE IMPORTED BRIDEGROOM AND OTHER STORIES OF YIDDISH NEW YORK, Abraham Cahan. Film Hester Street based on Yekl (1896). Novel, other stories among first about Jewish immigrants on N.Y.'s East Side. 240pp. 5⅜ × 8½.
22427-9 Pa. $6.95

SELECTED POEMS, Walt Whitman. Generous sampling from Leaves of Grass. Twenty-four poems include "I Hear America Singing," "Song of the Open Road," "I Sing the Body Electric," "When Lilacs Last in the Dooryard Bloom'd," "O Captain! My Captain!"—all reprinted from an authoritative edition. Lists of titles and first lines. 128pp. 5³⁄₁₆ × 8¼.
26878-0 Pa. $1.00

THE BEST TALES OF HOFFMANN, E. T. A. Hoffmann. 10 of Hoffmann's most important stories: "Nutcracker and the King of Mice," "The Golden Flowerpot," etc. 458pp. 5⅜ × 8½. 21793-0 Pa. $8.95

FROM FETISH TO GOD IN ANCIENT EGYPT, E. A. Wallis Budge. Rich detailed survey of Egyptian conception of "God" and gods, magic, cult of animals, Osiris, more. Also, superb English translations of hymns and legends. 240 illustrations. 545pp. 5⅜ × 8½. 25803-3 Pa. $11.95

FRENCH STORIES/CONTES FRANÇAIS: A Dual-Language Book, Wallace Fowlie. Ten stories by French masters, Voltaire to Camus: "Micromegas" by Voltaire; "The Atheist's Mass" by Balzac; "Minuet" by de Maupassant; "The Guest" by Camus, six more. Excellent English translations on facing pages. Also French-English vocabulary list, exercises, more. 352pp. 5⅜ × 8½. 26443-2 Pa. $8.95

CHICAGO AT THE TURN OF THE CENTURY IN PHOTOGRAPHS: 122 Historic Views from the Collections of the Chicago Historical Society, Larry A. Viskochil. Rare large-format prints offer detailed views of City Hall, State Street, the Loop, Hull House, Union Station, many other landmarks, circa 1904–1913. Introduction. Captions. Maps. 144pp. 9⅜ × 12¼. 24656-6 Pa. $12.95

OLD BROOKLYN IN EARLY PHOTOGRAPHS, 1865–1929, William Lee Younger. Luna Park, Gravesend race track, construction of Grand Army Plaza, moving of Hotel Brighton, etc. 157 previously unpublished photographs. 165pp. 8⅞ × 11¾. 23587-4 Pa. $13.95

THE MYTHS OF THE NORTH AMERICAN INDIANS, Lewis Spence. Rich anthology of the myths and legends of the Algonquins, Iroquois, Pawnees and Sioux, prefaced by an extensive historical and ethnological commentary. 36 illustrations. 480pp. 5⅜ × 8½. 25967-6 Pa. $8.95

AN ENCYCLOPEDIA OF BATTLES: Accounts of Over 1,560 Battles from 1479 B.C. to the Present, David Eggenberger. Essential details of every major battle in recorded history from the first battle of Megiddo in 1479 B.C. to Grenada in 1984. List of Battle Maps. New Appendix covering the years 1967–1984. Index. 99 illustrations. 544pp. 6½ × 9¼. 24913-1 Pa. $14.95

SAILING ALONE AROUND THE WORLD, Captain Joshua Slocum. First man to sail around the world, alone, in small boat. One of great feats of seamanship told in delightful manner. 67 illustrations. 294pp. 5⅜ × 8½. 20326-3 Pa. $5.95

ANARCHISM AND OTHER ESSAYS, Emma Goldman. Powerful, penetrating, prophetic essays on direct action, role of minorities, prison reform, puritan hypocrisy, violence, etc. 271pp. 5⅜ × 8½. 22484-8 Pa. $5.95

MYTHS OF THE HINDUS AND BUDDHISTS, Ananda K. Coomaraswamy and Sister Nivedita. Great stories of the epics; deeds of Krishna, Shiva, taken from puranas, Vedas, folk tales; etc. 32 illustrations. 400pp. 5⅜ × 8½. 21759-0 Pa. $9.95

BEYOND PSYCHOLOGY, Otto Rank. Fear of death, desire of immortality, nature of sexuality, social organization, creativity, according to Rankian system. 291pp. 5⅜ × 8½. 20485-5 Pa. $7.95

A THEOLOGICO-POLITICAL TREATISE, Benedict Spinoza. Also contains unfinished Political Treatise. Great classic on religious liberty, theory of government on common consent. R. Elwes translation. Total of 421pp. 5⅜ × 8½. 20249-6 Pa. $8.95

MY BONDAGE AND MY FREEDOM, Frederick Douglass. Born a slave, Douglass became outspoken force in antislavery movement. The best of Douglass' autobiographies. Graphic description of slave life. 464pp. 5⅜ × 8½.   22457-0 Pa. $8.95

FOLLOWING THE EQUATOR: A Journey Around the World, Mark Twain. Fascinating humorous account of 1897 voyage to Hawaii, Australia, India, New Zealand, etc. Ironic, bemused reports on peoples, customs, climate, flora and fauna, politics, much more. 197 illustrations. 720pp. 5⅜ × 8½.   26113-1 Pa. $15.95

THE PEOPLE CALLED SHAKERS, Edward D. Andrews. Definitive study of Shakers: origins, beliefs, practices, dances, social organization, furniture and crafts, etc. 33 illustrations. 351pp. 5⅜ × 8½.   21081-2 Pa. $8.95

THE MYTHS OF GREECE AND ROME, H. A. Guerber. A classic of mythology, generously illustrated, long prized for its simple, graphic, accurate retelling of the principal myths of Greece and Rome, and for its commentary on their origins and significance. With 64 illustrations by Michelangelo, Raphael, Titian, Rubens, Canova, Bernini and others. 480pp. 5⅜ × 8½.   27584-1 Pa. $9.95

PSYCHOLOGY OF MUSIC, Carl E. Seashore. Classic work discusses music as a medium from psychological viewpoint. Clear treatment of physical acoustics, auditory apparatus, sound perception, development of musical skills, nature of musical feeling, host of other topics. 88 figures. 408pp. 5⅜ × 8½. 21851-1 Pa. $9.95

THE PHILOSOPHY OF HISTORY, Georg W. Hegel. Great classic of Western thought develops concept that history is not chance but rational process, the evolution of freedom. 457pp. 5⅜ × 8½.   20112-0 Pa. $9.95

THE BOOK OF TEA, Kakuzo Okakura. Minor classic of the Orient: entertaining, charming explanation, interpretation of traditional Japanese culture in terms of tea ceremony. 94pp. 5⅜ × 8½.   £0070-1 Pa. $2.95

LIFE IN ANCIENT EGYPT, Adolf Erman. Fullest, most thorough, detailed older account with much not in more recent books, domestic life, religion, magic, medicine, commerce, much more. Many illustrations reproduce tomb paintings, carvings, hieroglyphs, etc. 597pp. 5⅜ × 8½.   22632-8 Pa. $10.95

SUNDIALS, Their Theory and Construction, Albert Waugh. Far and away the best, most thorough coverage of ideas, mathematics concerned, types, construction, adjusting anywhere. Simple, nontechnical treatment allows even children to build several of these dials. Over 100 illustrations. 230pp. 5⅜ × 8½.   22947-5 Pa. $7.95

DYNAMICS OF FLUIDS IN POROUS MEDIA, Jacob Bear. For advanced students of ground water hydrology, soil mechanics and physics, drainage and irrigation engineering, and more. 335 illustrations. Exercises, with answers. 784pp. 6⅛ × 9¼.   65675-6 Pa. $19.95

SONGS OF EXPERIENCE: Facsimile Reproduction with 26 Plates in Full Color, William Blake. 26 full-color plates from a rare 1826 edition. Includes "The Tyger," "London," "Holy Thursday," and other poems. Printed text of poems. 48pp. 5¼ × 7.   24636-1 Pa. $4.95

OLD-TIME VIGNETTES IN FULL COLOR, Carol Belanger Grafton (ed.). Over 390 charming, often sentimental illustrations, selected from archives of Victorian graphics—pretty women posing, children playing, food, flowers, kittens and puppies, smiling cherubs, birds and butterflies, much more. All copyright-free. 48pp. 9¼ × 12¼.   27269-9 Pa. $5.95

PERSPECTIVE FOR ARTISTS, Rex Vicat Cole. Depth, perspective of sky and sea, shadows, much more, not usually covered. 391 diagrams, 81 reproductions of drawings and paintings. 279pp. 5⅜ × 8½. 22487-2 Pa. $6.95

DRAWING THE LIVING FIGURE, Joseph Sheppard. Innovative approach to artistic anatomy focuses on specifics of surface anatomy, rather than muscles and bones. Over 170 drawings of live models in front, back and side views, and in widely varying poses. Accompanying diagrams. 177 illustrations. Introduction. Index. 144pp. 8⅜ × 11¼. 26723-7 Pa. $7.95

GOTHIC AND OLD ENGLISH ALPHABETS: 100 Complete Fonts, Dan X. Solo. Add power, elegance to posters, signs, other graphics with 100 stunning copyright-free alphabets: Blackstone, Dolbey, Germania, 97 more—including many lower-case, numerals, punctuation marks. 104pp. 8⅛ × 11. 24695-7 Pa. $7.95

HOW TO DO BEADWORK, Mary White. Fundamental book on craft from simple projects to five-bead chains and woven works. 106 illustrations. 142pp. 5⅜ × 8. 20697-1 Pa. $4.95

THE BOOK OF WOOD CARVING, Charles Marshall Sayers. Finest book for beginners discusses fundamentals and offers 34 designs. "Absolutely first rate . . . well thought out and well executed."—E. J. Tangerman. 118pp. 7¾ × 10⅝. 23654-4 Pa. $5.95

ILLUSTRATED CATALOG OF CIVIL WAR MILITARY GOODS: Union Army Weapons, Insignia, Uniform Accessories, and Other Equipment, Schuyler, Hartley, and Graham. Rare, profusely illustrated 1846 catalog includes Union Army uniform and dress regulations, arms and ammunition, coats, insignia, flags, swords, rifles, etc. 226 illustrations. 160pp. 9 × 12. 24939-5 Pa. $10.95

WOMEN'S FASHIONS OF THE EARLY 1900s: An Unabridged Republication of "New York Fashions, 1909," National Cloak & Suit Co. Rare catalog of mail-order fashions documents women's and children's clothing styles shortly after the turn of the century. Captions offer full descriptions, prices. Invaluable resource for fashion, costume historians. Approximately 725 illustrations. 128pp. 8⅜ × 11¼. 27276-1 Pa. $11.95

THE 1912 AND 1915 GUSTAV STICKLEY FURNITURE CATALOGS, Gustav Stickley. With over 200 detailed illustrations and descriptions, these two catalogs are essential reading and reference materials and identification guides for Stickley furniture. Captions cite materials, dimensions and prices. 112pp. 6½ × 9¼. 26676-1 Pa. $9.95

EARLY AMERICAN LOCOMOTIVES, John H. White, Jr. Finest locomotive engravings from early 19th century: historical (1804–74), main-line (after 1870), special, foreign, etc. 147 plates. 142pp. 11⅜ × 8¼. 22772-3 Pa. $8.95

THE TALL SHIPS OF TODAY IN PHOTOGRAPHS, Frank O. Braynard. Lavishly illustrated tribute to nearly 100 majestic contemporary sailing vessels: Amerigo Vespucci, Clearwater, Constitution, Eagle, Mayflower, Sea Cloud, Victory, many more. Authoritative captions provide statistics, background on each ship. 190 black-and-white photographs and illustrations. Introduction. 128pp. 8⅞ × 11¾. 27163-3 Pa. $13.95

EARLY NINETEENTH-CENTURY CRAFTS AND TRADES, Peter Stockham (ed.). Extremely rare 1807 volume describes to youngsters the crafts and trades of the day: brickmaker, weaver, dressmaker, bookbinder, ropemaker, saddler, many more. Quaint prose, charming illustrations for each craft. 20 black-and-white line illustrations. 192pp. 4⅝ × 6. 27293-1 Pa. $4.95

VICTORIAN FASHIONS AND COSTUMES FROM HARPER'S BAZAR, 1867-1898, Stella Blum (ed.). Day costumes, evening wear, sports clothes, shoes, hats, other accessories in over 1,000 detailed engravings. 320pp. 9⅜ × 12¼.
22990-4 Pa. $13.95

GUSTAV STICKLEY, THE CRAFTSMAN, Mary Ann Smith. Superb study surveys broad scope of Stickley's achievement, especially in architecture. Design philosophy, rise and fall of the Craftsman empire, descriptions and floor plans for many Craftsman houses, more. 86 black-and-white halftones. 31 line illustrations. Introduction. 208pp. 6½ × 9¼. 27210-9 Pa. $9.95

THE LONG ISLAND RAIL ROAD IN EARLY PHOTOGRAPHS, Ron Ziel. Over 220 rare photos, informative text document origin (1844) and development of rail service on Long Island. Vintage views of early trains, locomotives, stations, passengers, crews, much more. Captions. 8⅞ × 11¾. 26301-0 Pa. $13.95

THE BOOK OF OLD SHIPS: From Egyptian Galleys to Clipper Ships, Henry B. Culver. Superb, authoritative history of sailing vessels, with 80 magnificent line illustrations. Galley, bark, caravel, longship, whaler, many more. Detailed, informative text on each vessel by noted naval historian. Introduction. 256pp. 5⅜ × 8½. 27332-6 Pa. $6.95

TEN BOOKS ON ARCHITECTURE, Vitruvius. The most important book ever written on architecture. Early Roman aesthetics, technology, classical orders, site selection, all other aspects. Morgan translation. 331pp. 5⅜ × 8½. 20645-9 Pa. $8.95

THE HUMAN FIGURE IN MOTION, Eadweard Muybridge. More than 4,500 stopped-action photos, in action series, showing undraped men, women, children jumping, lying down, throwing, sitting, wrestling, carrying, etc. 390pp. 7⅞ × 10⅝.
20204-6 Clothbd. $24.95

TREES OF THE EASTERN AND CENTRAL UNITED STATES AND CANADA, William M. Harlow. Best one-volume guide to 140 trees. Full descriptions, woodlore, range, etc. Over 600 illustrations. Handy size. 288pp. 4½ × 6⅜.
20395-6 Pa. $5.95

SONGS OF WESTERN BIRDS, Dr. Donald J. Borror. Complete song and call repertoire of 60 western species, including flycatchers, juncoes, cactus wrens, many more—includes fully illustrated booklet. Cassette and manual 99913-0 $8.95

GROWING AND USING HERBS AND SPICES, Milo Miloradovich. Versatile handbook provides all the information needed for cultivation and use of all the herbs and spices available in North America. 4 illustrations. Index. Glossary. 236pp. 5⅜ × 8½. 25058-X Pa. $5.95

BIG BOOK OF MAZES AND LABYRINTHS, Walter Shepherd. 50 mazes and labyrinths in all—classical, solid, ripple, and more—in one great volume. Perfect inexpensive puzzler for clever youngsters. Full solutions. 112pp. 8⅛ × 11.
22951-3 Pa. $3.95

PIANO TUNING, J. Cree Fischer. Clearest, best book for beginner, amateur. Simple repairs, raising dropped notes, tuning by easy method of flattened fifths. No previous skills needed. 4 illustrations. 201pp. 5⅜ × 8½. 23267-0 Pa. $5.95

A SOURCE BOOK IN THEATRICAL HISTORY, A. M. Nagler. Contemporary observers on acting, directing, make-up, costuming, stage props, machinery, scene design, from Ancient Greece to Chekhov. 611pp. 5⅜ × 8½. 20515-0 Pa. $11.95

THE COMPLETE NONSENSE OF EDWARD LEAR, Edward Lear. All nonsense limericks, zany alphabets, Owl and Pussycat, songs, nonsense botany, etc., illustrated by Lear. Total of 320pp. 5⅜ × 8½. (USO) 20167-8 Pa. $6.95

VICTORIAN PARLOUR POETRY: An Annotated Anthology, Michael R. Turner. 117 gems by Longfellow, Tennyson, Browning, many lesser-known poets. "The Village Blacksmith," "Curfew Must Not Ring Tonight," "Only a Baby Small," dozens more, often difficult to find elsewhere. Index of poets, titles, first lines. xxiii + 325pp. 5⅜ × 8¼. 27044-0 Pa. $8.95

DUBLINERS, James Joyce. Fifteen stories offer vivid, tightly focused observations of the lives of Dublin's poorer classes. At least one, "The Dead," is considered a masterpiece. Reprinted complete and unabridged from standard edition. 160pp. $5\frac{3}{16}$ × 8¼. 26870-5 Pa. $1.00

THE HAUNTED MONASTERY and THE CHINESE MAZE MURDERS, Robert van Gulik. Two full novels by van Gulik, set in 7th-century China, continue adventures of Judge Dee and his companions. An evil Taoist monastery, seemingly supernatural events; overgrown topiary maze hides strange crimes. 27 illustrations. 328pp. 5⅜ × 8½. 23502-5 Pa. $7.95

THE BOOK OF THE SACRED MAGIC OF ABRAMELIN THE MAGE, translated by S. MacGregor Mathers. Medieval manuscript of ceremonial magic. Basic document in Aleister Crowley, Golden Dawn groups. 268pp. 5⅜ × 8½. 23211-5 Pa. $8.95

NEW RUSSIAN-ENGLISH AND ENGLISH-RUSSIAN DICTIONARY, M. A. O'Brien. This is a remarkably handy Russian dictionary, containing a surprising amount of information, including over 70,000 entries. 366pp. 4½ × 6⅛. 20208-9 Pa. $9.95

HISTORIC HOMES OF THE AMERICAN PRESIDENTS, Second, Revised Edition, Irvin Haas. A traveler's guide to American Presidential homes, most open to the public, depicting and describing homes occupied by every American President from George Washington to George Bush. With visiting hours, admission charges, travel routes. 175 photographs. Index. 160pp. 8¼ × 11. 26751-2 Pa. $10.95

NEW YORK IN THE FORTIES, Andreas Feininger. 162 brilliant photographs by the well-known photographer, formerly with *Life* magazine. Commuters, shoppers, Times Square at night, much else from city at its peak. Captions by John von Hartz. 181pp. 9¼ × 10¾. 23585-8 Pa. $12.95

INDIAN SIGN LANGUAGE, William Tomkins. Over 525 signs developed by Sioux and other tribes. Written instructions and diagrams. Also 290 pictographs. 111pp. 6⅛ × 9¼. 22029-X Pa. $3.50

ANATOMY: A Complete Guide for Artists, Joseph Sheppard. A master of figure drawing shows artists how to render human anatomy convincingly. Over 460 illustrations. 224pp. 8⅜ × 11¼. 27279-6 Pa. $9.95

MEDIEVAL CALLIGRAPHY: Its History and Technique, Marc Drogin. Spirited history, comprehensive instruction manual covers 13 styles (ca. 4th century thru 15th). Excellent photographs; directions for duplicating medieval techniques with modern tools. 224pp. 8⅜ × 11¼. 26142-5 Pa. $11.95

DRIED FLOWERS: How to Prepare Them, Sarah Whitlock and Martha Rankin. Complete instructions on how to use silica gel, meal and borax, perlite aggregate, sand and borax, glycerine and water to create attractive permanent flower arrangements. 12 illustrations. 32pp. 5⅜ × 8½. 21802-3 Pa. $1.00

EASY-TO-MAKE BIRD FEEDERS FOR WOODWORKERS, Scott D. Campbell. Detailed, simple-to-use guide for designing, constructing, caring for and using feeders. Text, illustrations for 12 classic and contemporary designs. 96pp. 5⅜ × 8½. 25847-5 Pa. $2.95

OLD-TIME CRAFTS AND TRADES, Peter Stockham. An 1807 book created to teach children about crafts and trades open to them as future careers. It describes in detailed, nontechnical terms 24 different occupations, among them coachmaker, gardener, hairdresser, lacemaker, shoemaker, wheelwright, copper-plate printer, milliner, trunkmaker, merchant and brewer. Finely detailed engravings illustrate each occupation. 192pp. 4⅝ × 6. 27398-9 Pa. $4.95

THE HISTORY OF UNDERCLOTHES, C. Willett Cunnington and Phyllis Cunnington. Fascinating, well-documented survey covering six centuries of English undergarments, enhanced with over 100 illustrations: 12th-century laced-up bodice, footed long drawers (1795), 19th-century bustles, 19th-century corsets for men, Victorian "bust improvers," much more. 272pp. 5⅜ × 8¼. 27124-2 Pa. $9.95

ARTS AND CRAFTS FURNITURE: The Complete Brooks Catalog of 1912, Brooks Manufacturing Co. Photos and detailed descriptions of more than 150 now very collectible furniture designs from the Arts and Crafts movement depict davenports, settees, buffets, desks, tables, chairs, bedsteads, dressers and more, all built of solid, quarter-sawed oak. Invaluable for students and enthusiasts of antiques, Americana and the decorative arts. 80pp. 6½ × 9¼. 27471-3 Pa. $7.95

HOW WE INVENTED THE AIRPLANE: An Illustrated History, Orville Wright. Fascinating firsthand account covers early experiments, construction of planes and motors, first flights, much more. Introduction and commentary by Fred C. Kelly. 76 photographs. 96pp. 8¼ × 11. 25662-6 Pa. $8.95

THE ARTS OF THE SAILOR: Knotting, Splicing and Ropework, Hervey Garrett Smith. Indispensable shipboard reference covers tools, basic knots and useful hitches; handsewing and canvas work, more. Over 100 illustrations. Delightful reading for sea lovers. 256pp. 5⅜ × 8½. 26440-8 Pa. $7.95

FRANK LLOYD WRIGHT'S FALLINGWATER: The House and Its History, Second, Revised Edition, Donald Hoffmann. A total revision—both in text and illustrations—of the standard document on Fallingwater, the boldest, most personal architectural statement of Wright's mature years, updated with valuable new material from the recently opened Frank Lloyd Wright Archives. "Fascinating"—*The New York Times*. 116 illustrations. 128pp. 9¼ × 10¾. 27430-6 Pa. $10.95

PHOTOGRAPHIC SKETCHBOOK OF THE CIVIL WAR, Alexander Gardner. 100 photos taken on field during the Civil War. Famous shots of Manassas, Harper's Ferry, Lincoln, Richmond, slave pens, etc. 244pp. 10⅝ × 8¼.
22731-6 Pa. $9.95

FIVE ACRES AND INDEPENDENCE, Maurice G. Kains. Great back-to-the-land classic explains basics of self-sufficient farming. The one book to get. 95 illustrations. 397pp. 5⅜ × 8½. 20974-1 Pa. $7.95

SONGS OF EASTERN BIRDS, Dr. Donald J. Borror. Songs and calls of 60 species most common to eastern U.S.: warblers, woodpeckers, flycatchers, thrushes, larks, many more in high-quality recording. Cassette and manual 99912-2 $8.95

A MODERN HERBAL, Margaret Grieve. Much the fullest, most exact, most useful compilation of herbal material. Gigantic alphabetical encyclopedia, from aconite to zedoary, gives botanical information, medical properties, folklore, economic uses, much else. Indispensable to serious reader. 161 illustrations. 888pp. 6½ × 9¼. 2-vol. set. (USO) Vol. I: 22798-7 Pa. $9.95
Vol. II: 22799-5 Pa. $9.95

HIDDEN TREASURE MAZE BOOK, Dave Phillips. Solve 34 challenging mazes accompanied by heroic tales of adventure. Evil dragons, people-eating plants, bloodthirsty giants, many more dangerous adversaries lurk at every twist and turn. 34 mazes, stories, solutions. 48pp. 8¼ × 11. 24566-7 Pa. $2.95

LETTERS OF W. A. MOZART, Wolfgang A. Mozart. Remarkable letters show bawdy wit, humor, imagination, musical insights, contemporary musical world; includes some letters from Leopold Mozart. 276pp. 5⅜ × 8½. 22859-2 Pa. $6.95

BASIC PRINCIPLES OF CLASSICAL BALLET, Agrippina Vaganova. Great Russian theoretician, teacher explains methods for teaching classical ballet. 118 illustrations. 175pp. 5⅜ × 8½. 22036-2 Pa. $4.95

THE JUMPING FROG, Mark Twain. Revenge edition. The original story of The Celebrated Jumping Frog of Calaveras County, a hapless French translation, and Twain's hilarious "retranslation" from the French. 12 illustrations. 66pp. 5⅜ × 8½.
22686-7 Pa. $3.95

BEST REMEMBERED POEMS, Martin Gardner (ed.). The 126 poems in this superb collection of 19th- and 20th-century British and American verse range from Shelley's "To a Skylark" to the impassioned "Renascence" of Edna St. Vincent Millay and to Edward Lear's whimsical "The Owl and the Pussycat." 224pp. 5⅜ × 8½.
27165-X Pa. $4.95

COMPLETE SONNETS, William Shakespeare. Over 150 exquisite poems deal with love, friendship, the tyranny of time, beauty's evanescence, death and other themes in language of remarkable power, precision and beauty. Glossary of archaic terms. 80pp. 5³⁄₁₆ × 8¼. 26686-9 Pa. $1.00

BODIES IN A BOOKSHOP, R. T. Campbell. Challenging mystery of blackmail and murder with ingenious plot and superbly drawn characters. In the best tradition of British suspense fiction. 192pp. 5⅜ × 8½. 24720-1 Pa. $5.95

THE WIT AND HUMOR OF OSCAR WILDE, Alvin Redman (ed.). More than 1,000 ripostes, paradoxes, wisecracks: Work is the curse of the drinking classes; I can resist everything except temptation; etc. 258pp. 5⅜ × 8½. 20602-5 Pa. $5.95

SHAKESPEARE LEXICON AND QUOTATION DICTIONARY, Alexander Schmidt. Full definitions, locations, shades of meaning in every word in plays and poems. More than 50,000 exact quotations. 1,485pp. 6½ × 9¼. 2-vol. set.
Vol. 1: 22726-X Pa. $15.95
Vol. 2: 22727-8 Pa. $15.95

SELECTED POEMS, Emily Dickinson. Over 100 best-known, best-loved poems by one of America's foremost poets, reprinted from authoritative early editions. No comparable edition at this price. Index of first lines. 64pp. 5³⁄₁₆ × 8¼.
26466-1 Pa. $1.00

CELEBRATED CASES OF JUDGE DEE (DEE GOONG AN), translated by Robert van Gulik. Authentic 18th-century Chinese detective novel; Dee and associates solve three interlocked cases. Led to van Gulik's own stories with same characters. Extensive introduction. 9 illustrations. 237pp. 5⅜ × 8½.
23337-5 Pa. $6.95

THE MALLEUS MALEFICARUM OF KRAMER AND SPRENGER, translated by Montague Summers. Full text of most important witchhunter's "bible," used by both Catholics and Protestants. 278pp. 6⅝ × 10. 22802-9 Pa. $10.95

SPANISH STORIES/CUENTOS ESPAÑOLES: A Dual-Language Book, Angel Flores (ed.). Unique format offers 13 great stories in Spanish by Cervantes, Borges, others. Faithful English translations on facing pages. 352pp. 5⅜ × 8½.
25399-6 Pa. $8.95

THE CHICAGO WORLD'S FAIR OF 1893: A Photographic Record, Stanley Appelbaum (ed.). 128 rare photos show 200 buildings, Beaux-Arts architecture, Midway, original Ferris Wheel, Edison's kinetoscope, more. Architectural emphasis; full text. 116pp. 8¼ × 11. 23990-X Pa. $9.95

OLD QUEENS, N.Y., IN EARLY PHOTOGRAPHS, Vincent F. Seyfried and William Asadorian. Over 160 rare photographs of Maspeth, Jamaica, Jackson Heights, and other areas. Vintage views of DeWitt Clinton mansion, 1939 World's Fair and more. Captions. 192pp. 8⅞ × 11. 26358-4 Pa. $12.95

CAPTURED BY THE INDIANS: 15 Firsthand Accounts, 1750–1870, Frederick Drimmer. Astounding true historical accounts of grisly torture, bloody conflicts, relentless pursuits, miraculous escapes and more, by people who lived to tell the tale. 384pp. 5⅜ × 8½. 24901-8 Pa. $8.95

THE WORLD'S GREAT SPEECHES, Lewis Copeland and Lawrence W. Lamm (eds.). Vast collection of 278 speeches of Greeks to 1970. Powerful and effective models; unique look at history. 842pp. 5⅜ × 8½. 20468-5 Pa. $13.95

THE BOOK OF THE SWORD, Sir Richard F. Burton. Great Victorian scholar/adventurer's eloquent, erudite history of the "queen of weapons"—from prehistory to early Roman Empire. Evolution and development of early swords, variations (sabre, broadsword, cutlass, scimitar, etc.), much more. 336pp. 6⅛ × 9¼. 25434-8 Pa. $8.95

AUTOBIOGRAPHY: The Story of My Experiments with Truth, Mohandas K. Gandhi. Boyhood, legal studies, purification, the growth of the Satyagraha (nonviolent protest) movement. Critical, inspiring work of the man responsible for the freedom of India. 480pp. 5⅜ × 8½. (USO) 24593-4 Pa. $7.95

CELTIC MYTHS AND LEGENDS, T. W. Rolleston. Masterful retelling of Irish and Welsh stories and tales. Cuchulain, King Arthur, Deirdre, the Grail, many more. First paperback edition. 58 full-page illustrations. 512pp. 5⅜ × 8½. 26507-2 Pa. $9.95

THE PRINCIPLES OF PSYCHOLOGY, William James. Famous long course complete, unabridged. Stream of thought, time perception, memory, experimental methods; great work decades ahead of its time. 94 figures. 1,391pp. 5⅜ × 8½. 2-vol. set.
Vol. I: 20381-6 Pa. $12.95
Vol. II: 20382-4 Pa. $12.95

THE WORLD AS WILL AND REPRESENTATION, Arthur Schopenhauer. Definitive English translation of Schopenhauer's life work, correcting more than 1,000 errors, omissions in earlier translations. Translated by E. F. J. Payne. Total of 1,269pp. 5⅜ × 8½. 2-vol. set.
Vol. 1: 21761-2 Pa. $11.95
Vol. 2: 21762-0 Pa. $11.95

MAGIC AND MYSTERY IN TIBET, Madame Alexandra David-Neel. Experiences among lamas, magicians, sages, sorcerers, Bonpa wizards. A true psychic discovery. 32 illustrations. 321pp. 5⅜ × 8½. (USO) 22682-4 Pa. $8.95

THE EGYPTIAN BOOK OF THE DEAD, E. A. Wallis Budge. Complete reproduction of Ani's papyrus, finest ever found. Full hieroglyphic text, interlinear transliteration, word-for-word translation, smooth translation. 533pp. 6½ × 9¼. 21866-X Pa. $9.95

MATHEMATICS FOR THE NONMATHEMATICIAN, Morris Kline. Detailed, college-level treatment of mathematics in cultural and historical context, with numerous exercises. Recommended Reading Lists. Tables. Numerous figures. 641pp. 5⅜ × 8½. 24823-2 Pa. $11.95

THEORY OF WING SECTIONS: Including a Summary of Airfoil Data, Ira H. Abbott and A. E. von Doenhoff. Concise compilation of subsonic aerodynamic characteristics of NACA wing sections, plus description of theory. 350pp. of tables. 693pp. 5⅜ × 8½. 60586-8 Pa. $13.95

THE RIME OF THE ANCIENT MARINER, Gustave Doré, S. T. Coleridge. Doré's finest work; 34 plates capture moods, subtleties of poem. Flawless full-size reproductions printed on facing pages with authoritative text of poem. "Beautiful. Simply beautiful."—*Publisher's Weekly*. 77pp. 9¼ × 12. 22305-1 Pa. $5.95

NORTH AMERICAN INDIAN DESIGNS FOR ARTISTS AND CRAFTS-PEOPLE, Eva Wilson. Over 360 authentic copyright-free designs adapted from Navajo blankets, Hopi pottery, Sioux buffalo hides, more. Geometrics, symbolic figures, plant and animal motifs, etc. 128pp. 8⅜ × 11. (EUK) 25341-4 Pa. $7.95

SCULPTURE: Principles and Practice, Louis Slobodkin. Step-by-step approach to clay, plaster, metals, stone; classical and modern. 253 drawings, photos. 255pp. 8⅛ × 11. 22960-2 Pa. $10.95

CATALOG OF DOVER BOOKS

THE INFLUENCE OF SEA POWER UPON HISTORY, 1660–1783, A. T. Mahan. Influential classic of naval history and tactics still used as text in war colleges. First paperback edition. 4 maps. 24 battle plans. 640pp. 5⅜ × 8½.
25509-3 Pa. $12.95

THE STORY OF THE TITANIC AS TOLD BY ITS SURVIVORS, Jack Winocour (ed.). What it was really like. Panic, despair, shocking inefficiency, and a little heroism. More thrilling than any fictional account. 26 illustrations. 320pp. 5⅜ × 8½. 20610-6 Pa. $7.95

FAIRY AND FOLK TALES OF THE IRISH PEASANTRY, William Butler Yeats (ed.). Treasury of 64 tales from the twilight world of Celtic myth and legend: "The Soul Cages," "The Kildare Pooka," "King O'Toole and his Goose," many more. Introduction and Notes by W. B. Yeats. 352pp. 5⅜ × 8½. 26941-8 Pa. $8.95

BUDDHIST MAHAYANA TEXTS, E. B. Cowell and Others (eds.). Superb, accurate translations of basic documents in Mahayana Buddhism, highly important in history of religions. The Buddha-karita of Asvaghosha, Larger Sukhavativyuha, more. 448pp. 5⅜ × 8½. 25552-2 Pa. $9.95

ONE TWO THREE . . . INFINITY: Facts and Speculations of Science, George Gamow. Great physicist's fascinating, readable overview of contemporary science: number theory, relativity, fourth dimension, entropy, genes, atomic structure, much more. 128 illustrations. Index. 352pp. 5⅜ × 8½. 25664-2 Pa. $8.95

ENGINEERING IN HISTORY, Richard Shelton Kirby, et al. Broad, nontechnical survey of history's major technological advances: birth of Greek science, industrial revolution, electricity and applied science, 20th-century automation, much more. 181 illustrations. ". . . excellent . . ."—Isis. Bibliography. vii + 530pp. 5⅜ × 8¼.
26412-2 Pa. $14.95

Prices subject to change without notice.

Available at your book dealer or write for free catalog to Dept. GI, Dover Publications, Inc., 31 East 2nd St., Mineola, N.Y. 11501. Dover publishes more than 500 books each year on science, elementary and advanced mathematics, biology, music, art, literary history, social sciences and other areas.